D0877312

1998

Tales of Wayward Girls and Immoral Women

SOCIAL & BEHAVIORAL SCIENCES   *Sociology*

36-3061   HV43   97-33863 CIP
Tice, Karen W. **Tales of wayward girls and immoral women: case records and the professionalization of social work.** Illinois, 1998. 260p bibl index afp ISBN 0-252-02397-8, $49.95; ISBN 0-252-06698-7 pbk, $26.95

   The social work profession in the US celebrates its 100th birthday this year, marking the centennial anniversary of the first specialized training course for American social workers held in New York in the summer of 1899. In this fascinating history of social work, Tice (Univ. of Kentucky) shows how case records and the use of narration were pivotal in both the development of the profession and the ascendancy of casework over social activism in practice. Case recording emerged in the late 1800s as part of the new Charity Organization Societies' efforts to make charitable giving more systematic and scientific. Investigation, documentation, and description of the needy were central features of the new approach. Case records served other purposes as well; for instance, they provided dramatic human interest stories that engaged the public and agency benefactors and documented professional successes. Prototypical case records were used extensively for professional training; case recording was and still is a central feature of the casework apprenticeship in social work education. Tice shows how, as historical documents, case records illuminate the life of the poor as seen from the professional's vantage point, as well as trace the development of casework practice. Highly recommended for students and scholars in social work and related fields. Upper-division undergraduates and above.—*B. A. Pine, University of Connecticut*

Tales of Wayward Girls and Immoral Women

Case Records and the Professionalization
of Social Work

Karen W. Tice

University of Illinois Press

Urbana and Chicago

© 1998 by the Board of Trustees of the University of Illinois
Manufactured in the United States of America

1   2   3   4   5   C   P   5   4   3   2   1

This book is printed on acid-free paper.

Library of Congress Cataloging-in-Publication Data
Tice, Karen Whitney, 1955–
Tales of wayward girls and immoral women : case records and the
professionalization of social work / Karen Tice
    p.   cm.
Includes bibliographical references and index.
ISBN 0-252-02397-8 (cloth : alk. paper).—
ISBN 0-252-06698-7 (pbk. : alk. paper)
1. Social case work—United States—History.
2. Social case work reporting—United States—History.
3. Social service—United States—Records and correspondence—History.
I. Title.
HV43.T43   1998
361.3'2—dc21   97-33863
CIP

To "Hazel," whose spirit and story started and sustained this project.

Contents

Acknowledgments

Throughout the course of writing this book, I have been fortunate in the encouragement I have received from many quarters and want to thank those who helped inspire and nurture my work. My warm gratitude and thanks goes to my friend and advisor Richard Angelo, who not only provided the initial encouragement in his graduate seminars and conversations but also generously spent many hours nursing and nudging this project along. Without his care, intellectual imagination, affirmation, humor, and toleration for my numerous bouts of doubt and derailment, this book would not have been written. I am also grateful to Wilburn Hayden, Beth Goldstein, Skip Kifer, Linda Worley, Allan DeYoung, and Lori Garkovich for their ideas and inspirations, especially to Ronda Connaway, whose commitment to women and social work influenced my early training as well as this volume.

This project would also not have been possible without the prodding I received from Patricia Rieker to submit it for publication and her ongoing help along the way. My special thanks go to my dear colleagues, Joanna Badagliacco and Monica Udvardy, for their sustenance. During our weekly dinner get-togethers they provided the ongoing friendship and support that were essential in overcoming many slumps and navigating stressful periods. I am also grateful for the support and assistance of my friend Alice Templeton, who raised many keen questions that I hope have sharpened the arguments made in this book. Many thanks as well to Jenrose Fitzgerald for her help, wit, insights, and infectious enthusiasm for writing and reading. Thanks as well go to Hillary Angelo, Mary Anglin, Susan Bordo, Francie Chassen-Lopez, Pat Cooper, Sharon Hamilton, Laurie Hatch, Jan Hurley, and Elaine Liberto.

I also thank the librarians and archivists whose assistance has been critical to my research. Terry Birdwhistell at the University of Kentucky Special Collections patiently provided help with archival research, as did Elizabeth Mock at the University of Massachusetts at Boston's archives and David Klaassen at the Social Welfare Archives at the University of Minnesota and the staff at the Salvation Army Archives and Research Center, Alexandria, Virginia. Karen Hewitt of the University of Illinois Press provided excellent editorial guidance, and anonymous reviewers who were vigilant in reading my manuscript offered helpful suggestions for revision.

Love and thanks especially are due Dwight Billings, who daily lived and labored with these words and pages as if they were his own and provided endless intellectual, emotional, and domestic nourishment. Without his care, inspiration, and loving companionship over the years, this book would not have been realized.

Introduction

Case Narratives and the Quest for Professional Authority—From the Soup Kettle to the Inkwell

Now things have changed rapidly in the last fifty years. Thousands of people are living where hundreds lived then. Some of them have come from so far that their language and customs are strange. . . . Social customs, along with the rest have altered so much that grandmother's kettle of soup is no longer the first aid used by a neighborly soul for even neighborliness has become complicated; and granddaughter is being trained in ways of modern social service.

∾Newton (1930)

We are coming to realize more and more that the written word plays a prominent part in this [the MSPCC] help program. Wasn't it Lloyd C. Douglas who said in his novel that "the only chemicals imperative to evolution are water, blood, and ink—and the greatest of these is ink."

∾Blake (1947)

The scientific charity organization movement in the later years of the nineteenth century was pivotal in reshaping benevolent practices in the United States. Pioneering charity organization experts sought to consolidate the burgeoning charitable domain by introducing a unified set of systematic techniques, widening control over a broad range of diagnostic and discursive fields, disseminating techniques borrowed from business and science, and articulating a distinctive core of services to promote professionalization in charitable work.

In their efforts to claim a place among the established professions and unify the many branches of charitable and reform activities, these pioneers challenged prior religious and neighborly approaches to benevolence as sentimental and indiscriminate. To increase their prestige (and even though most social workers were women) charity organization experts called into question nineteenth-century ideologies of women's special fitness for charity work by insisting upon neutered and more highly rationalized models of professionalism and science. They aspired to replace notions of what historian Peggy Pascoe (1990) terms the "moral authority" of benevolent grandmothers and neighborly women with the authority of professional experts trained in investigation, diagnosis, and, as I will stress in this book, keeping case records.

In a shift toward science, business, and a professionalized order and away from religious and feminized models of benevolence, the scientifically based charity organization society (COS) movement introduced practices for gathering and documenting facts about the poor and aberrant. First organized in Buffalo in 1877, local charity organization societies were established in twenty-five cities throughout the United States by 1890. They led in the early movement to professionalize charity endeavors by stressing the role of scientific investigation in establishing the worthiness of charity recipients, eliminating fraud and duplication of services, and promoting rehabilitation over relief, knowledge over sentiment (Kellogg 1893).

The pen, pencil, and typewriter emerged as quintessential tools in a professional practice that celebrated scientific description, documentation, and investigation. Meanwhile, soup kettles and almsgiving became potent symbols of archaic, discredited methods. Scientific charity leaders, including Mary Richmond, Zilpha Drew Smith, S. Humphreys Gurteen, Josephine Shaw Lowell, Amos Warner, Edward Devine, and John Glenn, introduced new discourses on waste, worthiness, and imposture as well as new techniques for efficiency. At the same time, they enlarged the vocabulary of transgressions. Business management techniques to facilitate intra-agency efficiency and prevent costly duplication, including "standardized forms, regular reports to 'stockholders,' and the use of 'cost/benefit' analysis" (Wenocur and Reisch 1989, p. 49), found warm welcome in professional charity work, especially within charity organization societies.[1]

Compatible with transformations in the larger socioeconomic order, calls by those who advocated charity organization societies reverberated throughout the many fields of social work practice (Wenocur and Reisch 1989) and anticipated trends that would come within the larger charitable enterprise during the early decades of the twentieth century. Although not immune to harsh criticism from social reform leaders such as Jane Addams, who spoke for other branches and methods of reform work, the movement's distinctive set of discourses and methods were a key departure point for the reorganization of charity in the United States. The charity organization society movement imparted the critical ingredients for the emergence of casework: a structure of professional processes for individualizing client problems and solutions that was the template for social work practice in the early twentieth century and the forerunner of contemporary "direct practice" (Leiby 1978; Leighninger 1987; Lubove 1973; Stadum 1992; Wenocur and Reisch 1989). By examining a fundamental tenet of casework that had become canonical in social work by the 1920s—record-keeping—I will argue that the investigative and documentation practices that the movement pioneered permanently reshaped discursive and institutional practices of benevolence as well as the social relations of charity workers, donors, and recipients from the 1920s to the present.

Case recording was pivotal in the battles to professionalize social work, tied as it was to the rising ascendancy of casework as the archetype for professional endeavor and the resultant waning of social reform.[2] By the 1920s, to be without case records, or to produce ones that were "deficient" (not all forms of record-keeping were considered professionally adequate), was to undermine social work's claims to scientific and professional practice and thus risk losing the endorsement and funding of local governments, charities commissions, chambers of commerce, and other professional and community standard-setting organizations. Through national professional networks of conferences, journals, and speciality associations, record-keeping not only became an integral part of child-placing, child-protective, and family welfare agencies, but it was also essential to the practice of medical, psychiatric, and school social work (Cabot 1919; Farmer 1921; Haskins 1923; Lyons 1920; Oppenheimer 1925; Swift 1934).

Historians writing "bottoms-up histories" have begun to make extensive use of case records, which have proven to be gold mines for scholars interested in social welfare history and the lives of stigmatized subjects. Studies by Broder (1988), Gordon (1988), Kunzel (1993), Lunbeck (1994), Meyerowitz (1988), Pascoe (1990), and Stadum (1992) make significant use of institutional records and case record materials to explore shifting fields of practice and representation around issues of mental hygiene, poverty, juvenile delinquency, single pregnancy and motherhood, gender and sexuality, and abuse. Several of these authors, however, acknowledge methodological uneasiness over using case material because of the unexamined influence of social work authors on the production of these materials (Kunzel 1995). Some have speculated that case records may reveal more about authors than subjects. These studies, however, have not concentrated on social workers as authors nor on the construction of social work authority and knowledge-building. They have not probed deeply into encounters between caseworkers and clients, and no study has highlighted the shifting conventions for constructing case records.[3]

By focusing on case records themselves and on the textual politics of caseworkers, I will explore the development and transformations of case-recording over the early decades of the twentieth century by analyzing not only the published writings of a broad spectrum of casework leaders but also, and just as important, the unpublished records of front-line caseworkers. As professional constructions, casewritings created clients, authorities, problems, and solutions. Caseworkers transformed clients' biographies into professional representations shaped by emerging professional interests. Caseworkers' distinctive relationship to clients, however, and their grounded approach to knowledge-building, resulted in case narrations that prevent easy generalizations about social workers, clients, and social agencies. Read through the professional agendas that directed them, these sprawling tales not only tell a great deal about what caseworkers actually did and thought but also reveal insights into the subjectivities of social work's clients.

Leslie Leighninger (1987) argues correctly that many accounts of the professionalization of social work overemphasize the degree of internal cohesion within the profession. In fact, unity among casework leaders was elusive when it came to how case records should be written. In professional literature, at conferences, and within national committees set up to define procedures for recording clients' lives, early social workers quarreled constantly over the appropriate tone for case record narratives. At the same time, they also sought to standardize methods of observation and interpretation. Debates over the social case record became prominent during the 1920s, a particularly fertile time in social work when practitioners searched for common paradigms and techniques to organize disparate fields of practice.[4] As a result of this search for a common foundation, social workers became well attuned to the problematics of vocabulary, representation, and conceptual systems. Case records provided the critical terrain for professional in-fighting about procedures for ordering, producing, and interpreting these case records and debating the narrative conventions for representing "facts."

Debates about the nature of case-recording reveal contradictory professional ambitions and afford an excellent vantage point on the early conflicts that accompanied the professionalization of charity work in the United States. Some social work leaders sought to achieve scientific objectivity in their narratives, whereas others hoped to preserve local color and human interest. Seeking ways to find regularities in the social world, scientifically inclined social workers argued that the case record story should be methodically standardized by the use of topologies, outlines, and questionnaires. Humanists, however, those most concerned with unique context, vividness, and human interest, argued for giving free rein to the imagination in order to approximate how a fiction writer or playwright might inscribe the lives of clients. Still other voices in these debates, although a minority, advocated sharing textual space with clients or using clients' "own stories," confessional documents, verbatim interviews, and informant narratives.

Battles over the making of case records, however, were not confined to social work. In an article appearing in the *Journal of Sociology and Social Research,* Helen Witmer, a professor of social work at Smith College, noted that by the late 1920s social case records had become the "storm center" of the social sciences (1930, p. 113). Perhaps not surprisingly, just as case-recording was beginning to assume paramount importance, case descriptions came to be regularly challenged by the better established fields of sociology, psychiatry, and psychology. Social workers were judged to be unreliable eyewitnesses of the social world and offered "fatherly" counsel to help them remove undesirable "subjective" and "feminine" presences in case records.[5]

Because of the centrality of case records to the project of profession-building, they soon came to be considered the most efficient pedagogical basis for social work training and the major means for conveying to new social workers what veterans knew and did. Case records were published regularly in the *Charity Organization Bulletin, The Family,* and the *Judge Baker Foundation Case Studies,* and presenters at national meetings drew upon case studies to suggest improvements in social work practice. In 1920 Porter Lee, director of the New York School of Social Work, urged social workers to upgrade and standardize professional education by employing the case method of teaching. Both Steiner (1921) and Hagerty (1931) echoed Lee's call, and Breckinridge (1924), Dixon and Browning (1938), Cannon and Klein (1933), Towle (1941), and Lowry (1939), among others, responded by publishing well-read collections of case records for teaching purposes. Social work leader Frank Bruno asserted that "case records of actual situations, edited for teaching purposes, furnished an all but exclusive method of teaching social casework, both to the employee receiving in-service training and to the student at school" (1957, p. 189).

Mary Richmond's *Social Diagnosis* (1917), the text most widely used in the early training of social workers, was based on the analysis of case records collected from agencies in five cities. Numerous other early books also relied heavily on case record illustrations (Burleigh and Harris 1923; Devine 1914; Joint Committee on Methods of Preventing Delinquency 1926; Marcus 1929; Richmond 1922; Sayles, ed. 1932; Southard and Jarrett 1922; Spaulding 1923; Walker 1937). Recognizing the widespread impact of such published case collections, Joanna Colcord, a leader in the field of family welfare and Mary Richmond's successor in the charity organization department of the Russell Sage Foundation, noted the large number of students of social casework who had "followed the travels of Albert Gough, anxiously considered the problems of Ames, the tuberculous hatter, and rejoiced in the prospect of better times ahead for Peter and Marie Costello" (Colcord and Mann, eds. 1930, p. 275).

But reading case records was not enough; social workers had to be trained to write them. Gordon Hamilton of the New York School of Social Work argued that case-recording and description should be solely the province of professionally trained experts. "In an ultimate sense only the trained diagnostician can write a good record," she contended, "for only he can pluck from the unending web of social experience the thread of probable significance" (1936, p. 184).

Reading and keeping records thus became integral parts of training new casework staff as well as supervising new cases, because making professional case narratives was considered a key casework responsibility (Lubove 1973, p. 138; Munro 1951; Wheeler 1925).[6] Lubove notes that students at the New York School of Philanthropy studied case records at the COS district office.[7] Many schools of social work required coursework in case-recording methods (Braungard 1929). The Russell Sage Foundation and professional associations such as the American Association of Hospital Social Workers and the National Committee on Visiting Teachers distributed standardized case record forms to social service agencies in many cities, and numerous how-to books and articles on case-recording and record-keeping appeared during the early decades of the twentieth century (Bristol 1936; Farmer 1921; Hamilton 1936; Lewis 1931; Ralph 1915; Sheffield 1920; Solenberger 1910). Staff social workers at a variety of agencies were also instructed first to consult local Confidential Exchanges (inter-agency clearinghouses and archives of case files) in order to read records from other agencies before visiting "cases." Social workers who ignored such records, according to Francis McLean, superintendent of the Brooklyn Bureau of Charities and later field secretary for the Russell Sage charity organization department, would never be anything but "bunglers," remnants of the "typical old fashioned charity which organized charity was supposed to supplant" (1908, p. 106).

Typewriters, dictaphones, and stenographers were quickly made imperative by changing casework practices that demanded more than the curt ledger entries of an earlier era. Workers at the Minneapolis Family Welfare Association in 1912, for example, spent 48 percent of their time sending out written and verbal reports (Annual Report 1912, p. 7). At the fiftieth anniversary of this agency in 1934, workers joked about high cost of their first typewriters, as opposed to the costs of absenteeism resulting from writer's cramp (Stadum 1987, p. 112).

Case records were seen as an essential tool for training and a valuable source of information vital to policy-oriented research across disciplines. They were not only textbooks for social workers but also the laboratory material for research, because they were "mines of facts" (Hamilton 1923). Other disciplines agreed upon the potential research value of case records. Carol Aronovici, director of the Philadelphia Bureau for Social Research, for example, noted that sociology "must not disregard the record as a source of information for sociological research. Buried in the scores of thousands of records of welfare agencies of this country are first-hand, accurate sociological data gathered without bias and without a preconceived point of view" (1916, p. 470).

Almost incidentally, case records were also said to be good for social work's clients. Their object was "to ensure efficiency in treatment with the subordinate object of saving clients from unnecessary inquiry" (Bruno 1916, p. 453). Promoting diagnostic thinking on the part of social workers, sparing clients the necessity of telling their stories over and over again, and making transitions smoother when workers or clients moved were among the benefits frequently thought to accrue to clients (Bristol 1936; Hamilton 1936; Richmond 1925; Sheffield 1920). Maurice Karph noted that case records were the "basis for all policy-making on cases" and were "frequently looked upon as the personification of the client himself" (1931, p. 144).[8] Case records not only described but also represented clients and their situations, thus forming the basis for decisions about interventions and, ultimately, clients' well-being.

Finally, case records and their rich tales of "loose living, of disease, of twisted minds, of groping souls, of hysterical seeking for the joy of life" (Stern and Stern 1923, p. 287) also proved invaluable as social workers asserted professional expertise and pleaded for public support. Through human-interest stories in newspapers and books, case records proved to be a vital documentary source for those intent upon communicating a worldview that championed their preferred solutions to social ills. The assistant director of the New York Charity Organization Society, Clare Tousley, observed that social workers would always need case stories "to light our facts and figures" and "to tell [our] story to Main Street" (1927, pp. 175–76). Case records, it was soon discovered, could be reshaped to serve as professional tales of accomplishment, highlighting professional social workers as rescuers and saviors. At the same time, they could be used effectively to arouse public sympathy, because they conveyed the emotional human drama that social workers faced in everyday reform work. In the retelling of valiant struggles against life's circumstances, social work case stories provided moral lessons that validated the rewards of virtue, industry, and restraint.

Convinced of their ultimate publicity and persuasive value, many social workers cultivated the art of human interest story-writing to popularize their efforts (Tousley 1920). The New York Charity Organization Society went so far as to train staff members to be "cub reporters" in order to write casework stories for annual reports, journals, and newspapers. Early professional social work associations sponsored case story contests (Warner, Queen, and Harper 1930; Whipple 1927), and trade books and magazine articles written by social workers and based on case records retold to a general audience proliferated during the 1930s as part of the expansion of social documentary literature. To popularize emerging professional ambitions and visions, social workers experimented with a variety of dramatic forms for presenting professional tales: exhibits, plays, pageants, and street fairs. Powerful reform organizations such as the Russell Sage Foundation and the National Child Labor Board organized departments of exhibits to display new forms of social work expertise, and many local reform organizations hired publicity agents to assist in building professional credibility.

Record-keeping thus played a key role in the legitimation of social casework. Early social work leaders clearly acknowledged the importance of case records for consolidating professional knowledge. At the 1917 meeting of the National Probation Association, for example, Mary Richmond argued that social workers were "going to have to depend largely upon the study of full and accurate case records for our own advancement in skill, in the first place, and for the advancement, in the second place, of the body of knowledge that we social workers hold in common" (Colcord and Mann, eds. 1930, p. 403). Embracing this philosophy, the New York School of Philanthropy defined case-recording as one of the "fundamental techniques of social work" and an integral part of professional education (Warner, Queen, and Harper 1930, p. 565).

Yet despite early professional emphasis on the importance of case records, scholars have not used them to examine the project of social work professionalization. Their significance has also largely been overlooked in social welfare historiography. Yet the study of case records as professional constructions is essential for exploring the process of profession-building and legitimation in social work and the consolidation of social workers' professional identity. By failing to consider early debates about case records, as well as their production by front-line social workers, historians have overlooked considerable diversity and complexity within this profession-building project. More than just a barometer of the progress toward professionalization, case records were a central site for contesting the roles of science, art, representation, objectivity, realism, and gender in organized charity and reform. Tracing the shifting definitions, forms, and uses of case records, as well as the cross-currents among professional discourses about them, yields not a neatly linear story of the construction of social work but rather a plural, circuitous account that reveals the complexities of professionalization and narrative authority. An examination of case record writing practices in early social work will perhaps stimulate renewed reflections about the politics of contemporary writing in the field.

Professional Textual Practices

> But when they [social workers] go into the pots and look at what you are cooking and take a spoon and stir it and say it smells good and look out the corner of their eye you feel uncomfortable. . . . *And always they have their book and pencil in hand!*
>
> ∾Wannamaker (1925)

Professional writing is a calculated act informed by professional norms that ironically both limit and extend the possibilities of professional practice. As Bazerman and Paradis (1991) note, professional texts perform an essential role in constructing versions of reality and play, as Dorothy Smith (1990) argues, an essential part in the making and remaking of facts and worlds.[9] They structure relations among professions and help organize perceptions. Thus, by understanding textual dynamics within a particular profession it is possible to understand how professions constitute themselves through the clustering of people, activities, tropes, and language, as well as how texts contribute to profession-building by socializing outsiders to professional paradigms and thereby advancing the scope of expert authority.

Case records, as both professional acts and professionally framed versions of reality, were designed to advance the goals of social casework. They enabled social work leaders to establish boundaries and critical relevances for writing about their clients, and they located people as sites of professional actions. The story of the professionalism of social work is not a story of the discovery of transparent and unsullied facts nor of simple documentary realism divorced from professional interests. Rather, it is a story about how professional power shaped the interpretation, narration, and representation of social reality and clients' lives, as well as how particular narrative elements came to be accepted as factual.

Representation is "never a simple act of discovery," and representations are always "mediated," the "product of interpretation" (Alcoff 1991–92, p. 9). As a professionally shaped set of expectations and operations, record-keeping is a formalized way of knowing and rewriting that potentially subdues and transforms individual biography into professionally translated and abridged versions.[10] As Donnelly notes in relation to medicine, case histories are "made" not "taken" (Monroe, Holleman, and Holleman 1992, p. 50). Even the most succinct medical case report requires selection, interpretation, and ordering to "conceptually enclose narration, constrain signs to mean only one thing, and tie utterances down to unalterable meanings" (Charon 1992, p. 118). Yet patients' narratives "open possibilities."

This process of displacing individuals' unique experiences with generalized professional narratives has been important to the rise of social work professionalization, even though social work has not traveled as far down that troublesome road as some other professional disciplines.[11] Professional conventions for rendering the lives and experiences of clients in social work too often result in distorted truncations. Reported accounts are controlled by professional categorizations that make over, tidy, and shape clients into professionally recognizable types, thus disclosing only those pieces that fall into prefigured slots. As Byron Green notes, professional texts "construct individuals as documentary facsimiles, not as situated presences" (1983, p. 2). Too often social work tales result in problem-saturated ways of knowing and representing those persons judged to be on the margins, ignoring their complexity, strengths, and dreams.[12]

Greater attention to the politics of professional writing about others is sorely needed in social work so as not to turn clients into caricatures and privilege the voice of expert authority. Social work need not forsake its professional storytelling, but it should interrogate professional textual practices more vigilantly. With-out such reflexivity, seemingly factual texts such as case records achieve what Green calls "constitutive innocence" (p. 13) through the obliteration of the professional interests that go into their production. When this erasure occurs, the ethical di-lemmas that necessarily accompany narrative authority fail to be acknowledged and addressed.

Although much of modern social work practice is still spent translating client experience into professional texts, social work literature has largely ignored issues of representation, the politics of interpretation and meaning, disparities between the writer and the writer's subjects, the nature of expert narrative authority, and the impact of gender, race, class, and professional authority on the construction of knowledge. Questions about textual practices are not merely aesthetic. A nar-rative is "an act of social interaction, a positioned intervention" (Duggan 1993, p. 794). Narrative practices involve power and intervention and thus have profound implications for modes of thinking and writing that have silenced poor people, immigrants, people of color, women, gays and lesbians, and other historically mar-ginalized groups. Narrative practices also create opportunities for dialogue, self-representation, and more participatory ways of knowing. Yet such questions are given too little attention within contemporary social work.[13]

Gender, Professional Proximity, and Narrativity

In addition to issues of textual and interpretative power, the topic of gender should be explored more fully in studies of social work professionalization. The growing body of scholarship that has begun to address the roles of women and gender ide-ologies in social reform practice and policy has suggested a portrait of reform that is more multifacted than are traditional interpretations that neglected gender (Abramovitz 1989; Frankel and Dye, eds. 1991; Ginzberg 1990; Kunzel 1993; Mun-cy 1991; Pascoe 1990; Peiss 1986; Stansell 1987). In addition to simply noting the significance of gender, these studies move social welfare history beyond reductive and monolithic characterizations of women reformers by avoiding essentialized and universal categorizations. New studies show that class, ethnic, regional, and racial differences among women reformers created a variety of styles of benevo-lence (Brown 1989; Gordon 1991, 1994; Guy-Sheftall 1990; Hewitt 1990; Lasch-Quinn 1993; Neverdon-Morton 1989; O'Donnell 1994; Salem 1990).

By focusing not only on the relations between women and men but also on dif-ferences among women reformers, complexities of race, class, ethnicity, and power that shaped professional representation, the care relationship and transformations in models of benevolent practice gain new significance in studies of the history of American charity work and reform activism. Recent studies also note the importance of gender for understanding many of the battles for control of benevolence (Ginzberg 1990; Kunzel 1988, 1993; Tice 1992).[14] Attention to such battles debunks conventional assumptions of a unitary social work ethos and the notion of discrete stages of professional development while highlighting the continuing importance of gender in social welfare history.

Gender was not only a fundamental ingredient in the historical battles to professionalize reform work but also a major influence on the textual practices of social work because of the gendering of professional proximity (the distinctive depth of relationship between many caseworkers and their clients). Gender influenced the experiences upon which professionals based their writings, as well as the way that their narratives were received. What brought middle-class observers and reformers into the daily lives of the poor was the practice of home-visiting, a long-standing procedure of nineteenth-century benevolent slum work and twentieth-century professional casework. Christine Stansell (1987) has shown that religiously motivated explorations that searched for those in the throes of odious circumstances gave rise to home visits, which took men and women out of church confines and into slum homes. The formulaic situations, casts of stock characters, and ritualized conversations of home visitor accounts came to constitute a narrative genre in and of itself. Home visitor narratives of "last ditch repentance (on a deathbed of rags)" and stock characters such as the "fallen woman, starving seamstress, and ragged match girl" appeared in the annual reports of tract societies as well as in published fictional sketches at the end of the nineteenth century (Stansell 1987, p. 66). "Bible women," however, were not the only visitors to zones of poverty and social ills. Increasingly, large numbers of middle-class women reformers, including visiting teachers, caseworkers, and health visitors, also went to the "wrong side of town," thereby claiming slums as spaces appropriate for them and their charitable ministrations.

The accounts written by women reformers often employed many of the same distancing figures of speech as those their male counterparts wrote; they also reflected many of the same class biases. Women's accounts were nonetheless more "aural than visual," because unlike many casual male explorers these women spent many hours listening to the stories of working-class and impoverished women and children (Ross 1993). It is important not to imagine that the differences between aural and visual narratives, for example, reflected essential gender differences. Rather, the differences in narrative styles that scholars such as Ross have observed reflect differences in how highly gendered reform and care-giving professions were organized.

In the following chapters, I argue that carrying on versions of religiously inspired home-visiting in the form of casework forced social workers to stay in close contact with the everyday lives of clients, a professional mandate that profoundly shaped how they wrote professional narratives. Early social workers were well aware of the distinctive nature of their relationship to clients. Thus Katherine Hardwick (1922) acknowledged that nearness, not remoteness, was both the strength and weakness of social casework. Casework demanded "an absorbing sharing in the lives of others." Practically, it meant "a certain amount of taking babies to the hospital, ordering family groceries, playing basketball with Willie, and buying Suzie's hair ribbons" (p. 246).

The comparison of early social work with psychiatry illustrates well how variations in proximity between professionals and clients influenced the narratives of gendered professions. Arguing for the advantage of social workers' proximate viewpoint over that of psychiatry, Jessie Taft (1918), director of child study at the Seybert Foundation, pointed out that psychiatrists' diagnostic horizons were limited by the confining nature of their contacts with patients in hospitals. Unlike social workers, who were exposed to "life in the raw," psychiatrists' "false" detachment led to views of "misleading simplicity" about clients. Later, Taft criticized the typical psychiatrist for "abstracting his patient from life and putting him in an artificially simplified environment" (1922, p. 372). In contrast, she claimed, "only the case worker leaves the hospital, clinic, office, and laboratory behind and observes the individual in action, at home, at work, in school; playing, loving, toiling, hating, fearing, striving, succeeding, failing, an organic part of social context."

A dramatic illustration of differences in professional proximity to clients is found in *The Kingdom of Evils* (1922) by E. E. Southard, a psychiatrist, and Mary Jarrett, a psychiatric social worker. In this study of one hundred case histories drawn from the Boston Psychopathic Hospital, 4,901 hours were reported as being spent with patients. Out of that number, physicians spent 674 hours, psychologists spent 94, and social workers spent 4,133. Social workers' contact accounted for fully 84 percent of total contacts.[15]

Because the profession of social work requires listening to, talking with, and maintaining sustained personal contact with clients, caseworkers not only saw more than did their counterparts (most of whom were male) in psychiatry and mental hygiene, but they also knew the domestic side of poverty better. As a result, women in social work often produced "truths" from their explorations that differed significantly from those of allied fields. The distinctive patterns of relationships rarely yielded stories that had tidy resolutions, unlike the diagnostic, conceptually ordered, and abstract descriptions of psychiatry. Psychiatrists' writings were perceived as more professionally prestigious, whereas the writings of women in social work were often thought of as marginal.[16] Social work narratives, nonetheless, were characterized by considerable diversity that precluded essentialized, static conclusions about caseworkers' relationships with clients, caseworkers' professional writings, and the impact of gender on social work.[17]

Chapter Overviews

> If you want to understand what a science is you should look in the first
> instance not at its theories or its findings, and certainly not what its
> apologists say about it; you should look at what the practitioners of it do.
>
> ∾Clifford Geertz, quoted in Van Maanen (1988)

This study is based not only on the writings of a quarrelsome group of early leaders in social work, sociology, and psychology and on paradigmatic case records published in professional literature for pedagogical purposes, but also on social workers' case records collected from a variety of casework agencies. I have analyzed 150 case records and examined many others from the Massachusetts Society for the Prevention of Cruelty to Children and the Minneapolis Child's Protective Society (child protective societies); the Associated Charities/Family Welfare Association of Minneapolis (a family casework-relief agency); and the Minneapolis Citizen's Aid Society Girls' Department and the Boston Children's Aid Society (child-placing agencies).[18] A summary of information on dates and the durations of cases sampled appears in the appendix.

Because many of these case records also incorporate records from schools, courts, psychiatric hospitals and clinics, industrial schools, and institutions for the "feebleminded," they not only allow for a comparative reading of textual practices across professions but also furnish opportunities to explore the impact of differing agency missions on the reported activities and techniques of caseworkers and their effects on relationships with clients. The records provide a proximate view of daily encounters and relationships between early social caseworkers and their poor and immigrant clients. Attending to such records counteracts the tendency in social welfare history to focus on social work leaders rather than on practitioners and clients.

Many records I studied span several decades, reporting observations of and interactions with clients over many years. Some records yielded hundreds of pages of narrative chronicling the lives of clients during the early decades of the twentieth century, especially during the 1920s. They document the multiplicity of dialects and accents that caseworkers spoke in numerous interactions with clients at home, at school, at work, at dinner, and at play. They also uncover much of the range of normatively determined judgments that social workers from a variety of agencies routinely made about personality, housekeeping, employability, character, sexual behavior, dress, cuisine, parenting, and leisure. These case records thus inscribe the perspectives of a wide range of informants and provide a close-up view of the professional knowledge that social workers constructed from bodies and testimony. Finally, they tell a different story about the early history of social work practice than the one that can be gleaned solely from discourses that the profession's leaders have produced. Thus they provide a concrete view of the convolutions of casework knowledge-building and practice throughout the early decades of the twentieth century.

Chapter 1, "I'll Be Watching You: The Advent of the Case Record," traces the emergence of the practice of case-recording in the charity organization society movement, which, beginning in the late nineteenth century, defined case-recording as an indispensable part of its new scientific practice of charity. Through a case study of a child protective society, the chapter focuses on the evolution of this key practice within social casework. It also explores how the diffusion of case-recording to other sectors of the social reform enterprise achieved increased hegemonic status throughout the profession.

Chapter 2, "The Construction of the Case Record and Professional Legitimation," explores the rich debates—both within social work and between social work and other professions—that ensued over the writing of case records. The 1920s were a busy time for embellishing COS descriptive methods, and social workers profoundly questioned the politics of professional narrativity. They argued about representation, vocabulary, conceptual systems, and fact-finding and debated the relative emphasis that science or art should have in guiding professional narrations.

Chapter 3, "The Rescue of 'Juvenile Fragments': The Case of Hazel," analyzes the records of one young woman placed under the professional jurisdiction of social work and psychology. Her position as the subject of two versions of professional writing practices provides a comparison of the two professions' conceptual and narrative practices. Unlike the records from a child guidance clinic that produced a tightly organized set of theoretical etiologies and diagnostics about Hazel, the sprawling record her social worker wrote lacked the conceptual tidiness provided by the mental hygiene paradigm and allowed traces of Hazel's subjectivities to be apparent. Although the tale of Hazel was by no means an innocent textual construction, the social work version of her story illustrates the differences between professional expertise in social work and psychology and reveals that a distinctive kind of knowledge was produced in social work, primarily a women's field of endeavor.

The next two chapters are based on my reading of case records written by a wide range of social workers. Chapter 4, "To Make a Case: Tales of Detection," explores the process of "making a case," whereby social workers descended into a world they describe as nightmarish—that of wayward, wily, and willful clients. Once there, they positioned themselves in the narratives as saviors of public morality who shielded communities from the contaminating influences of supposedly malignant clients. In these menacing accounts, social workers constructed a vast array of portentous signifiers to denote moral and sexual disorder, writing tales replete with signs of women's conduct disorders: vermilion lips and arched eyebrows, ruptured hymens, dirty kitchens, unsupervised children on city streets, liquor bottles, and mysterious men hanging about. Gathering and displaying testimony and probative evidence were the key elements in this genre of case stories. To obtain such evidence, social workers talked to a wide variety of persons, including landlords, neighbors, and storekeepers, to fashion rumor, gossip, and innuendo into professional knowledge.

Chapter 5, "Tales of Protection: The Gentler Touch," examines a rosier genre of case stories that describe the propitious relationships social workers forged with the special clients who took their advice and followed preferred pathways toward upright lives. In these accounts the clients were more likely to bloom with modesty than makeup. Instead of merely employing and narrating sleuthlike methods for procuring incriminating testimony, tales of protection were built around intimate talks, pleasant walks, and gentle nudges by social workers who wrote hopefully of the likelihood of being able to refashion the habits and lives of promising clients in ways both amenable and indebted to social work. Hinting at yearnings for an alternative, cross-class relationship, the writers clung to a seasoned set of beliefs in a "benevolent femininity" that could unite them and clients in sisterly bonds that would transcend class differences and ultimately purify the unchaste and ill-bred.[19] Although these social workers may indeed have yearned for, and in some cases achieved, forms of intimacy unparalleled in male-dominated professions, the relationships they narrated were never innocent of the privileges embedded in class standing and the power that issued from professional authority. Chapter 5 thus examines the contradictions in this complex project of building and sustaining cross-class, power-laden relationships that navigated between the often differing dreams and ambitions of social workers and those of clients.

Case records were not meant to gather dust in central office filing cabinets, nor were they to be read only by social work apprentices. Instead, they were believed to be useful for dramatizing social work situations with vivid characterization, drama, and moral significance in order to arouse public sympathy and support. Both case records and the investigations social workers conducted that contributed to them formed the basis for many human interest stories, popular fiction, and scholarly studies of the poor. Chapter 6, "Tales of Accomplishment: Social Work and the Art of Public Persuasion," provides an overview of social work's adventures with publicity and persuasion and examines the variety of tropes social workers have used to represent both clients and professional agendas in battles to popularize their field.

The diverse strategies caseworkers used to constitute a domain of expert knowledge included how they defined, observed, and represented client populations as well as the dynamics of textual authority in an emergent profession. In this book I will use case records to tell an admittedly untidy story but perhaps one that rescues the rich texture, drama, and complexity that characterized the battles to professionalize casework in the early twentieth century and points to enduring issues that deserve the attention of contemporary educators and social workers.

1

"I'll Be Watching You": The Advent of the Case Record

Every breath you take
Every move you make
Every bond you break
Every move you make
Every step you take
I'll be watching you

∾The Police (1983)

This is the day of organization; the tramps, beggars, and criminals are organized; they have signs, gripes, passwords, and even newspapers. It is time for organized charity.

∾Osborne (1904)

So in philanthropy we have come more and more to the scientific method of procedure. Charity organization societies have led the way to this by the emphasis they have placed upon making and studying the case record.

∾Taylor (1912)

Case records played a significant role in social work knowledge-building and professionalization, beginning with the charity organization society (COS) movement that arose during the 1870s. Indeed, the movement still continues to influence conceptions of professional social work. Tied to socioeconomic upheavals that followed the Civil War and the depression of 1873–77, the scientific charity organization movement and its network of professional problem-solvers responded to a multifarious array of social anxieties. Large-scale industrialization, massive immigration, and migration from rural to urban places were among the forces reshaping social arrangements in the United States. Cities had begun to dominate the nation's political, social, and economic life. Urban growth, increasing numbers of the poor, proliferating labor strikes, concerns about venereal disease and tuberculosis, and the specter of widespread class conflict and gender disorder all generated anxiety in an increasingly anxious American middle class (Boyer 1978;

Wenocur and Reisch 1989). These fears were consolidated around a conviction that cities were the source of pathology, "Sodoms and Gomorrahs of sexual excess and sybaritic indulgence, Babels of conflicting languages, religions, and customs, chaotic, ungovernable" (Smith-Rosenberg 1986, p. 172). The great cities "epitomized the foreign, the unknown, and the dangerous."

New sensibilities about the menace of urban pathology, the poor as its virulent vortex, and heightened perceptions of urgency about the containment of disorder fueled the efforts of late-nineteenth-century reformers. Alarms about the iniquitous and duplicitous nature of the poor were heard more frequently than characterizations of them as virtuous and pious.[1] The poor were increasingly perceived throughout the nineteenth century as the specific locus of threat and pollution because they "never did anything. They did not converse, or cook, or do laundry, or discipline their children; mostly they just peered out from their 'fever nests,' an exhausted and depleted species. Crowded together, the pathologies of the 'pariah inhabitation' fed on each other. The festering cancer threatened to contaminate the whole body social" (Stansell 1987, p. 201).

Armed with powers of *parens patriae,* the culmination of a multitude of trepidations about the perversion and unruliness of the poor, a middle-class version of proper domesticity became the preferred solution to a wide range of plagues infecting the urban social space. According to middle-class reformers, a middle-class domestic space—and a properly virtuous female within it—were crucial for healing a wide variety of social and economic ills. Reformers hoped that poor and immigrant women in particular would approximate an idealized model of the middle-class household by sheltering themselves from the harmful influences that lay in waiting just beyond the confines of the home. It was women's special duty to restrain inner pathological desires, to ensure that their husbands stayed sober and thrifty, and to safeguard their children by keeping them off the streets and comfortably ensconced at home. At the same time that middle-class women reformers urged domestic responsibilities upon poor women, however, they also used rhetorics of special morality to increase freedom of movement outside their own homes.

This belief that women possessed unique moral virtues sustained by the sheltered domestic sphere they occupied, an ideology Lori Ginzberg calls "benevolent femininity," infused antebellum Protestant descriptions of society and prescriptions for progress. The widespread conviction that women have unique responsibilities and natural abilities for disseminating virtue and morality had also carried the expectation that women's influence should, like the "dew of heaven" (Ginzberg 1990, p. 35), act in divine ways. That mandate had permeated a broad spectrum of antebellum reform movements, including the New York Female Moral Reform Society and numerous local industrial schools and rescue homes for the wayward and widowed throughout the country. The uniqueness of being female, and the benevolent work such uniqueness legitimated, led to beliefs that gender differences predominated over other distinctions and that the ultimate fulfillment of women's mission would dissolve class boundaries, at least among virtuous women.[2]

Ginzberg, among others, argues that postbellum reform organizations, although not fitting into a single category, were clearly distinguishable from their predecessors in terms of shifting discourses of class, gender, and morality. The scientific charity organization movement in particular played a pivotal role in this postbellum shift by significantly reshaping and enlarging the field of charity work. In moving away from religiously based reform to a scientific model of neutered and trained expertise, the charity organization society movement helped unravel longstanding assumptions of female moral authority. Ginzberg notes that reform organizations such as charity organization societies helped usher in new sensibilities that emphasized the similarity, not moral superiority, of women to men. They also perpetuated notions that class position was a moral condition and that the middle class was synonymous with virtue. Questions about gender sameness and differences plagued early social workers, however, and longstanding assumptions about gender-appropriate behaviors in the home and in the profession coexisted with emergent notions of neutered benevolence.

Charity organization reformers asserted secular, scientific, and class-based claims to authority, thus repudiating, at least in part, notions of women's moral authority. Social science expertise, business efficiency, and systematic techniques for fact-finding and prolonged character study were increasingly pursued within the discourses and practices of scientific charity (Lubove 1973). Professional charity organizations vigorously sought to discredit traditional religious approaches and benevolent femininity as sentimental, promiscuous, and indiscriminate and to reshape them as a domain of trained experts. S. Humphreys Gurteen, a member of the clergy, founded the first charity organization society in Buffalo in 1877 and argued that the "redemption of the poor would never be achieved by the pulpit or platform oratory," but must come in part from the "business and professional men" of the community (Boyer 1978, pp. 148–49).

Legitimized by scientific ideologies and disciplinary techniques, new views of charity and the depravity of the poor thus gained ascendancy over older worldviews of benevolence anchored in religious understandings and romantic ideals.[3] Charity organization societies played an integral role in this shift and were thus integral components of the rising tide of disciplinary professionalism in the United States. As part of the tide, the widening reach of empirical science produced new impulses toward narrative realism. Realism was a "product of the sense that past and present had become 'discontinuous,' that the inherited cultural traditions no longer applied to current reality, so reality must be sought in what was 'existing, comprehensible, visible, palpable; the scrupulous imitation of nature'" (Ross 1991, p. 58). A turn to the presumably transparent realism of hard facts and empirical science promised reassurance in a world where older certainties, especially religious understandings, were seemingly in shreds. Naturalistic approaches such as Darwinism, eugenics, and the method of taxonomy were increasingly used in the service of reestablishing order. Such impulses were also registered in social work as fact-gathering, classification, microscopic inspection, bureaucratic consolidation, and exhaustive documentation. Archiving the lives of the poor and deviant became a hallmark of the movement's practice.

Religiously based reform activity did not completely disappear in the postbellum period, nor was charity organization the only game in town. Settlement house workers, missionaries, political reformers, and others vied for attention and support. The rhetoric and practices of scientific charity, however, remapped the organization and practice of benevolence. Not only did the charity organization movement significantly change the discursive and institutional practices of benevolence, but it also profoundly reshaped social relationships among charity workers, donors, and recipients with in ways still felt: the notions of waste, duplication, and fraud; the division of the poor into such binary categories as "worthy/unworthy"; and individualistic and characterological explanations of poverty.[4] More than any other legacy to current practice, the case record remains an enduring memorial to the scientific charity movement.

The Scientific Charity Credo

> It is for Charity Organization to strike the note of alarm as the storm-clouds of pauperism and crime gather on the distant horizon of the apparently calm sea of a self-contentment born of wealth, success, and selfishness.
>
> ∾Holt (1891)

Advocates of the charity organization society movement attacked traditional practices of charity and almsgiving as being sentimental and indiscriminate. They were seen not only to multiply the numbers of the poor but also to cause poverty (fig. 1). A display advertisement for the Minneapolis Community Fund, for example, succinctly concluded that the operation of old charity was indiscriminate, "like watering a garden to kill the weeds" (Stillman 1927, p. 189). Soup lines, bread lines, holiday dinners, and direct handouts were defined by Lexington, Kentucky, advocates of the movement as "small change charity," outmoded techniques likely to produce chronic pauperism, weaken the character and moral fiber of the poor and multiply their numbers, and in general create community chaos rather than solve the problem of poverty (Tice 1992).

To solve the problem of poverty, character flaws and moral illnesses of the poor had to be weeded out and replaced with virtue, industry, and thrift. Hostility to almsgiving was based on the belief that character defects and the degenerate impulses of the poor caused poverty. Although Amos Warner, a prominent spokesperson for charity organizations, acknowledged some social causes of degeneration, he argued that the organizations should not be diverted by giving attention to "those changes in industry which have displaced large numbers of individu-

WHICH IS BETTER?

THIS OR THIS

HELPING THE POOR HELPING THE POOR

IN   OUT OF

THEIR POVERTY   THEIR POVERTY

Figure 1. "Which Is Better?" 1915. Scientific charity condemned indiscriminate almsgiving. Associated Charities of Lexington and Fayette County, *The Vanguard* (report of fourteenth year)

als" or to "the undue power of class over class" (1922, p. 113). These sociological problems were of secondary importance to the primary problems of character and morality. To illustrate his point, Warner asked readers of his classic text *American Charities* to imagine a second Robinson Crusoe stranded on the same desert island, facing material conditions identical to those the fictional Crusoe faced: "Suppose he spent his time distilling some kind of liquor, and subsequently got drunk; suppose he allowed his mind to wander in dreamy and enervating revery upon debasing subjects; suppose that in consequence of these habits he neglected his work, did not plant his crop at the right time, and failed to catch fish when they were plentiful" (1922, p. 39).

Alexander Johnson, associated with charity organization societies in both Cincinnati and Chicago and secretary of the National Conference of Charities and Correction, likewise described charity work as the "science of weak beings." For all who come under the purview of social work, Johnson argued, it is "weakness not strength that brings them . . . which makes them objects of our 'correction'" (1923, p. 130).[5]

An emphasis on cross-class professional relationships and friendships became a predominant and distinguishing part of the practice of casework. The key player was to be the "friendly visitor," a person who would impart the virtues of middle-class sensibilities and life-styles to clients who otherwise were "weak beings." Under the motto "not alms, but a friend," first adopted by the Boston Charity Organization Society, the contributions of friendly visitors were to impart "knowledge, courage and cheer—knowledge how better to run a house . . . courage and cheer to face the numberless complications of every life" (Watson 1922, p. 151). As the New York Charity Organization Society warned, "If we do not furnish the poor with elevating influences, they will rule us by degrading ones" (Fifth Annual Report, Jan. 1, 1887, p. 38, quoted in Lubove 1973, p. 5). Mary Richmond argued that "social contact with all sorts and conditions of men" was essential to civilization, and she urged social workers to "get back into genuine relations with people of smaller incomes" (1907, p. 309). By the early 1890s, more than four thousand visitors, many of them unpaid, sought to establish "genuine" friendships in slums across the country, causing Charles Kellogg to hope that an army of such visitors would, with time, wash through the slums "like a tidal wave . . . flooding every part" with "sweetness and order and light" (Boyer 1978, p. 151).[6] By the middle of the next decade, according to Wenocur and Reisch (1989), the difficulty of finding sufficient volunteers, and the perceived need for specialized expertise, led to the preponderance of paid workers over unpaid visitors.

From the standpoint of the charity organization movement, charity work—despite its friendly aspect—had to be redefined as a scientific, businesslike practice that would organize the philanthropic resources of a community efficiently, provide centralized administration and documentation of relief cases, and investigate every case to weed out unworthy applicants for relief. The language of scientific rationality and efficiency, along with engineering metaphors, became common in charity organization reports. A typical one from Lexington, Kentucky, in 1915, described "old charity" as "an engine with no destination, no engineer, no rail to run on, no brakes, too much steam. It needs systemizing, harmonizing, and modernizing. Old relief was based on the story the person could tell. The new is based on discovered and real need" (Associated Charities of Lexington and Fayette County 1915, p. 7).

A passion for case-recording and social investigation, the litmus tests for scientifically assessed worthiness, characterized the charity organization society movement's practice of benevolence, as social workers rallied under the slogan of "charitable efficiency." The Associated Charities of Boston defined their mission as being able

> to aid every private person. To give alms only to the worthy poor, or rather to give with knowledge. To lessen the labors of the relieving agencies, by giving to each the knowledge of the others. To stop imposture so that the occupation of living on relief may cease. Registration notifies every lazy tramp to quit Boston or go to work. The main object is to make sure relief is adapted to real needs. This will lessen relief for the unworthy. But for the really worthy and most suffering poor it should make relief more full and prompt and tender. (First Annual Report [1879], quoted in Gordon 1988, p. 325)

George Holt boasted that the relationship of a charity organization to a community was "plainly one of knowledge—knowledge of the causes that effect ruin and disaster to society" (1891, p. 121). Edward Devine, secretary of the New York Charity Organization Society, compared the methods of charity organization to the "broad sunlight of knowledge" and concluded that to "give without knowledge is not only unwise: it is wicked" (1901, p. 323).

Charity organizations sought not only to manage the poor but also to reduce sentimental and spontaneous acts of individual giving. The Rev. H. L. Wayland, founder of the New Haven, Connecticut, Charity Organization Society, argued that "we must reform those mild, well-meaning, tender hearted, sweet voiced criminals who indulge in indiscriminate charity" (Bremner 1956b, p. 170). From this perspective, charity was to be disentangled from religion and reorganized as a scientific business endeavor in the hands of unsentimental experts.

To accomplish those goals, charity organization societies introduced a vast new array of surveillance practices, including investigation, registration, observation, and classification. As early as 1893, Charles Kellogg, secretary of the Philadelphia Society for Organizing Charity, had noted that the procedures of registration and investigation "form a sieve that separates with a practical justice, cases entitled by misfortunes to material aid from those who would pervert such aid to the prolongation of self-ruinous habits" (p. 73).

Members of charity organizations designated new areas of pathology as well as new ways of ordering, arranging, and knowing people. Keeping systematic case records was essential so that "problems may be brought down in human terms . . . not in sweeping generalizations but in piled-up actualities" (Paul Kellog, quoted in Young 1939, p. 22). Amassing facts and "giving with knowledge" thus became central components of a charity organization's project of reorganizing benevolent efforts. According to a conference of the Associated Charities of Boston in 1886, the quest for facts was fueled by the belief that "two-thirds of the error in charity work arise from misinformation or lack of information. In thorough preliminary investigation, followed by sympathetic searching into the facts on the visitors' part, lies our chief strength as a practical body of scientific workers" (Lubove 1973, p. 20).

This new approach to fact-gathering demanded that charity be reconstituted as casework and carried out in a highly individualized, case-by-case manner (fig. 2). Such individualized investigation and documentation constituted an instance of what Foucault conceptualizes as the modern disciplinary "gaze," a technique of power or knowledge that creates new forms of controlling visibility (fig. 3). As a form of power or knowledge, the gaze is more deeply penetrating than earlier forms of power because it "leaves no zone of shade" (Foucault 1979, p. 177). Unidirectional and asymmetrical, the gaze requires a detailed observation of individuals, their habits and histories, and the redefinition of persons as cases, objects, sights,

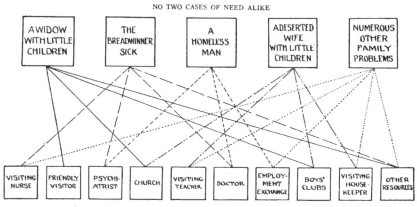

Figure 2. "No Two Cases of Need Alike," 1922. The casework advocated by charity organization society movement leaders called for individualized investigation and treatment. Watson (1922, p. 141)

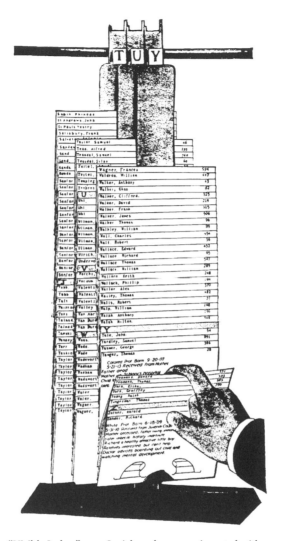

Figure 3. "Visible Index," 1915. Social workers experimented with a variety of techniques to increase the visibility of their clients and heighten their own ever-more-deeply penetrating professional gaze. Ralph (1915, p. 140)

and appearances—not subjects in a dialogical relationship—whereby they are controlled and arranged. For Foucault, a case is mute: "He is seen, but does not see, he is the object of information, never a subject in communication" (1979, p. 201).

In an address to the National Conference of Charities and Correction in 1888, H. L. Wayland celebrated the protracted gaze the charity organization society movement had fixed upon the poor: "Where the Old Charity gave a shilling and lost sight of them [the poor], the New follows them, and sees where they sleep and eat, are born and die" (Watson 1922, p. 277). J. T. Mastin, general secretary of the State Board of Charity and Corrections in Virginia, echoed these sentiments when he hailed the following approach: "Seek to know them, to get a record of their lives, and of their family histories, file these for future reference, and especially study them in order to become informed as to hereditary evil tendencies that should be guarded against" (1912, p. 49). Comprehensive investigation and case history documentation would allow charity workers to discern inherited predispositions for destructive family patterns.

The efficiency of the prolonged gaze, documentary accumulation, and investigative knowledge were routinely and uncritically celebrated by members of charity organizations.[7] This emphasis on investigation, however, provoked strong, ongoing censure from other members of the charity and reform enterprise.[8] For example, Jane Addams of Hull-House spoke of the "sentimental" and "unscientific" qualms raised when many "see the delay and caution with which relief is given, these do not appear as conscientious scruples, but the cold and calculating action of selfish man" (Lubove 1973, p. 10). But Mary Richmond warned that workers must not be "swept away by enthusiastic advocates of social reform from that safe middle ground which recognizes that character is at the very center" of social disorganization and demoralization (quoted in Lubove 1973, pp. 9–11). She also asserted that, in fact, the poor were not left to starve, because "trained" workers were "promptly" ferreting out the complexities of the situation. Nothing, she added, "hurts a trained worker more than thoughtless charity" (1901, p. 328). Social workers trained in the investigative techniques of the movement and attentive to problems of character were perceived as the remedy to the perceived chaos of the charitable dominion. Furthermore, reorganizing charity work as the province of trained workers would help promote its professionalization.

The movement's ardor for comprehensive case knowledge, protracted fact-finding, and extensive paper trails dovetailed with the nineteenth-century lust for knowledge of the other. Stansell (1987), Meyerowitz (1991), Ross (1993), Nord (1987), and Walkowitz (1992) assert that throughout the nineteenth century there existed longstanding traditions of exploration, spectatorship, and interpretation of the urban badlands and those who lived there. These traditions provided important precursors for charity organization society movement approaches and their accounts of the poor and deviant. Slum exploration, a genre of popular fiction, journalism, and scholarly studies, employed the tropes of degeneration, contagion, and gender disorder while chronicling the brave excursions of the middle class into vile and perilous regions of the city. The poor were caricatured in a variety of ways: as a primitive race apart from the national community, as frightening and calculating villains, as passive victims of sullied surroundings and predatory men, and as pathetic waifs and widows. Deborah Epstein Nord has observed (1987) that urban explorers developed a repertoire of interpretative images for the urban poor and made analogies between them and the primitive, swarthy, threatening people of other lands. Stallybrass and White argue that the repudiation of the "socially peripheral other" by the dominant "top" of society was paradoxically accompanied by the heightened symbolic importance of the other (1986, p. 5). This ambivalence resulted in two poles in reference to lowly others: "repugnance and fascination" (p. 5). As urban investigators distanced themselves from their subjects of study, they felt compelled to possess a comprehensive knowledge of the other by violating borders in what Stallybrass and White call a "poetics of transgression" (p. 202). The charity organization society movement was no exception.

Charity organization society reformers constructed a variety of binary social and spatial divisions to organize their interpretations of the slum and its inhabitants. They carried on conventional rhetorical traditions by employing and refining polarized images of good/bad, virtue/vice, darkness/light, center/periphery, worthy/unworthy, high/low, and primitive/civilized in case histories and newspaper reportage. John Van Dyke, for example, argued that there was a sharp division line and "violent contrasts" between the "Upper and the Nether" zones of the city. Not only did the Nether zone "reek and roar," but "the opposite poles of humanity are likewise represented" (1909, p. 241). It became possible to discern a "gap between the highest intelligence and social rank and the lowest animal existence."

Scientific charity also ushered in language for a variety of new classifications of people judged defective. Here, too, as in their use of binary contrasts and metaphors of business and engineering, the charity organization society movement approach both mirrored and elaborated the cultural expressions of its era. Beginning in the nineteenth century, the "obsession with deviation and control" lead to a proliferation of labels "that may have engendered vastly more kinds of people than the world had ever known" (Hacking 1986, p. 226). Classification created new ways for people to be and new ways of "making up people." As "new modes of description" come into being, "new possibilities for action come into being as a consequence" (p. 231). Carroll Smith-Rosenberg has also noted the emergent fascination with taxonomy that "transposed the amorphous qualities of the socially disorderly into specific forms of sexual deviance." Proliferating categories and cross-classifications of sexual deviance and otherness "fictively contained and controlled social disorder" (1986, pp. 267–68).

Movement leaders were similarly ingenious at enlarging the vocabulary of transgression. They authorized new types of ominous others and developed taxonomies for making up and arranging people. Mary Conyngton (1913), for example, was devoted to finding those persons categorized under the rubric of "false poor" and provided a detailed survey of popular ways to stage poverty, such as "crust throwing," "cripple appeals," and "begging letters." She then subdivided the broad categories of "tramps," "beggars," and "thieves" into such highly nuanced taxonomic arrangements as the "tomato can variety," the "yeggman," "tramp propers," and "tramp impostors." "Fallen women" and "wayward girls," however, provided the best sources for new categories of description, including various classifications under the rubrics of "feeblemindedness" and "mental inferiority," as well as such conduct and personality disorders as "constitutional psychopathic personalities," "constitutional psychopathic inferiors," "constitutional affective disorders," "semi-prostitutes," and "semi-delinquents."

The poor was not the only group to receive the prolonged gaze of benevolent experts. The charity organization society movement also championed new scientific methods for finding, documenting, and knowing those who were wayward, insane, vicious, feebleminded, and criminal. Investigations of ancestry and "constitution" were essential components of the ascendant scientific methodology for knowing the poor and all those treated as others. As reliance on heredity as a cause of otherness intensified, extensive investigation and documentation of family histories became customary.

Abundant literature flourished that was based on the sociological menace posed by poor constitutions, degenerate stocks, taints, and the various contagions believed to inhabit the "nether regions" of city slums. Boyer (1978) has noted the widespread use of "public health analogies" among those who belonged to charity organizations, including discourses on "moral infections, contagions, and plague spots" that constructed slums as dangerous labyrinths and the poor as a menacing, multiplying maelstrom threatening middle-class civilization and community. Leon Stern, for example, wrote the following description of the Bilder Clan, a socially menacing stock: "They present the peculiar problem of socially degenerating groups. . . . They, themselves, form a secret sort of community . . . a secret community spreading out its tentacles and thriving lustily after its own fashion. To dig into the records of their social life is to dig into an ulcer in the community that is spread and ramified. They are like weeds growing sturdily and waxing strong wherever their seed may fall" (1922, p. 188).

Many alarmist studies of hereditary degeneracy such as that posed by the Bilder Clan were published throughout the late nineteenth and early twentieth centuries. Richard Dugdale's *The Jukes: A Study in Crime, Pauperism, Disease, and Heredity* (1875) was a popular, sordid saga of murders, illegitimacy, beggary, theft, pauperization, and prostitution that surrounded an impoverished family in upstate New York. By Dugdale's account, the Jukes reproduced more than 1,200 individuals, either by descent or marriage, including seven murderers, 130 criminals, 310 paupers, 440 "defectives," and countless prostitutes. Dugdale noted that when all such pauperism, harlotry, and crime was considered, the Jukes had cost the community more than a million and quarter dollars. Arthur Estabrook updated their appalling and costly legacy in a follow-up study in 1915.

Tales of degenerate stocks such as the Jukes confirmed the importance of the charity organization society practice of case documentation and registration, which allowed social workers to monitor chronic problems and individuals and recognize patterns. Oscar McCulloch's *The Tribe of Ishmael* (1888), for example, grew out of a charity organization worker's recognition that one particular family was recurrent in his cases. Additional studies of degenerate stocks were published, including Goddard's *The Kallikak Family* and Estabrook and Davenport's *The Nam Family*. Fears of poor ancestry and "primitive types" would appear in many later accounts as well.[9] The investigation of ancestry and constitution thus became a canonical part of both charity organization societies and their numerous progeny. The Boston Children's Aid Society (BCAS), for example, recommended that eugenic charts be made for each of its cases because "the strains and taints of families when plotted out in such a way stand out strikingly" (Lawton and Murphy 1915, p. 168).

A fear of poor genetic stocks governs much of the writing of charity organization workers, and their accounts are also filled with the looming perception that gender trouble was brewing. James Tufts, for example, observed that "industrialization, conditions of city life, the progress of higher education, and a general movement towards the emancipation of women have combined so as to change both the controlling conditions of human life and the mental attitudes and temper of men, women, and children" (1914, p. 25). A decreasing birth-rate among the middle class, increased numbers of women working outside their homes, shifting patterns of recreation and sociability, and the prevalence of "social diseases" all intensified anxieties about the conduct of women of all classes (D'Emilio and Freedman 1988; Meyerowitz 1991; Pascoe 1990; Peiss 1986; Smith-Rosenberg 1986; Stansell 1987; Walkowitz 1992). Traditional narratives about the snares and pitfalls that could befall innocent women—sullied environments and brutal men, for example—were enlarged to include new sensibilities about brazen, predatory women and unfit mothers who threatened the moral life of American communities.

Feeblemindedness, inebriety, love of pleasure, and frivolity were among the enlarged constellation of characteristics that women who threatened society displayed. Maude E. Miner warned (1915, p. 261) that she found "pleasure-craving girls whose love of amusement had found outlet only in dangerous dance-halls and pleasure halls . . . young girls who labored long at grinding, monotonous, mechanical work for a low wage whose utter fatigue lessened their power to resist temptation." "Pleasure-craving" and "fatigued girls" not only produced accelerating consternation among middle-class social workers but also spawned generational clashes within working-class and immigrant communities. The shifting patterns of pleasure and work experienced by their daughters propelled many working-class parents to turn to reform agencies for help in managing them. Such requests refutes a simple social control thesis that presents only "Dickensian images of the heartless state hauling off weeping protesting children from their humble, helpless parents" (Brenzel 1980, p. 206).[10]

In tune with the preoccupations of the era, charity organization society workers and their progeny became preoccupied with women's sexual morality and misconduct. They revised the long tradition of efforts to rescue and protect indigent and immigrant women that had directed much of the work done in evangelical maternity homes and protective residences for working women. Instead, they focused upon saving society from "morally tainted" women and girls thought to be capable of "infecting its members with a moral evil more hideous than physical disease" (Francis 1906, p. 142). Josephine Shaw Lowell, founder of the New York Charity Organization Society, wrote that "one of the most dangerous causes of crime, pauperism, and insanity is the unrestricted liberty allowed vagrant and degraded women" (quoted in Abramovitz 1989, p. 153). Lowell saw women as particularly dangerous sources of physical contagion and moral decay because they were the "visible links in the direful chain of hereditary, pauperism, and disease." George Bliss also warned that pre-pubescent girls, especially "moron girls," constituted a particularly portentous menace because they "almost certainly [became] the mothers of defectives, and, given a chance, [were] capable of founding famil[ies] like the Jukes" (1916, p. 265). Likewise, Vida Francis concluded that "the cost to the state of even one bad girl in her far-reaching influence for social evil is incalculable" (1906, p. 145).

Women and girls came to occupy starring roles as the primary objects of investigation, classification, and documentation by the charity organization society movement and their casework descendants. A preoccupation with controlling the menace of what was called "feeblemindedness" was evident in the campaign of the Boston Children's Aid Society to expand institutions for the containment of feebleminded girls who "spelled horror and disaster to good families. . . . They have broken up certain homes by successfully tempting men into immoral sex relations and they have falsely charged innocent men . . . and they become mothers of illegitimate children whom they do not love and grossly neglect" (1914, pp. 20–21). Consequently, the female capacity for social evil resulted in more severe punishment for women and girls than for men, as reflected in the greater frequency and length of institutionalization for females than for their male counterparts (Hobson 1987; Pleck 1987; Schlossman and Wallach 1978; Schnieder 1980).

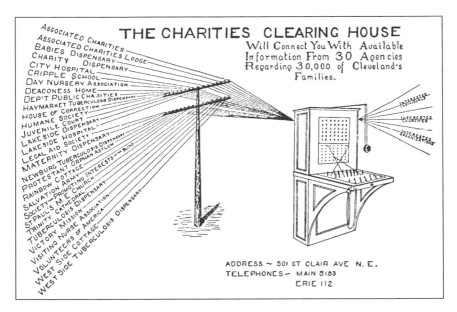

THE CHARITIES CLEARING HOUSE

Will Connect You With Available Information From 30 Agencies Regarding 30,000 of Cleveland's Families.

Associated Charities
Associated Charities Lodge
Babies Dispensary
Charity Dispensary
City Hospital
Cripple School
Day Nursery Association
Deaconess Home
Dep't Public Charities
Haymarket Tuberculosis Dispensary
House of Correction
Humane Society
Juvenile Court
Lakeside Dispensary
Lakeside Hospital
Legal Aid Society
Maternity Dispensary
Newburg Tuberculosis Dispensary
Protestant Orphan Asylum
Rainbow Cottage
Salvation Army—Promoting Interests of the Blind
Society—M.E. Church
St. Paul's Cathedral
Trinity Cathedral
Tuberculosis Dispensary
Victory Mission
Visiting Nurse Association
Volunteers of America
West Side Cottage
West Side Tuberculosis Dispensary

INTERESTED INDIVIDUALS
INTERESTED CLUBS
INTERESTED ORGANIZATIONS

ADDRESS ~ 501 ST CLAIR AVE N. E.
TELEPHONES ~ MAIN 5183
ERIE 112

Figure 4. "The Charities Clearing House," 1922. The confidential exchange, a tool for the systemic exchange of case information among agencies, played a significant role in the rationalization of charity. Watson (1922, p. 141)

The Confidential Exchange

Confidential exchanges, central registration bureaus for interagency information-sharing, were indispensable in the new practice methodology and a force that helped consolidate the institutionalization of case-recording (fig. 4). Dubbed by Mary Richmond as "joint traffic agreements" among agencies, exchanges were clearinghouses for all "factual" records on individual cases. They were touted as efficient means by which to conquer the chaos that had earlier characterized the charity field through the systematic exchange of case information and histories among cooperating agencies.

Exchanges were seen as a vital source of information for social workers, who were urged to consult an exchange even before meeting with clients. According to Laura Woodberry (1924), secretary of the Boston Exchange, they were good "for the primary purpose of checking fraud and duplication" as well as "to coordinate the service units through their case work" (p. 51). Eugene Lies, superintendent of the United Charities of Chicago, advocated the exchange concept as a "potent preventer of waste" (1914, p. 67). Exchanges were perceived as being good for clients because they made grilling to ascertain personal data unnecessary. Exchanges also allowed social workers to avoid offering conflicting advice that would evoke a "bewildered and often dazed condition of the mind" of a client (Watson 1922, p. 126).

By the mid-1890s the New York Charity Organization Society held case files on 170,000 individuals. Chicago, the nation's largest registration bureau, had 555,000 family names recorded in its files. Although dubbed "confidential," such case material was circulated widely, not only to charitable agencies and interested organizations but also to prospective employers, landlords, banks, and the police, as well as to cooperating member charitable agencies and interested individuals. Some exchanges published monthly confidential bulletins similar to the commercial ratings of worthy and unworthy credit applicants published by commercial credit-rating agencies.

In 1916 the Boston Children's Aid Society suggested a "black list" and registry for alcoholics (Annual Report 1916), and soon afterward Alexander Johnson organized a national network of charity organization society workers to keep track of traveling mendicants through the printing of a weekly confidential listing. Johnson boasted that such mendicants "found themselves confronted by advance knowledge of themselves. To be told the history of their lives and schemes for years past, and given twenty-four hours to leave town or be arrested was very disquieting" (1923, p. 289). In the 1930s, Pauline Young (1935, p. 176) likened case records and exchanges to banks. She urged social workers when encountering "the chiseler," the 1930s' version of the unworthy pauper, "to inform the individual that relief agencies are operated to some extent like banks and corporations and the records kept indicate when he has forfeited his credit."

The confidential exchange also became a central element of what Alan Sekula has characterized as the "grandiose clerical mentality" (1986, p. 56) that emerged during the late nineteenth century. The rise of case documentation, constituting dossiers, and clearinghouses of client information were essential devices for arranging the disorderly and dangerous others within administrative power relations. As a member of one charity organization put it, "A clearinghouse could help reestablish orderly and effective relations among the city's various elements" (Boyer 1978, p. 150). Holt likened exchanges to an "index to a vast ledger of accounts . . . a guide to the lost traveller at the fork of the road or a compass to a storm-tossed mariner," the result of "accumulated experiences of lives ill or well spent" (1891, pp. 120–21). Boyer notes that "the sheer mass of dossiers offered deceptively tangible assurance that the complex and disturbing human reality [social workers] had documented had somehow been subdued and rendered manageable" (p. 150).[11]

By 1919, when the National Association of Social Service Exchanges was formed, the confidential exchange had become a vital professional compass. Amelia Sears of the United Charities of Chicago warned that "unless social workers are to continue flying around in futile motion . . . they must consult the confidential exchange for it contains the bibliography in case work analogous to that in the field of science" (1921, p. 251). Woodberry similarly applauded the "composite efficiency" that confidential exchanges produced and warned of the chaos that would befall social workers who neglected the exchange: "It cannot be when the root is neglected that what should spring from it will be well ordered" (1924, p. 51). If nothing else, the exchange gave the semblance of containing disorder.

The Spread of the Charity Organization Society Movement

By 1890 charity organization societies had been established in more than a hundred cities throughout the United States. Wenocur and Reisch (1989) and Lubove (1973) argue that a variety of forces resulted in the prominence of the movement in charitable endeavors. The movement's focus was in accord with the ideological status quo that extolled the conjunction of individual responsibility and administrative organization as the panacea for the poor. Its standardized and "unified methods of practice," including investigation, record-keeping, and registration, also helped ensure that it eventually surpassed other, more reform-oriented approaches. The concept of social settlements, for example, lacked a "distinct, unique service commodity or a distinctive organizational form" (Wenocur and Reisch 1989, p. 42). Ironically, the actual—and perceived—challenges of settlements to the established order of things, as well as settlement work's more egalitarian, less expert-based notions of benevolent relationships, helped catapult the charity organization society movement into the professional limelight. Although settlement rhetoric and practice never disappeared, the dance of professionalization was increasingly choreographed by the movement.

Educational institutions, foundations, and professional associations played roles in advancing the movement's approach by propagating its discourses and techniques. Journals such as *Charities Review, Lend-a-Hand,* and *Charities Record* as well as the National Conference of Charities and Correction also provided prominent forums. By the end of the 1890s the Associated Charities of Boston had adopted a plan whereby it paid people to learn the techniques of charity organization. In 1898 the New York Charity Organization Society organized a training class, which became the New York School of Philanthropy in 1904. Ensuing decades brought a web of schools of social work, a majority of which braided their curriculum and field experiences with movement techniques, thus ensuring that new recruits to reform were properly schooled (Lubove 1973).[12] In 1905 the New York Charity Organization Society established a field department to help spread the principles and methods of the movement nationally, the art of case-recording in particular. The field department also instituted a series of forwarding centers through which community agencies that lacked charity organization societies might secure investigative evidence for decision making and case documentation.

Within this context, the Russell Sage Foundation was essential in promoting the professionalization of charity and reform by awarding nearly $5.8 million in grants between 1907 and 1931. The charity organization society movement was the favored child of the reform family, and almost a third of the $1.8 million in grant money the Russell Sage Foundation allocated from 1907 to 1917 was given to the New York Charity Organization Society (Wenocur and Reisch 1989, p. 57). In 1909 the foundation established a charity organization department primarily devoted to extending the methods of the movement nationally through publications and field agents. Also in 1909, the New York Charity Organization Society National Publications Committee was reorganized, and *The Survey* magazine was launched with backing from Russell Sage to an initial readership of about ten thousand (Leiby 1978).

Charity organization, of course, was not the only model for social reform during these early years of social work experimentation. A variety of benevolent movements existed alongside scientific charity organization, including the settlement house movement. Although settlements varied widely in their activities, a unifying requirement of settlement work was co-residence in poor neighborhoods. Bertha Capen Reynolds (1963, p. 27) argued that the requirement profoundly distinguished settlement house work from charity organization "visiting." Observing that members of charity organizations saw "people only when they are in trouble and at their worst," Reynolds argued that settlement workers "live with them in their good and bad times and see them at their best. It makes our attitudes different."[13] Significantly, the Russell Sage Foundation ignored the settlement house movement, choosing instead to support scientific charity organizations almost exclusively, and settlements found no other comparable foundations upon which to draw for support (Wenocur and Reisch 1989).

The Russell Sage Foundation also supported efforts to present the message of charity organization to the general public. As part of a social survey and exhibit in Springfield, Illinois, for example, in 1915 the foundation funded and published a three-act play entitled *A Bundle or a Boost?* (fig. 5). The performance was designed as a visualization of how to give advice over material aid, a preferred charity organization society movement practice. The cast included the villainous "Father Springfield," whose primary task was to hand out bundles of provisions. In contrast, "Mr. Better Way," the charity organization hero, had no bundles to distribute but "more to give," so ultimately the poor would receive "help so that they won't need relief." The play ended with Mr. Better Way surrounded by a cheerful throng of deserving poor who had been referred to the society by a teacher and truant officer.

THE PLAYHOUSE OF AN EXHIBITION

Two or three times during each afternoon and evening session of the Springfield Survey Exhibition a twenty or thirty minute play on one of the survey topics was presented in the playhouse. This was an attractive pavilion facing the entrance to the hall. (See diagram on page 98c.) Frequently a three to five minutes' introductory talk or "interpretation" helped to prepare the audience for the lesson of the little play.

The scene here is taken from "A Bundle or a Boost," a short play dealing with almsgiving versus constructive charitable work.

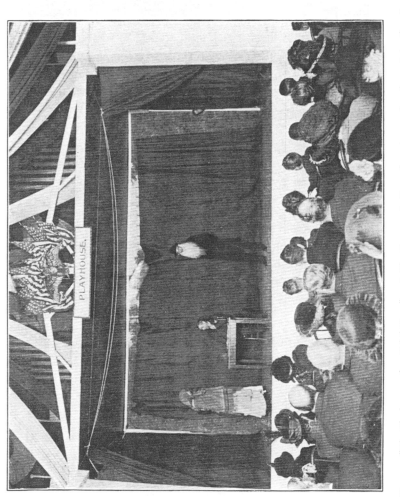

Figure 5. "The Playhouse of an Exhibition," 1918. Charity organization advocates employed a variety of methods to publicize their preferred approaches to poverty, including plays such as *A Bundle or a Boost*, which was given at the Springfield Survey Exhibition. Routzahn and Routzahn (1918, p. 86a)

In 1911 the National Association of Societies for Organizing Charities (later re-named the American Association for Organizing Family Social Work) was estab-lished, with a membership of 142 societies. Membership was contingent upon the employment of a full-time paid agent, the maintenance of individual case records, and an agreement to answer inquiries from, and make investigations for, associ-ated charities in other cities (Watson 1922, p. 346). By 1919 the association had in-creased its membership to 180, and by 1925 it claimed 220 agencies and had launched a national magazine, *The Family.*

Gradually, the techniques of the charity organization society movement prevailed in a variety of social work settings and profoundly shaped the fortunes of numer-ous benevolent organizations. Under the banner of standardization, efficiency, and cooperation, charity organization societies were given power in many municipali-ties to oversee benevolent work of all types, thereby disciplining a variety of alter-native approaches, including religious and mutual aid societies (Stewart 1916; Strong 1910). In 1917, for example, a charities survey conducted by the American Associa-tion for Organizing Charity in Lexington, Kentucky, to guide the allocations of public funds recommended no funding for the City Missionary Society. Funding was also denied to the Colored Orphans Home, a mutual aid program managed by a board composed of African American women. One of the reasons given for doing so was the fact that their records were perceived to be faulty.[14] Charity organization societ-ies in Kansas City and Milwaukee likewise refused to endorse the evangelical rescue work of the Salvation Army. In Los Angeles the Municipal Charities Commission also refused to endorse the Salvation Army, stating that the Army's program did not attain a "reasonable standard of efficiency." Subsequently, four Army employees were placed under arrest in Los Angeles for operating without a permit from the com-mission, the *Salvation Army War Cry* reported on October 10, 1914.[15]

Charity Organization and Prevention

Throughout the late nineteenth and early twentieth centuries the charity organi-zation society movement underwent a variety of face-lifts. Changing social cli-mates, massive economic dislocations, and criticisms of the unfeeling red tape and third-degree investigative practices of organized charity propelled the movement to enlarge and modify its organizing project.[16] Although neither forsaking con-cerns of character or heredity nor its techniques of investigation and documen-tation, the movement added environmental and preventive concerns, making for a paradoxical vocabulary and an ambiguous mix of practices.

As the movement matured, it muted its emphasis of the terms *deserving* and *worthy* and made a rhetorical shift toward a vocabulary that embraced the social causes of poverty and championed prevention (Watson 1922). James Edward Hagerty (1931, p. 67) thus noted that a new metaphor for charity work had begun to be discussed at social work conferences. Social workers evoked images of "old charity" as an ambulance at the foot of the cliff, designed to care for those who had fallen over. New "preventive charity," by contrast, did not build preventive fences, but rather educated people to build fences for themselves "at the top of all cliffs wherever danger awaits the unwary."

Since the 1890s, the movement had more frequently branched out and taken on such social issues as child labor, tuberculosis, and housing reform. In 1919 the American Association for Organizing Charity enlarged its focus to include not just "destitute families but disorganized families" as well (Watson 1922).[17] The turn toward prevention, Watson proudly observed (p. 333), was a "progressive evolution" that followed the lead of more established professions, including medicine. Significantly, he credited the movement's pioneering use of case records as an important catalyst in the evolution: "It has been the charity organization societies with their *records of flesh and blood* supplying abundant illustrations with which to reinforce cold arguments in behalf of measures of prevention that has brought about a social awakening in many communities" (p. 540, emphasis added).

The movement's emphasis on accumulating comprehensive knowledge through the case study of clients was augmented by the amassing of new forms of diagnostic evidence introduced by new specialties in medical and psychiatric social work. In addition, the publication of Mary Richmond's *Social Diagnosis* in 1917 helped introduce casework, a twentieth-century form of the movement's philosophy, as the fundamental component of social work practice. Social casework and diagnosis, a set of expert techniques for the collection, accumulation, and interpretation of evidence, were clearly successors to methods the movement had long cherished. They became the dominant framework for social work practice throughout the 1920s (Leighninger 1987; Lubove 1973; Wenocur and Reisch 1989).

Beginning in 1923, the Milford Conference, an annual gathering of casework leaders from diverse specialties, met to determine whether there was a methodology that unified disparate fields of social work practice. A final report in 1928 concluded that a generic casework did indeed exist across specialty areas and that declaration helped consolidate a universal technical focus for practice. Although the 1920s brought together many currents of social work practice under the rubric of generic "casework," doing so was by no means a placid process. Social workers wedded to social action, social policy concerns, and the orientations of social settlements continued to clamor for alternative forms of practice and reform, a shouting match that characterized the history of the discipline's professional development (Chambers 1963; Leighninger 1987).[18]

Case Records in Their Infancy: A Case Study

Fueled by charity organization societies, realistic description and systematic record-keeping became the flesh and blood of casework practice in the early decades of the twentieth century as these techniques spread to diverse social work and reform organizations, including child-placing, family welfare, child protection, child guidance, and psychiatric, school, and medical social work. By the 1920s, case record-keeping practices had ripened fully, and debates around the construction of case records became vociferous, both within social work itself and among its neighboring fields such as sociology and psychiatry.

Before the 1920s, case records had been meager, terse, and haphazard. Early styles of case record-keeping consisted predominantly of short, diarylike entries of interventions taken by social workers, along with their quick diagnoses of clients. Case records from the Lexington, Kentucky, Associated Charities, such as in the following example from 1911, are typical of the abrupt style and brief verdict of client worthiness: "W.P. and his wife reported sick. Called and found home if it can be called such in a state of extreme want, filth, and squalor—fruit boxes used for furniture—swarms of flies—a bed so dirty that you couldn't tell the print of the cloth—told them when they cleaned up help would be given. Called two days later and was refused admittance" (Madeline Breckinridge Papers, box 693). Deep descriptions of the clients' history and heredity were not a standard part of practice.

The record-keeping practices of the Massachusetts Society for the Prevention of Cruelty to Children (MSPCC) in 1901 were typical of the era. They consisted of a ledger-book entry of a client's name, residence, parents, children, and a few brief remarks. The latter tended to consist of quick one-liners: "is profane," "is shiftless," "below the mental standard," "is ignorant," or "girl has no shame at her situation and is lacking in moral sense." Descriptions of the social worker's activities were also vague and abbreviated, as, for example, "gave advice," "warned and advised him," or "wrote a warning."

The MSPCC's case records from this period tended to describe only one or two contacts with clients and were at most a page in length. "Officer reports mother lives with her mother who has a fair home," one reads. "Officer thinks the child is not properly cared for and mother is immoral. Will watch for evidence" (1901). Another case was described in only one entry: "Father is a colored laborer and mother is dead. The daughter is feebleminded. The house is filthy and only has two rooms. The bedding is filthy. Wrote to the Overseer of the Poor to get to investigate with a view to make a case of feeble-mindedness."

By 1906 the MSPCC had begun to develop a case file system and had introduced standardized coversheets that listed not only demographic information but also habits and referral sources. With the arrival of Carl C. Carstens, formerly of the

New York Charity Organization Society, as the new director of the MSPCC in 1907, the emphasis on record-keeping intensified. According to Carstens's stenographer Maggie Blake, "In Mr. Carstens' mind dwelt the fact that every child handled by the society should be a subject of a record" (Blake 1947, p. 14). Soon afterward, case narratives began to grow dramatically in length and detail. Coversheets provided more and more of the kinds of categorical information considered important for diagnosis and treatment, and summary paragraphs recounting clients' initial problems and social workers' sense of the resolution of such problems became standard.

The Boston Children's Aid Society also mandated a new policy in 1914: At the end of each calendar year, caseworkers were to add a summary of their work with each individual client to the client's case record. The records could then be "scanned for defects in our work with individuals just as an accountant scans for defects in the administration of funds" (Boston Children's Aid Society 1914, p. 14). The narrative section of the agency's records grew proportionally, often to several hundred typed pages. In accordance with the more highly "individualized" involvement and the in-depth investigation that the evolution of casework implied, the time caseworkers devoted to their cases and recording also expanded dramatically.[19] By 1912 the society asserted that one of the "essential steps to good work" lay in keeping full case records and boasted that "full records, clearly indexed are kept. Important decisions, observation, experiments with their success and failure are fully and faithfully recorded, making a complete and living history of each child, its surroundings, and influences brought to bear on it. A research worker is collating and comparing these experiences and making them available for instruction as to methods and for a study of causes and tendencies" (Boston Children's Aid Society 1912, p. 40). Case records thus became as much about social work practice and professional instruction as about clients.

Traditionally, protective societies such as the MSPCC were distinguished from their reform counterparts by the limited number of women on their staffs.[20] In 1908, however, Carstens added five stenographers to a total staff of seventeen. One of these stenographers, Maggie Blake, the author of an informative unpublished history of the MSPCC, noted that the "importation of us females into the office routine was primarily for the purposes of building up the record system" (Massachusetts Society for the Prevention of Cruelty to Children 1947, p. 51). The stenographers' "womanly flair for details" was viewed as necessary for clerical tasks formerly done, somewhat episodically, by male staff members (1947, p. 46).[21] By 1947 the MSPCC had enlarged its clerical staff to nearly fifty. The trend toward hiring stenographers and recorders was characteristic of many such reform organizations at the turn of the century. The Boston Children's Aid Society, for example, expanded from two stenographers in 1909 to five by 1916.[22]

By the 1920s, however, social work leaders argued that these early attempts at record-keeping were inadequate. For example, Ada Eliot Sheffield of the Boston Bureau of Illegitimacy noted, "These old records reflect case treatment that would not be regarded as individualized in the modern sense" (1920, p. 6). Gordon Hamilton of the New York School of Social Work characterized early records as lacking precise scientific information and exhibiting a "certain roughness of the eye and awkwardness of hand" because they were constructed on the basis of "observation of surface facts and judgements of the eye" (1923, p. 334). According to such practice, "one glass of beer might render a home unsuitable forever" (p. 336).

Staff of the MSPCC would agree as well that their earlier records had been crude by 1920 casework standards. Throughout the 1920s, all new social workers employed by the agency were trained in the art of making case records, and an extensive study of the existing records was an important aspect of doing that (Braungard 1929; "Growing Pains" 1934; Waite 1926). Within three months of being hired, new case-workers were also required to read Ada Eliot Sheffield's *The Social Case History: Its Construction and Content* (1920), a how-to manual for constructing case narratives.

Throughout the first two decades of the twentieth century, agencies such as the MSPCC had been busy revising both face sheets and narrative sections to include new diagnostic and treatment innovations, changes that allow contemporary readers a view of shifting emphases in agency practice. In 1923, for example, the MSPCC added masturbation to its list of presenting problems, and by the mid-1920s the agency had developed a special form, "Case Work Appraisal," to be filled out at the closure of a case. At both the MSPCC and BCAS, case records disclose a growing emphasis on physical as well as mental examinations, IQ testing for mental defects, and the growing closeness of both agencies to the mental hygiene approach of the influential Judge Baker Foundation, a child guidance agency in Boston. Child protective and placing societies and family welfare agencies were by no means idle while new ideas for practice began to ripen and became available for harvest.

Case Records Become Hegemonic: A Case Study

> Oh, there were plenty of faults in organized charity—plenty, Ann sighed. It had too much red tape. Often, complete records of families in distress were considered more important than relieving the distress. And charity workers did become hard, from familiarity with misfortune. But so did surgeons, and no-one was suggesting that surgery be handed over to the sympathetic spinsters and grandmothers of the parish.
>
> ༄Lewis (1933, p. 27)

Among the many battles for the control of benevolence characterizing the early years of social work, one of the most virulent and therefore revealing battles nationally was that which ensued between professionally identified charity organizations and the Salvation Army. The two employed distinct sets of discursive practices, institutional forms, and reform methods, each legitimized by distinct sources of authority. The conflict between the Salvation Army and scientific charity was also a battle between two worldviews—an older world in decline and anchored in religious understandings and a rising, empiricist worldview legitimated by a new scientific ideology and such disciplinary techniques as case record-keeping.

The practices of the Salvation Army were at odds with the emergent ambitions of scientific charity. Investigation, case documentation, and ongoing case supervision were lacking. The vice president of the Newark Associated Charities vividly expressed the fundamental tensions between the Salvation Army's evangelical project of social and spiritual redemption and the professionals' task of expert social management through scientific methods. The Army, he asserted, did not "reach the right people and they do not reach them in a way as to permanently reform their character. If the Salvation Army was in dead earnest about the salvation of souls and the reconstruction of character, would it not follow up even the bums and strive to elevate them and make it hard to gouge the public by using their free beds and living like vampires upon the public?" (Rose 1906, p. 506).

In addition to being a contest between old and new methods and worldviews, the battle between the charity organization movement and the Salvation Army also formed along class and gender lines. As they sought to bring spiritual conversion to the homeless, the drunkards, and the unfed, as well as to raise donations for their work, the Salvation Army's "Hallelujah Lassies," many of whom were from working-class backgrounds, flaunted and stretched the normal spatial confines of charity work that reflected customary gender and class boundaries and exclusions. Not only did the Lassies, as they called themselves, impinge upon the customary space of class superiors, but their methods were also far from genteel. They were ready to court ridicule and use sensational ploys to bring their message of redemption before the public. Unlike the charity organization society movement's practitioners, who moved sleuthlike throughout the slums and avoided incident and spectacle, the Salvation Army was intent on creating fanfare to spread its message. Members were known to lie in the snow, or in coffins, until an audience gathered and then arise to give a stirring address. Violating the spatial norms and proprieties honored by middle-class women reformers, the Hallelujah Lassies marched boldly into saloons and other dens of vice to issue invitations to Army meetings.[23]

In her study of the maternity home movement, Regina Kunzel (1993) has noted that evangelicals differed profoundly from professional social workers in their approach to charity recipients. Evangelical workers sought to "reach down and clasp the hand of some sister and help her struggle up" (Kunzel 1988, p. 24). Professional social workers sought to redefine rescue homes as places of treatment and replace sisterly ties and the salvation of souls with a more detached casework relationship, difficult as that might have been in practice.[24]

In contrast, Evangeline Booth, who assumed command of the Salvation Army in 1906, attributed the success of the Army to its ability to establish familial relationships with those it served, noting that in "Army homes" workers never spoke of "fallen women" but rather of "sisters," never "cases" but always "our girls or sisters who have stumbled" (Magnuson 1977, p. 86). Many evangelical women were by no means silent about their criticisms of professional casework and its preferred methods. In part, their resistance was based on professional demands for case-recording. Kunzel cites one rescue worker who described her resistance as being "a reluctance to dissect sin or to closely investigate the career of the sinner" and quotes another worker who said that "Jesus had no 'survey committee,' no place for records for the past of the individual" (1993, p. 133).

Charity organization society workers, however, were vociferous, even vicious, in their battles for benevolence. Madeline Breckinridge of the Lexington, Kentucky, Associated Charities waged a twelve-year campaign to drive the Salvation Army from her community and eventually sued to prevent the city from funding it (Tice 1992). Married to the editor of the *Lexington Herald* and a great-granddaughter of the Kentucky statesman Henry Clay, Breckinridge had at her command the class privileges of the southern gentry and also a newspaper column with which to shape public opinion. To discredit the Salvation Army's social work, she argued that its methods were sentimental, unscientific, inefficient, and sure to create chaos and disorganization by encouraging "no-accounts" to flock to Lexington. The Salvation Army's free soup kitchen was "a soft snap for the impostor and for the fraud, and the no accounts who find pauperism easier and more pleasant than working, and who will come [to Lexington] like flies to the honey pot" (Breckinridge 1921, p. 173).

The Army's lax record-keeping practices became a target of Breckinridge's ire, and she repeatedly attacked the records as inadequate. They did not contain "a plan to lift a family out of poverty. They show no occupation, no record of families and friends who can help and no answers to the question of have they been helped before," she wrote in the *Herald* on August 29, 1917. And in an editorial on August 17 of the same year, she had observed, "Of the thirty-four people who the Salvation Army recorded as receiving some material aid, twenty-four have comprehensive and conclusive histories at the Associated Charities. Some of their record cards date back to 1908 and show considerable investigation. All were judged not to need material aid as the right treatment. One case in particular that the Salvation Army said was trustworthy, a woman who made and sold aprons, had, in fact many entries as 'adept beggar, not assisted, chronic beggar.'" On June 1 she had remarked that "not even the recording angel himself, used as he is to tangled and devious records, could tell with the Salvation Army books what has been done in the way of relief," and on June 9 she complained that the benevolent public was being "duped and hypnotized by the lull of the tambourine."

Because of its initial recalcitrance, the Salvation Army's eventual nationwide conversion to charity organization society methods of case-recording and its use of the social service exchange are perhaps the best illustrations of the movement's tenacity and success in ushering in a textual revolution in social work. The movement's legacy is found in the widespread diffusion of the new techniques of case-recording and the investigations those techniques championed. By the 1930s, not only did Salvation Army training courses and manuals include curricular material borrowed from professional social casework but improving relations with the social work profession had also become a top priority.

Lecture notes from a Salvation Army training course mention that workers "should be constantly revising our language and improving our records (Salvation Army Social Welfare Work, Family Relief, ca. 1930s, p. 54). The anonymous author noted that part of the Army's historical aloofness to social work had been because of the perception that professional social workers were cold and impersonal and because of the movement's role in having Army social workers jailed. Other barriers included the fact that professional social workers perceived Army workers as ignorant of scientific social work, handing out indiscriminate relief, and not cooperating with other charity agencies. By the 1930s, however, this divide was crumbling. Anita Robb, the Salvation Army's first professionally trained and identified social worker, applauded concurrent meetings of the Salvation Army's Southern Territory Council and the National Conference on Social Work by saying that such meetings "helped to demonstrate to our staff officers that social workers would not bite and were perfectly harmless" (Anita Robb Papers, undated, p. 7).

In 1933 the Salvation Army developed an introductory course in social welfare work. According to the course's manual, "real" social workers do not "infringe on the rights and personalities of others," "ask too many personal questions before rendering any service," or emphasize the keeping of records over the "heartbreaking problems of human beings" (*An Introductory Course*, p. 12). Some Army members began to argue that, to keep up with the times, the organization should adopt the language and many of the methods of social work, especially case-recording. Typical weaknesses in the social work of the Army, as identified in the training course, had included the lack of case records and investigation: "our personnel of years ago had more heart than head . . . and love for humanity rather crowded out the much needed investigation of cases upon which so much really depends . . . the personnel of today believes in thorough investigation, actual facts, collateral visits" (p. 12). Army workers also boasted of a "marked improvement in individual case records. . . . The Army now has it on paper, whereas a few years ago the work was done and the results were there in the flesh and blood, but not in the card indexes or letter files" (Anita Robb Papers, undated, "Replies to Your Questions," p. 3).

Robb and other Salvation Army officers repeatedly called for workers to keep better case records. In a lecture on how that could be accomplished, she called case narration one of a caseworker's most important tasks. Failure was compared to "considering your dress finished if you did everything but put in the hem" (Anita Robb Papers, lecture 11, undated, p. 1). Especially because social work was vastly more complicated than it had been thirty years earlier, Army trainers argued that "he who does modern case work, must of necessity prepare carefully records of his work or find himself hopelessly bogged in the mass of details involved" (*An Introductory Course* 1933, p. 77). By the mid-1930s all Salvation Army personnel used standardized cover and narrative sheets.

The Army had become devoted to case documentation by the 1930s and was fully immersed in the same debates about science, art, and representation that commanded the attention of professional social workers. Army workers were instructed to be scientific when narrating case records but to avoid "a long string of hard cold facts [which] usually leave the record frozen and unappealing to the reader": "A good record will have life, movement, and vividness. Certainly the officer or case worker does not want to paint with loud colors, yet his record must tell the story in an interesting and fascinating manner. It is said that even scientists must understand the act of expression and certainly the case worker needs the same knowledge" (*An Introductory Course* 1933, p. 79).

The tension between writing vivid, colorful, and dramatic case records that would appeal to the heart or quantitative, objective, and factual accounts was a significant aspect of the feuds that occurred within social work and among social workers, sociologists, and psychologists. Their battles to redesign and modernize charity organization society movement protocols and practices, especially concerning the production of case records and the nature of professional textual representations, were common throughout the 1920s and will be examined in chapter 2.

The Legacy of Charity Organization

Charity organization society methods of documentation, record-keeping, and investigation inspired criticism from a variety of quarters. Watson (1922, p. 494) observed that attacks had come from a variety of groups, including "mudslinging journalists," "radicals who feel that all charity is merely palliative and out of place in the modern world," and the "lay public," which felt that charity had lost its "warmth" and been replaced by needless red tape and public exposure of the poor. Writing in 1890 to the *Arena,* a reform magazine, one critic urged readers to "consider the torture endured by needy families upon discovering that their relief applications had caused their names, history, and troubles, to be spread in a written record to be coddled and gossiped about" (Boyer 1978, p. 154). In a similar letter in January 1924 to the editor of the *Lexington* (Kentucky) *Herald,* a citizen criticized that city's charity organization society by saying: "Many hardened wretches would rather freeze or starve than be investigated and run the risk of getting into public print." The Lexington chief of police stated in 1917 that he rarely referred clients to the Associated Charities because the poor "don't want to go where they are going to be asked about themselves or make any investigation as to whether they are objects of charity" (Madeline Breckinridge Papers, box 698, p. 50). Finally, clients themselves condemned the investigative and recording practices of charity organization agencies as invasive. One described such practices as a "feminized third degree" (Kunzel 1993, p. 135), another as "public slander" (Devine 1914, p. 262). Yet despite such criticism, the keeping of case records became firmly entrenched as a fundamental tenet of professional casework practice.

Although charity organization society practices were being gradually adopted by such recalcitrant groups as the Salvation Army, some social welfare historians have argued that those practices eventually faded from popular use. Michael Katz (1986, pp. 80–83), for instance, argues that the movement went "from the vanguard to the backwaters of social policy" as social work broadened its approach. By failing to stress the centrality of the movement's practices of comprehensive investigation and case documentation to the profession, however, Katz greatly underestimates the continuing influence of charity organization society methodology. Its core practices of casework and recording revamped social reform work in lasting ways. By the 1930s, for example, Pine Mountain Settlement School in Kentucky, by no means a champion of charity organization society methods during the 1920s, had mandated a visit to student homes and a comprehension record of each home and family. Students had to submit a five-page self-history before being accepted into the settlement school (Pine Mountain Settlement School Archives, reel 3).

In contrast to Katz, Wenocur and Reisch (1989) argue that through exceptional resources, organization, and the introduction of standardized service practices such as investigation and registration, the charity organization society movement established hegemony over the unruly field of social work. These authors, however, also overlook the fundamental bequest the movement left: case-recording. Later social workers did not forsake the movement's commitments to keeping case records and to investigation. In fact, these practices remain canonical among all social workers.

Some social work leaders of the past also argued that other discourses eclipsed the charity organization society movement and transformed case-recording (Hamilton 1923). By 1930 Virginia Robinson of the Pennsylvania School of Social and Health Work contended that social case records had progressed so that "a layman, with no knowledge of social work, would be struck by the great difference in subject matter, emphasis, and method. . . . They may find the newer records more humanely interesting" (pp. 94–95). My examination of case records written throughout the early decades of the twentieth century, however, suggests that social workers, in their descriptions as well as their interventions with clients, did not abandon, break, or forsake the movement's methods and preoccupations. Rather, they elaborated upon them. Far too readily, social welfare historians have interpreted the project of constructing social work authority as a tightly ordered expedition, a series of abrupt departures and breaks in discursive practices and methods. From a textual practice perspective, however, the development of social work can be seen as far more kaleidoscopic and continuous. It is the conflation of a multitude of diverse theories, rhetorics, and practices unified by a shared commitment to record-keeping.

Social workers have not forsaken the movement's devotion to the concept of "I'll be watching you." Instead, they have embellished the many ways of watching and describing. Writing case records had, by the 1920s, become a primary disciplinary obligation. Professional arguments no longer centered on winning support for encyclopedic case documentation; that point had been won. Instead, debates focused on how best to assemble case stories.

2

Case Records and Professional Legitimation

Social workers fought a variety of internal and external battles over the proper pathways to professionalization, and they faced a multitude of obstacles: formidable external challenges from other professions, academic disdain for their hands-on approach, and the long history of women's voluntary ministrations. They had to win public approval and sanction for their work among the poor, a group not seen as important given the hegemony of corporate values and class politics in the United States (Ehrenreich 1985). The fledgling profession also had to be responsive to changing market opportunities and constraints, fashion a distinctive "commodity," control its production and consumption, and attract elite sponsors (Wenocur and Reisch 1989).

The challenges did not stop there, however, for social work itself remained a variegated body of disparate fields of practice and was beset by intergroup disputes and differences. As Leighninger (1987) points out, some histories of social work professionalization tend to overemphasize internal cohesion while ignoring the pivotal role of internal debate among subgroups on the professionalization process.[1] While constructing a distinctive body of knowledge and fashioning methods for professional writing as well as standards for professional training and membership, social workers argued vehemently among themselves. Consequently, early pioneers in the field forged no linear or single pathway to professional legitimacy.

Furthermore, in the pursuit of expert authority and professional recognition, the gendered character of social work was never far removed from the issue of legitimation. Early spokespersons such as Tufts (1923) and Walker (1928) observed that the proportion of men to women in the field was usually estimated to be about one to ten. Women far outnumbered men in positions involving personal visiting and stenography, whereas men were more likely to hold executive positions.

Both authors concluded that from the point of view of professional standing and public confidence it was clearly a disadvantage that so few men worked in the field.

Gender was prominent in the way social work was perceived, even though interpretations of exactly how gender status hindered the young discipline differed widely. In some cases, social workers were judged to be unduly sentimental, meddlesome, sexually abnormal, or to be women who made gender trouble of one sort or another.[2] An early study of public opinion and social work reported that social workers were commonly perceived as "un-sexed humanitarians who [were] attempting to sublimate their parental instincts" (Bowman 1923, p. 482). Another study (Bing 1923, p. 486) reported that one respondent contended that a social worker's greatest liability was "simply that she's always a woman" who should remain in the confines of her own home. Elon Moore (1934, p. 505), a sociologist, noted a colleague's alliterative description of social work as a "mobile mob of maidens meditating matrimony," while George Preston, a physician, pointed out that many medical practitioners viewed social workers as "half-baked young girls running around trying to tell other people how to manage their affairs [when] what they need is a family of their own" (1927, p. 234).

Throughout the late nineteenth century, social workers increasingly denied that women were better suited for social work than men, despite public perceptions of the profession as the province of "half-baked young girls." Revising the ideology of "redemptive femininity" and "female moral authority" that earlier had legitimated women's role in benevolence, some early-twentieth-century social workers sought more neutered precepts for reconstituting the reform community in order to obtain the "broader cultural authority of professional legitimacy" (Kunzel 1993, p. 63).

They argued against traditional myths about women being uniquely fitted to dispense benevolence and aspired to establish a more gender-neutral, scientifically based professional authority. "Emphasizing femininity in an already feminized profession would only reinforce the subordinate status of social work in the professional hierarchy" (Kunzel 1988, p. 23). Thus, some social workers sought to end the era when true womanhood or motherhood was the primary qualification for benevolent work and supplement it with professional expertise (Kunzel 1993; Ladd-Taylor 1994). With what must have been a sigh of relief, Joseph Choate, a member of the New York State Charities Aid Association, argued that his organization deserved official state endorsement because it had discarded flimsy notions of benevolent femininity and replaced them with a muscular scientific professionalism: "Now, it might be supposed by some that the SCAA is a mere gathering of sympathetic women who go to these institutions to condole with the paupers, and carry them gingerbread and tracts, and lavish a little weak sentiment on them . . . not so; the SCAA has proved itself free from weak or sickly sentiment" (Ginzberg 1990, p. 195).

Yet many reformers would continue to emphasize women's special role and fitness for social welfare work, glorifying the unique qualities that legitimated women's participation in public life (Ladd-Taylor 1994; Muncy 1991). At the same time, throughout the country many social welfare organizations, such as the Lexington, Kentucky, Associated Charities, reshuffled roles and responsibilities according to traditional notions of a gendered division of labor. Chastising the Lexington organization because its board of directors "had an unduly proportion of ladies," the American Association for Organizing Charity recommended a reconstitution that would include mostly men, who were thought to excel at leadership and knowledge of civic and political affairs. The large number of "ladies" on the board might better serve on the case committee, where "sympathy and personal interest are most needed" (American Association for Organizing Charity 1918, pp. 12–13).

National efforts to make men more prominent within the profession included the establishment of a committee by the American Association for Organizing Family Social Work to recruit males. Some women in social work, however, criticized recruitment efforts that offered special inducements to men; they were also critical of male dominance in administrative positions (Deardoff 1925, p. 642).[3]

Overall, such attempts produced paradoxical results. On the one hand, social workers were subjected to an unrelenting barrage of external criticism for practicing what was perceived by sociologists, psychologists, and psychiatrists to be defective science. On the other hand, in the public mind, social work's embrace of science and professionalism fueled popular characterizations of social workers as unfeeling, cold busybodies, more attuned to machinery and red tape than to dispensing generosity and womanly kindliness.

In addition to social work's traditional identification as a women's field, its professional legitimation was also diminished by the academic transformation of late-nineteenth-century universities, whereby "objectivity" took precedence over advocacy as a basis for respect, thus discrediting practical vocations such as social work (Bulmer, Bales, and Sklar 1991; Ross 1991). Howard Odum (1923, p. 491), a sociologist who established the social work program at the University of North Carolina, suggested how far the profession had to go to win academic respectability. He pointed out the widespread resistance to social work in universities and noted that even teachers of education seemed to have forgotten the hostility that their professional training had received, because they also attacked social work. Odum observed that the adage "those who fail in other pursuits may teach or farm had been updated to include social work." In 1929 Dorothy Kahn reminded social workers that they were still classified by the Census Bureau as "semiprofessionals," a group made up primarily of "mediums, fortune tellers, and chiropractors" (p. 514).

The intimate involvement of social workers in the daily lives and domestic affairs of impoverished and immigrant clients also found disfavor among academicians and the better-established professions. Dorothy Ross's argument (1991, pp. 308–9) that "the conventional gentry culture of the academic professions discouraged the kind of direct contacts and sympathetic associations that were demanded by urban realism," especially when these led to "advocacy," can easily be extended to explain the hostility social workers encountered in the academy. As Bulmer (1991, p. 310) suggests, the "autonomous realm of 'expert' activity conducted by social scientists" in the early twentieth century was marked by "disinterestedness and detachment from the political and reform issues of the day." This academic culture erected masculine boundaries within sociology and psychiatry that denigrated social work and belittled concrete reform activity (Ross 1991).[4]

Demands for detachment and objectivity were among the most perplexing challenges to the masculinizing ambitions and professional aspirations of early social work. As Kunzel argues, "While social work theorists proclaimed the importance of professional detachment, practicing caseworkers struggled to negotiate the contradictory imperatives demanded of women and of professionals: maternal sympathy and nurturance on one hand, and objectivity and dispassion on the other. Gordon Hamilton, a social worker, likely spoke for many when she asked in 1937, "*What, in fact, is a professional friend?*" (1993, p. 141, emphasis added). In a memo on case studies and course outlines Bertha Reynolds, a psychiatric social worker and Smith College School of Social Work educator, described the quandary over detachment versus friendly visiting for teachers of casework. Their students would face many dangers in their relationships with clients, including "falling between two extremes . . . impersonality and sentimentality." Reynolds also pointed out that the mixed ambitions of social work were reflected in the "desire of the young student to see herself in a grand role as a benefactor, wielder of destinies, scientific expert . . . who magnifies the mysterious remoteness of professional procedures." She recommended that students stay "close to the reality of everyday experience avoiding the formation of professional haloes," and that they "come to see as a scientist or professional person" (Edith and Grace Abbott Papers 1927). Issuing a similar mixed message, Margaret Cochran Bristol (1936, p. 53) argued that it was imperative for social workers to develop the "ability to mix judiciously the necessary sympathetic understanding with the cold, calculating, disinterested objectivity of the scientific worker."

Social work's perceived failure to live up to scientific canons of objectivity formed the basis for a vociferous crusade led by sociologists to ridicule the profession's scientific aspirations (Burgess 1928; Eliot 1928; Moore 1934). Such crusades were examples of what Thomas Gieryn (1983, pp. 791–92) describes as "boundary-work," a rhetorical style used ideologically to demarcate science from non-science and distinguish among disciplines within science. "Boundary-work is a likely stylistic resource for ideologists of a profession or occupation: a) when the goal is expansion of authority or expertise claimed by other professions or occupations, boundary-work heightens the contrast between rivals in ways flattering to the ideologists' side; b) when the goal is monopolization of professional authority, boundary-work excludes rivals from within by defining them as outsiders with labels such as 'pseudo,' 'deviant,' 'or amateur.'" By challenging the textual objectivity of social workers as witnesses and recorders of empirical reality, sociologists used them as foils for constructing a "social boundary that distinguished nonscientific intellectual or professional activities" from their own (p. 791).

Psychiatry and psychology also engaged in border wars with social work. Both fields veered far out into waters long navigated by social workers and both shared knowledge and techniques with social work. In an informative study of the role of gender in the growth of psychiatry, Elizabeth Lunbeck (1994, p. 38) maintains that psychiatry's stance toward social work was simple: "Psychiatry was science, and science was masculine; social work was sentiment and sentiment was feminine." Psychiatrists reacted to social workers in a multitude of ways, including pronouncing them "incapable of exercising executive authority," belittling them as merely "useful intermediaries," and complimenting them for having the "grace" not to claim their efforts as scientific.

Yet psychiatrists also relied heavily upon social workers for a firsthand knowledge of clients, as well as for case-recordings to further the work of psychology and child guidance. In many organizations, social workers worked alongside psychiatrists and psychologists. Through referrals, jointly attended case conferences, and shared case records they often found themselves in the same company.

Social workers, however, had to work to overcome their standing as useful but circumscribed handmaidens to the more reputable, powerful, and male-dominated fields of psychiatry and psychology. Their feminized, personal knowledge of clients, although recognized as valuable in psychiatric study, nonetheless undermined their claim to professional authority. As E. E. Southard, a Harvard-trained pathologist and director of the Boston Psychopathic Hospital, summed up his image of psychiatric social workers, "She remains liquid. She is the ideal being, a universal solvent. She proves herself to be a useful intermediary in whatever field her path finally arrives" (Southard and Jarrett 1922, p. 389).[5]

Other psychiatrists, however, sought to distinguish themselves from what they perceived as a professionally immature field and its chaotic, gendered knowledge. Bernard Glueck (1919, p. 602) thus observed that although "the temptation" to relegate the task of taking life histories to psychiatric social workers was great, there was "danger" nonetheless in turning over such practices to "lay person[s]." Yet some saw allowing social workers to write psychiatric histories as a time-saving practice (Thom 1922). According to Southard (1919, p. 584), doing so allowed psychiatrists to maintain a professional distance from clients' "compensation tangles and domestic details" without sacrificing professional control over interpretation or having their authority undermined.

Social work thus faced many impediments to professional legitimacy: its checkered past grounded in a religious ethos of "redemptive femininity," the large proportion of women in the field, its intimate involvement with the poor, and hostility from professional neighbors in sociology and psychiatry. Although substantial disagreement existed over how best to respond to such challenges, social case records proved to be a main access for entry into the brotherhood of professions. Observing that medical diagnosis relied upon recording a glut of details while "searching for facts and factors," Carol Aronovici (1916, pp. 468–69) concluded that "if this method of recording cases is essential in medicine, which is surely on its way towards becoming a positive science, it is easily conceivable that in the field of social service, this method of recording is imperative."

In an infamous and inflammatory speech before the National Conference of Charities and Corrections (NCCC) in 1915—titled "Is Social Work a Profession?"— Abraham Flexner, M.D., answered that question negatively by asserting that "a profession must find a dignified and critical means of expressing itself in the form of a periodical which shall describe in careful terms whatever work is in progress; and it must from time to time register its more impressive performances in a literature of growing solidity and variety" (p. 590).[6] I contend that case records had a double purpose: they were practitioners' "periodicals" as well as the foundations for tales of professional accomplishment and virtuosity. Before case-recording could become a pathway to professionalization and a dignified means of professional expression, however, many debates about the place of science, art, subjectivity, and representation in the practice of case-recording would occur.

The Debates

In 1922 Frank Watson, a social worker, observed that "the art of case recording is still in a stage that [did] not permit dogmatism" (p. 472). Within social work, as in sociology and anthropology, no firmly established paradigm existed for the production of professional texts. As a result, the 1920s proved to be a fertile and active period for experimenting with different forms, methods, and rhetorical devices for what today is referred to as "representing others" (Marcus and Fischer 1986; Ross 1991).

Infighting about how to report, arrange, and interpret facts and extend the knowledge base in case records spawned another level of strife. For example, Ada Eliot Sheffield, an eminent social work leader, observed (1910, p. 36) that social work needed to go beyond merely reporting and accumulating factual information to develop "key conceptions which would give facts significance."[7] There was no "more urgent task before the reflective social worker than that of bringing to light the vagueness at innumerable important points in our social thinking." "Vagueness," according to Sheffield, was manifested in a variety of ways, including deficiencies in interpretative and diagnostic vocabularies and shaky attempts to conceptualize the origins and outcomes of client difficulties. She urged social workers to develop "definiteness of expectation or familiar acquaintance with meanings" so "definite attitudes of response would lead us, without reflection, to anticipate certain possible consequences" (p. 39). Accordingly, many turned their attention to constituting a technical language and conceptual tools to guide case-recording.

There was more to be done during the 1920s, however, than merely standardize language, conceptual tools, recording practices, and observational methods. Perceived by many as a professional vagrant, social work also had to convince other professions that its procedures and protocols had been sufficiently disinfected of subjective and feminine influences. In medicine, psychiatry, and sociology, the documentation of reality and significant "facts" was relatively nonproblematic compared to the concerns raised over social workers' descriptions and representations of the factual world. As Geertz (1988, p. 79) puts the problem in another context, "To be a convincing 'I-witness,' one must, so it seems, first become a convincing 'I.'" The challenge to become a creditable "I" sent social work in a multitude of directions in the search for authority.

For many, science was the correction that social work required. Arthur Todd celebrated the wonders of scientific spirit for doing away with what he termed "obtrusive personality." "Scientific self-immolation" he said, "pours a healthy astringent upon one's ego" (1919, p. 81). Many early social workers assumed the guise of detached, impartial scientific recorders and observers of facts. Unlike their more literary counterparts, they believed their descriptions to be mirrorlike and self-evident. J. Harold Williams, editor of the *Journal of Delinquency* and director of the California Bureau of Juvenile Research, for example, described (1922, pp. 66–67) the scientific approach in social work as "an attitude of mind associated with the ability and desire to make systematic observations and draw rational conclusions there from. Science does not make facts. It merely collects them in sufficient quantities and arranges them in order so that any person who sees them may be free to draw such conclusions as they seem to warrant. . . . It is an attempt to describe what is already known to exist, but to describe it without prejudice or partiality." Edward Devine (1939, p. 69) boasted that the records of charity organizations at the turn of the century provided more documentary evidence about the poor than could be found anywhere else, because they were written "with no special program of reform in mind, with no sensational or sentimental motive whatsoever; visitors had nevertheless learned to put down in black and white the facts." Along the same line, Helen Wallerstein of the Russell Sage Foundation asserted (1925, p. 113) that "the case history is of course the mirror of life in a sense that a work of fiction could never be . . . its essence is truth laid bare of all furnishments whatsoever."[8]

The story of the professionalism of social work, however, was not a story of the discovery of transparent and unsullied facts, nor of simple documentary realism divorced from professional contingencies. Rather, it is about how professional power shaped the interpretation, narration, and representation of social reality and constructed particular elements as factual and significant. Yet many social workers believed they could put an end to their vagrant professional status by emulating the "science" of sociology and later, throughout the 1920s, the "science" of psychology. The National Conference of Charities and Correction, for example, held a symposium on record-keeping, with presentations from Aronovici (1916), Bruno (1916), Hewins (1916), and Johnson (1916), some of whom advocated that social case records could be improved by modeling them after sociological research reports.

More than a decade later, social workers met jointly with sociologists to discuss improving social case records for research purposes. Those who were scientifically inclined sought to increase the "research value" of casework by promoting questionnaires, outlines, and topologies as methodological guidelines in constructing case records. Issues of comparability and generalization preoccupied them as they searched for regularities and types in the social world. Some members of this scientifically oriented cohort argued that advancement in psychology in particular was opening new areas of significance and that case records should be revised accordingly—for example, to tell new tales of inner psychological drama.[9]

Not all social workers were ardent devotees of science. Some turned to the literary world for models of how to write case records that would imitate the art of dramatic writing and highlight the conflict, tension, pathos, and tragedy found within case histories. Clare Tousley (1927) of the New York Charity Organization Society, for example, urged social workers to imitate a playwright when writing or speaking, and Frank Bruno (1928, p. 534), one-time director at the Minneapolis Family Welfare Association and a prominent social work educator, stated, "If the case worker were to study the method of drama, especially of dramatic writing, she would find a tool more adaptable for her purpose than any literary device yet invented."

Still others advocated more far-reaching methods, including sharing textual space with clients and personalizing authority by addressing the parts social workers themselves played in interactions with clients. Bertha Reynolds anticipated contemporary concerns about the partiality of truth and the relativity of various standpoints when she declared that "truth is not an absolute entity which one finds or one does not. . . . The relativity of it is very apt to be brought out by the students themselves in discussion when they sense, for instance, the difference that racial customs of politeness may make" (Abbott Papers 1927). Documenting personal participation could complicate and broaden the truth of social work knowledge.

Other social workers, however, had different reasons for how they positioned themselves in case records. In tune with the growing influence of psychology and its emphasis on such therapeutic issues as transference and identification, many turned to recording their own "process," including personal elements, during interactions with clients. Here, recording process did not guarantee the same depth of scrutiny given to the politics of privileging certain voices and locations and the healthy skepticism about the capacity to represent others fully, which can be found in contemporary debates over speaking, writing, and representation. Social workers rarely went so far as to interrogate their narrative authorities or doubt their representations of facts or interpretative stance. Yet some did foster opportunities for client self-expression in order to produce more intimate portrayals of clients' lives. Such efforts are similar to many contemporary sensibilities that politicize representation and embark on collaborative models for textual production.

The range of issues that occupied social workers around the construction of case records has not yet been exhausted. They also focused on problems related to bulk, organization, and ease of reference and sought a judicious blend of science and art by arguing that social case records could be improved from both directions by tinkering with their form and organization rather than content. Such recommendations were primarily utilitarian, designed either to advance the art or science of case-writing. The concerns, however, received much attention and occupied an important place in professional discourses on narrative methodology.[10] In tracing the course and content of these debates, social work leaders never disputed the need for professional recording but rather argued vehemently about the amount and kinds of literary and scientific additions to be added.

Writing Science: Outlines, Typologies, Factors

> Not all social workers can be Galileos, but some can and will make discoveries of equal importance to his, and all social workers who have the scientific point of view can and will contribute toward the ultimate formulation of the laws which control the human social machine.
>
> ∾Williams (1922)

Shifting discourses about science characterized early social work. As Thomas Gieryn suggests, "'Science' is no single thing," its boundaries are "ambiguous, flexible, historically changing, contextually variable, internally inconsistent, and sometimes disputed" (1983, p. 792). In differentiating scientific charity work from its religious and feminine antecedents, members of charity organization societies embraced a version of science based primarily on empirical fact-finding. Seeking to supplant what they perceived to be the nonscientific, subjective, and sentimental judgments of their predecessors, the documentation of "actual, concrete, discoverable facts" became the cornerstone of an emergent social work empiricism (Taylor 1912).

In ensuing years, however, some social workers worried that the mere reporting of facts was deficient science, because facts could neither stand alone nor speak for themselves and needed professional analysis. Factual case records had to be arranged, tidied, interpreted, and correlated. Tables, outlines, and typologies were perceived as essential for the advancement of scientific research and professionalization as documentation of causality and conditioning factors became the hallmarks of scientifically sophisticated social workers. Thus by 1931 Maurice Karpf, director of the Training School for Jewish Social Work, could argue that scientific social work now demanded "an open mind, objectivity, a search for basic causes, avoidance of undue and hasty generalizations, a passion for verification, and belief in control and improved technique" (p. 368).

Social workers seeking to advance the science of the discipline were preoccupied with increasing the research value of records, and many agencies, for example, the Boston Children's Aid Society, added research workers to their staffs during the second decade of the twentieth century. As early as 1908, John Koren, chair of the NCCC's Committee on Statistics, urged the "adoption of uniform and complete records with the main facts consistently and comparatively recorded; so that systematic knowledge might be available for general purposes" (p. 217). At the 1916 NCCC symposium on record-keeping, concern with improving the uniformity and research value of social case records resurfaced when Katherine Hewins argued that a face sheet was the obvious place to start to standardize case records because it contained information easily displayed in a tabulated format.

Knowing what to do with the narrative sections, however, proved more problematic. From the perspective of social workers who championed the art and drama of record-writing, attempts by scientifically inclined individuals to reshape the narrative portion of the record were fraught with danger. Frank Bruno (1916, p. 459), for example, argued that "any general plan in which we attempt to follow an imaginary outline kills the life of the narrative. To write a good narrative one must recreate the incident dramatically so that it lives again in the writer's mind and he puts down in the record the incident as a living organism." Not convinced by Bruno's arguments, Hewins (1916) concluded that facts within the narrative section should also be arranged with an orderliness to satisfy the demands of statisticians.

The call to order facts for statistical and research purposes was sounded from many quarters. Richard Cabot, M.D., reminded social workers (1919, pp. 36–37) that because "order is heaven's first law," they must be methodical in their writing. He proposed the application of a "mental rake" to case records, noting that "we must attack our task with a tool in our hand, a mental tool fitted to rake out the mass of confused ideas, certain significant facts. That rake is a logical schedule of questions. . . . Whenever you think well, you think with a schedule. . . . If you pack a trunk well, you pack it using a list, a schedule of things that ought to go into that trunk. Our printed social face card helps us to think and question with a schedule before us, to think in an orderly way."

Mental rakes in the form of outlines to guide the construction of case records were indeed devised by social work leaders. Mary Richmond, for example, formulated a series of questionnaires to increase the orderliness of case records. Her profoundly influential *Social Diagnosis* contained a series of questions for use with "Any Family," "The Immigrant Family," "The Insane," "The Feebleminded," and "The Unmarried Woman." Although Richmond warned that such questionnaires were clumsy and riddled with dangers, she nonetheless suggested they could bring "suggestive leads" to case recorders.[11] Helen Witmer (1930, p. 120) acknowledged that although dangers were associated with such outlines, even greater dangers were associated with unedited and untidy client narratives. Cautioning that "descriptions must not wander about unguided, determined only by the facts which the client or informant reveal in a free-flowing confession," she recommended that social workers institute indexing systems for the narrative portions of their records.

Harold Phelps (1927, p. 106), a sociologist, was firm in his advocacy of the need for outlines because "case records abound with random observations, which are practically worthless, because no uniform plan was used in their collection or classification and, therefore, is destructive of scientific advancement in treatment and analysis." Frances Price (1929, p. 517) also argued that record forms should be standardized in order to replace the "loosely constructed chronological record that allowed the worker to write down whatever facts she considers important and neglect those she has not thought to see." Until records were written that would allow comparison and generalization, Price contended, scientific treatment would remain outside the reach of social work.

Conditioning Factors

Scientifically minded social workers were not appeased with the use of mental rakes in the form of outlines, questionnaires, and face sheets. Identifying conditioning factors and recurrent client types was also seen as another way to move case records and practice toward higher scientific levels. Ada Eliot Sheffield (1920) argued that social workers needed "to frame a hypothesis as to what a fact means, and then search for confirmation or disproof in recurrent instances" (p. 38), and that the "storiette sequence" of case records must be edited by "marking off an integrative group of factors." Such scientific editing would help social workers to recog-

nize "type likeness[es]" and variations among clients, introduce order in thinking about variables, and help clarify causative relations (Sheffield 1931, p. 469).[12]

Sheffield was not the only one who advocated factoring as the basis for scientific knowledge-building and case-recording. Gordon Hamilton (1923), for example, also urged social workers to think in terms of conditioning factors. Helen
Witmer (1930, p. 119) likewise conceded that factoring and the discovery of types
were important for professional advancement: "It is a fact not always recognized
in an age that elevates science that psychiatrists and social workers practice an art;
they deal with individual cases, and to them the idiosyncrasies of the case are of
greater importance than the uniformities that run through cases of a given type.
But the advancement of their art must depend to some extent on the discovery of
types and uniformities."

Had case records been plotted to discover and delineate "types and uniformities" under the guise of science and objectivity, the result would have been reductive stories in which clients appeared simply as the compilation of conditioning
factors and uncomplicated types. Although other forms of professional writing
also essentialized clients, scientific writing was especially prone to abstraction.
Nonetheless, social workers were under heavy pressure to pursue that method for
telling their tales in the battle to win professional regard.

Sociology's Scientific Instruction

Beginning in 1926, the American Sociological Society established a section on
sociology and social work. At the four annual meetings that focused primarily on
the content and construction of case records sociologists had opportunity to instruct and advise on the proper scientific methods of recording. But social workers proved far from ideal pupils. As one sociological participant, Erle Young, observed, "The ease with which the discussion tends to become polemic and to make
more difficult the development of cooperative enterprises" (1930, p. 364).[13] Sociologists, nonetheless, persevered in their instructional efforts. Young, for instance,
described a procedure for isolating and determining the significance of factors in
a complex problem:

> 1) Decide upon a list of assumed unitary factors. . . . 2) List the factors identified in each
> case noting date of first appearance, of change, and of disappearance. 3) Segregate the
> cases into single-factor, two-factor, three-factor cases and so on and determine the rela-
> tive frequency with which each factor occurs separately and in combination with other
> factors. The combined strength of each factor can thus be determined. . . . Study the
> relation between the presence and absence of various factors in determining the *ultimate
> outcome of the case, noting adjustment rates, adjustment periods, and eventually perhaps
> adjustment costs.* (1930, pp. 361–62, emphasis added).

Young's approach was a precursor to trends now heralded as cost-efficient and toward basing case management decisions on computer-generated probabilities of likely outcomes (Campbell 1992). The loss of client complexity and subjectivity in such accounts, along with the disempowering effects of such professional operations to clients, are regrettably not factored in as costs.

Another important topic at these meetings was the implementation of methods for erasing what Ernest Burgess (1928, p. 528) referred to as the "personal equation of the social worker" from case records. Many sociologists applauded Eliot's suggestion that "quotation marks in the district office should have more exercise . . . so as to let the dramatis personae speak for himself" (1928, p. 539). Quoting clients directly was seen as a way of remedying the problem of social work's feminine (and, by extension, subjective) intrusions in case records.

Remedial scientific instruction for social workers by sociologists persisted long after their joint meetings ended. Elon Moore (1934, p. 507), for example, equated social work's "truth" to "folk wisdom" and complained that the "very nature of social work" results in a variety of errors and "inaccuracies" in social work records. After observing that the majority of social workers were of the "opposite sex," Moore argued on the basis of controlled experimentation that women's narrative recall abilities were significantly different from men's. Women's memory tended to excel over men's only for "disconnected material" or when items of "scandal or notoriety" were present. Speaking as one who taught social workers, Moore concluded that his "indictment of limitations" regarding them and their case records was not "intended to disparage that profession, nor to suggest that her records are without value." He had been "too closely associated with the early preparation of workers to permit such emphasis." Still, his comments reveal that social work's critics associated a nonscientific narrative form with gender ideologies.

Local Color Writing

Social work has held the faith of Emerson that "the only vulgar people are they whose poetry has not been written."
∾Wood (1925)

The case worker is nothing if he has not a broad human view based on the close, and one may say, loving interest in the drama of existence.
∾Hamilton (1936)

Social workers who sought a more artistic rather than scientific description of the poor, deviant, and criminal had many literary precursors to emulate.[14] Throughout the mid-nineteenth century, popular fiction, journalism, and drama had increasingly turned to the poor for story material. The result was a popular genre of urban exploration literature that frequently emphasized the sensational aspects of poverty, vice, and crime and reflected middle-class fears of the breakdown of race, class, and gender boundaries. Such writing claimed to embrace factual descriptions of excursions to the seamy other side of urban life, viewed as the breeding ground of criminality, madness, immorality, and ignorance.

Not all popular turn-of-the-century fiction, however, dealt with only the dark side of the city "wilderness." Edward Harrigan, for instance, took a different tack in popular comedies that emphasized the familiar rather than the lurid. He viewed human nature as being the same across classes, yet "it thins out and loses all of its strength and flavor under the pressures of richness and luxury. It is most virile and aggressive among those who know only poverty and ignorance. It is also then the most humorous and odd" (Bremner 1956a, p. 97). Paul Leicester Ford wrote in *The Honorable Peter Stirling* that "there is more true romance in a New York Tenement than there ever was in a baron's tower—braver battles, truer loves, nobler sacrifices. Romance is all about us, but we must have eyes for it" (Bremner 1956a, p. 86).

Robert Bremner, a historian, has observed (1956a, p. 170) that beginning in the 1890s, "The important matters in literature as in life, were romance, comedy, tragedy, and nobility of character. . . . If they were discoverable among people in humble walks of life, so much the better, for the locale was relatively new, the material fresh and interesting. The poverty of the characters although incidental to the main theme of romance, contributed atmosphere, poignancy, and a pathetic quality to the narrative." Thus numerous writers searched for virtue, heroism, and romance among the poor. Alice Rice, author of *Mrs. Wiggs of the Cabbage Patch,* a novel about a widow struggling to raise her children in Louisville, Kentucky, stated that "looking for nobility that lay hidden in the most unpromising personalities became for [her] a spiritual treasure hunt" (Bremner 1956a, p. 167).

Stansell has observed that evangelical women reformers were especially noteworthy contributors to the genre of storytelling that centered on the "female victim, a gentle and wounded spirit who partook of the piety and deference of the traditional worthy poor . . . 'poor yet industrious, modest quick neat,' frail, vulnerable, timid, and self-sacrificing" (1987, p. 72). In "The One White Lamb," for example, Elizabeth and Leon Stern (1923, p. 162) narrated the heroic goodness of a poor women and her social worker, "who seemed like a modern Madonna in a tailored suit." It is a tale of a noble and staunch black woman "at the stove [who] moved in the gray mist like a ghost of some large prisoner condemned to eternal work. In the steam, her face, big and kind, shone out with gleams of silver on its dark skin; that was the sweat pouring down." Three out of her four children had taken to wickedness, while the fourth, an "idiot," was saved from commitment to an institution by the social worker, who was impressed with the quiet suffering of his mother. The social worker had also learned that the boy was soon to die.

Despite occasional stress on nobility, however, social depravity and the vicious poor still occupied a vital place in urban exploration narratives, which positioned the poor as wanton agents of menace rather than as innocent and courageous victims. Elaine Showalter (1990) has argued that psychoanalytic case histories and turn-of-the-century fiction both began to question notions of a stable Victorian ego, thus adding to the growing abundance of fictional narratives on the criminal and aberrant. She points out that Freud's case studies of hysterical patients such as Dora as well as fictional works such as Robert Louis Stevenson's *The Strange Case of Dr. Jekyll and Mr. Hyde* (1886) were expressions of an emergent fascination with sexual scandals, deviancy, and abnormality. The confessions of beggars, thieves, and bums enjoyed widespread popularity. This fascination with unpredictable others, when combined with Progressive Era's documentary impulses, ensured that the poor and aberrant in fiction, social research, and social work case study would remain in the limelight, as, for example, in Theodore Dreiser's *Sister Carrie* (1901), Frank Norris's *The Octopus* (1901), and Upton Sinclair's *The Jungle* (1906).

Documentary realism became popular during the 1920s when nonfiction outsold fiction, which in turn gravitated toward realism. The trend continued during the 1930s. "The documentary motive was at work throughout the culture of the times in the rhetoric of the New Deal and the WPA arts projects; in painting, dance, fiction, and theater; in the new media of radio and picture magazines; in popular thought, education, and advertising" (Stott 1973, p. 4).

Social workers of all philosophies contributed to this massive documentation of social life. Stern and Stern (1923, p. 305) described social workers as the "new actors on an old stage, . . . outside the story, and yet moving the characters in it as a skilled and wise director moves his players; telling them to go here, to do this, to speak now, and when to be silent." Unlike those social workers preoccupied with questions of scientific factors and tables, a large group was concerned with artistry and color. In portraying clients, they aspired to convey the pulsating dramas of human presence rather than pulverized scientific abstractions. Not content with an orderly recital of neutral facts with the "tears wiped off," they sought instead to infuse their writing with picturesque, vivid coloring (Paradise 1923, p. 321).[15]

Many social work leaders thus reminded caseworkers that they had a plenitude of splendid material at their fingertips for dramatic and colorful narratives. Etta Hamilton (1925) suggested that "beauty and aesthetic interest" could be found in such unexpected places as slums. Viola Paradise (1932, p. 578) maintained that social workers "must cope with nearly every plot and passion known to literature. . . . What can one find in literature more crucial and dramatic than the bankrupt moment when an individual family or individual, unable to forge ahead on its own momentum, must call in outside aid? In that moment there are two wolves at the door, and one is as ready to devour the spirit as the other the flesh." Paradise argued that she could easily have selected a more dramatic social work moment than this routine investigative query on the need for relief, yet even such an ordinary investigation had much to offer to would-be artists. Social work material, she concluded, "is the very stuff of life—raw, bleeding, brutal, or tender and glowing; bitter and ironic, or grotesque and humorous" (1932, p. 580).

Many social work leaders thus turned to novelists and playwrights for instruction and inspiration, urging case-writers to read fiction and incorporate its techniques in their work. Paradise (1932, p. 583) suggested that social workers read widely, because all good literature that interprets life is of professional value. She recommended Ernest Hemingway's "The Killers," for example, for its lesson that "these characters might have begun as delinquents with whom you are working with today," and Gustav Flaubert's *Madame Bovary* because "the passion one of your cases feels for a man not her husband are of the same stuff." Virginia Robinson (1926) urged social workers to strive for the detailed and intimate pictures found in the novels of May Sinclair, D. H. Lawrence, and Dorothy Canfield Fisher, whereas Helen Wallerstein (1930, p. 27) found Henry Handel Richardson's trilogy *Ultima Thule,* a microscopic examination of the mental collapse of a character named Richard Mahoney, to be a "masterpiece of case recording." Anna Beattie (1925) published a must-read fiction list for social workers, and Arthur Todd (1919, p. 128) argued that "good books were like alpenstocks in our efforts to climb . . . and books on efficiency and detective stories share honors with the bible" when it came to general reading for social work.

Those who advocated the study of fiction as a way to deepen professional understanding of human behavior naturally saw literature as instructive for constructing case records. Wallerstein (1925, p. 114) noted that Dorothy Canfield Fisher's novel *The Homemaker* was an example of a flawless case history, although she thought "a case conference of experts was woefully needed" to rewrite the ending of the novel. Katherine Hardwick (1922), Mabel Hazelton (1927), Helen Wallerstein (1920a), and Lorine Pruette (1928) each held that drama and fiction provide important exemplars for social workers to improve character study and the art of expression. "A common basis of all records is the art of writing—to which little attention is paid," Hazelton (1927, p. 284) maintained, and Porter Lee (1920) lamented that social work education was impaired by the lack of artistry in case-recording.

Allegiances to colorful writing were especially predominant in the publicity and persuasion campaigns that social workers addressed to the general public (chapter 6). Many refashioned case stories as bases for fiction and wrote about illustrative cases for magazine and newspaper articles; others staged plays and pageants to stimulate interest in the profession and its clients. Tousley (1927, p. 176) argued that social caseworkers imitate playwrights by picking out a central theme when telling a "story of casework to Main Street or Broadway." After reading 250 entries submitted to a social work short story contest, she concluded, "These stories showed a marvelous understanding of life's tone and color and convinced me that many case workers can learn to write effectively if they will learn the elements which govern this field. So many times a beautiful story was worked up to a breathless climax only to have the worker leave us bumping along on a flat tire because, without rhyme or reason, she goes off to see the relatives or former employer." But, Tousley complained, social workers' elementary literary mistake was the tendency to "tell all." The profession would be better understood were they to "paint for those who know little of social work just the big outstanding things in the picture— a hill, a tree, and a sunset; details can be filled in later" (p. 175). Stuart Queen, a sociologist, contended (1927, p. 459) that the public wanted more than "a moving little tale about the Widow Jones or Orphan Annie," but Tousley argued that a sob story would always have an important role to play in illuminating the work of the profession.

The art of dramatic storytelling was also highly revered by a long-term nemesis of scientific charity: the Salvation Army. Maestros of public spectacles and sensational publicity, Army members also demonstrated a flair for colorful writing. One noteworthy example was "Salvation Army World's Mirror—What It Is Doing Is Shown by the Story of Diamond Dolly." Published in *The War Cry* in July 1912, the tale recounted the sad story of Diamond Dolly's downfall:

> In Louisville's underworld, she was just Diamond Dolly. "Diamond" because her hands, her head, and even her clothes glistened with gems. . . . The girl's advent into dance hall society was remarkable . . . Diamond Dolly captured them all—the gilded youth and the big saloonist. . . . Each hour, each day, each week brought the girl closer to her end. Too much wine, too many cigarettes and the heavy air of the night worked the shortening of her dynasty. . . . Dolly's diamonds disappeared one by one. The beautiful gowns disappeared one by one. The sunken eyes and pallid cheeks were symbols themselves of misery and of Dolly's passing. Dolly had the "con"—tuberculosis.

Although professional social workers typically sought to distance themselves from such groups as the Salvation Army, an uneasy truce existed on the issue of writing. Mary Richmond and Ada Sheffield each argued that the art of conveying "color" was important in general case-recording, although they both advocated color writing that was more measured than that of their publicity-seeking colleagues and the Salvation Army. Richmond (1917, p. 94) nonetheless argued that when social workers followed the "rule of nothing but the facts" they produced colorless records resembling "unstrung beads." She quoted (1917, p. 94) an unnamed critic who reportedly said after examining many case records that "whenever the 'only the facts rule' applies, the tendency is for every fact, big and little, to occupy about the same space in the record. Everything is brought to a dead level."

From a different angle, in another widely read social work text, *The Social Case Record,* Sheffield (1920, pp. 190–91) argued that those who wrote records would benefit by reading the fiction of "real masters of character portrayal such as John Galsworthy and Joseph Conrad which can sensitize [the social worker's] mind to the observation of subtle and significant traits and at the same time enrich her descriptive vocabulary." She warned, however, that a record-writer is more restricted than an artist, because "she is a specialist, reporting on such character facts as they bear on specific maladjustments. Not picturesqueness but precision is what she should strive for; not amateur 'portrayal' such as one that imputes a connection between full lips and warm emotions, close-set eyes and jealousy, erect carriage and pride, but professional interpretation, that chooses its words responsibly." Precision in the selection and interpretation of facts was more important than gratuitous description.

Sheffield (1920, p. 182) distinguished between "relevant and irrelevant color," reminding social workers that they were writing to "further treatment and not for the entertainment of drama seekers." Irrelevant color, she observed, was to be found in the writings of social workers who "individualized" clients by describing their appearance regardless of its significance. Even if such social workers were "writing novels instead of case records, a description which has no bearing on the plot would be out of place" (p. 183). By contrast, Sheffield found the following description of a wayward girl to be indicative of "relevant color": "The girl was of medium height, very dark, complexion clear, black hair, glittering eyes, bridge of nose somewhat flattened, teeth good and have been taken care of, shows evidence of negro blood. She laughs constantly and seems to be in excellent spirits" (p. 184). Such descriptive facts were relevant for treatment because of the "evidence of negro blood with its bearing on character . . . the appearance of the face, figure, manner, and dress of any young girl or woman client in so far as it is a factor in her attractiveness to men . . . and if she was a girl likely to run away, the height would be relevant for police identification" (p. 184). Specific detail that served social work's goal was commendable.

The tendency to record spectacular incidents in a client's life merely to enhance story interest constituted another problem for Sheffield. She argued (p. 195) that as "tempting as it is to repeat entertaining incidents," these must not distract either social workers or readers from the professional problem at hand. It was possible, however, to keep dramatic incidents for later publicity purposes, even if they did not shed light on current treatment. Two years later, in *Case Study Possibilities* (1922, pp. 7–8), Sheffield positioned herself more firmly within the scientific pole of the profession by noting that although reading fiction may afford "hypotheses for behavior, their validity would still have to be tested out through instances from actual life. In a scientific sense, no one could know that things happen typically as they do in this or that novel."

In later works such as Margaret Cochran Bristol's *Handbook of Social Case Recording* (1936, p. 74), Sheffield's preoccupation with technical rules for the exclusion of colorful material was further elaborated. Although many records were "lifeless, colorless, and devoid of those elements which give readers a feeling that the client and his associates actually lived," Bristol suggested that social workers' injection of local color be "measured" to avoid making the record colorful at the expense of brevity.

Many who sought to enhance the drama of case records, however, never forgot that the real business of social work was science. Even Claire Tousley, an ardent social work publicist, noted (1927, p. 176) that "we should not fail to hail the new developments of research and statistics with loud acclaim and bared heads for it is giving us a dignified peg on which to hang social work interpretation." Some social workers such as Frank Bruno, however, never resolved this quandary. On the one hand, Bruno argued that statistics and objective validity were indispensable. On the other hand, he believed (1926, p. 186) that ultimately social work's "means of description are subjective evaluations," and that the "real objective test of social work [was] an honestly and dramatically described case story."

Just as they had attacked the scientific aspirations of social workers, sociologists also attacked their writing ambitions. Sociologist Thomas Eliot, for example, criticized social work case records on the grounds that they lacked color and human presence. A case record, he complained (1928, p. 541), "has all the juice squeezed out, and is displayed, like a botanical specimen, from which even a soaking cannot revive a semblance of the original in its ecological setting." Eliot admitted that "occasionally, *The Survey* or *The Family* publishes a vivid but doubtless accurate thumb nail sketch of a case" (p. 542) but believed that in general social work's literary aspirations were not realized: "twice [he had] placed [cases] in the hands of fiction writers without a flash of response."

Although local-colorists advocated less abstraction in case narratives than did their scientific colleagues, they nonetheless produced stripped-down, sanitized accounts of clients' lives. Clients, in the local color genre, were generally presented as singularly heroic, romantic, or pitiful and thus deprived of complexity. Local color narratives, like those in the scientific mode, were heavily processed and purified and too often used to pursue professional ambitions at the cost of suppressing clients' perspectives and aspirations. In both cases, the imprint of professional authority was distinct.

Although traces of the client-subject were never completely erased from case records (chapter 3), the selection and editorial activities of social worker authors in both modes were omnipresent. A few, however, moved closer to, and made explicit, the commendable goal of finding more collaborative models for telling client tales by sharing textual space and promoting opportunities for letting the client speak.

Sharing Textual Space? Own Stories, Life Histories, and Verbatim Interviews

> I sometimes wonder what would happen if suddenly they [case histories] were to start talking. What sounds would issue from that cabinet! Children's cries, women's moans, resounding blows, quarrels, obscenities, recriminations, interrogations, hasty decisions, false testimony, administrative platitudes.
>
> ❧Konrad (1978)

Octavia Hill, a British charity organization society movement leader and housing reformer, was influential in advancing the project of slum supervision and reclamation efforts in England during the 1860s. She contended that social reconciliation necessitated a detailed, distinctive knowledge of the poor: "By character more is meant than whether a man is a drunkard or a woman is dishonest; it means knowledge of the passions, hopes, and history of people; where temptation will touch them, what is the little scheme they have made of their lives, or would make, if they had encouragement" (Richmond 1917, p. 30).

Mary Richmond insisted that Hill's approach to inquiry "was a conception so sound and so inspired that science came later not to correct it but to fulfill it" (p. 370). Although that proximate view of the intimate life of the poor was undoubtedly born of class privilege and professional power, Arthur Wood (1925, p. 64) argued nonetheless that the "democratic impulses" of social work generated a "faith in backward peoples." As a result, social workers were urged to seek to "enlarge their opportunities for [client] self-expression" and embark upon a variety of different courses for obtaining knowledge of these clients' "passions, hopes, and history."

The Americanization studies carried out around World War I by social workers under the auspices of the Carnegie Foundation were an early part of a tradition of knowledge-building that was unique because it allowed clients to speak for themselves. In a Chicago study, for example, an Italian family of nine's daily adjustments to life were extensively documented, and professional editing was conspicuously absent throughout the narration. Because such social investigation did not subject the words and attitudes of family members to extensive professional bowdlerization, its story of American ethnocentrism and the difficulties of cross-cultural travels—not conditioning factors or professional interpretations—formed the heart of the account:

The father tells of the difficulties of making it under the industrial system here. He has not been successful here. Luck in his opinion is responsible for success and it is more of an element than perseverance or industry. He thought the government should force the profiteers to cease their actions. He notes that while Americans brag about what a wonderful country they have, they overlook the fact that other countries have poetry, literature, scenery, and forms of government equal to America. The father is sure there is race prejudice against Italians and deplores the use of epithets like Wop, Dago, and Polack and hopes that the hate in our hearts will disappear. He thinks that anyone not born in the US can never be a real American. The schools have not been satisfactory for there is discrimination . . . if teachers could become more personally acquainted with the homes of their children, there might be more sympathy and interest. (Sophonisba Breckinridge Papers)

An example of early experimentation with giving textual space to clients, Americanization studies were important precursors to later efforts to elicit "own stories" and client self-expressions devoid of professionally generated rules of causality and signification.

In 1917 the *Charity Organization Bulletin* inaugurated a version of own stories that was called the "case monograph." This form of case-recording was thought to provide "more atmosphere and a deeper reality" and was assumed to differ from conventional case records. "Necessarily, the case record is without perspective; necessarily it chronicles the operations of social workers and detracts from the supreme theme of personality of the subject. The monograph, on the contrary, gives our subject in the round, sinking the social practitioners in the background. The one is filled with detached facts and only half-explained contradictions; the other is saturated with atmosphere and with a sense of origins" (Case Monographs of South Italians 1917, pp. 98–99). A case monograph was thought to more effectively convey a multidimensional client by deemphasizing the activities of the social worker author.

In a precursor to the case monograph that was also published in the *Charity Organization Bulletin,* Ida Hull (1914) noted that her work was designed to reveal "old country background" and provide better acquaintance "with the marked individuality behind a general type, and assistance in helping to rid social workers of stereotyped notions of foreigners" (p. 98). The editors of the monograph series asserted that "case stories are not new things—we are always writing them to illustrate some technical point or prove some thesis such as that immigrants should not be kept out of our country or should not be admitted in. The writer of this monograph had no such brief" (p. 99).

Despite touting the "lack of a brief," many entries were laden heavily with the perspectives of their social worker authors, resulting in documents vastly different from the uncensored accounts produced by those involved in Americanization studies. For example, Hull judged that:

> [Southern Italians] have a curious way of attributing great food value to some things such as imported macaroni cheese and oil just because they knew them and valued them in the old country. (p. 109)

> Mrs. M's mental processes are curiously slow. She does not think about anything abstract or not directly associated with her daily life. One can almost hear her wheels creak when she makes an unusual mental effort. (p. 120)

> It is not generally known that her upbringing was different from her neighbors of peasant stock, but she makes a better impression on Americans than do most Italians. Even the overseer of the poor noticed how attractive she was. (p. 127)

It is evident that a great deal of staging and framing went into this presentation as well as the free play of cultural stereotypes and class prejudices. Despite the purported effort to "sink the social practitioner in the background," the passages, compared with Americanization studies, reveal vastly different themes and significations that resulted in accounts that were both oppositional and adversarial.

Charity organization society case monographs and Americanization studies by no means exhausted the ways in which early social workers experimented with alternative forms of inquiry and recording. The variety of strategies for sharing textual space with clients included paraphrasing, direct quotations, verbatim interviewing, life histories, own stories, and clients' confessional writings to enhance client presence and build intimate knowledge of their passions and hopes. Linton Swift, an executive at the Family Welfare Association of America, for example, encouraged (1928, p. 537) social workers to allow clients to write their "own words" and provide a self-analysis. "Is it not possible that the impulse towards self-explanation and perhaps towards literary composition might be aroused with interesting results? The document might not always be truthful . . . even the lapses from truth should often be revealing. As with the confessional documents used by psychologists, the revelations would lie as much between the lines as in the words themselves." Laura Keiser (1927, p. 20) advocated an approach based on a free-floating discussion of attitudes so clients would have the chance "to relieve emotion through purging their minds." Lila Kline, who worked with former servicemen, noted (1922, p. 99) the value of letting clients tell their stories in their own ways, especially stories about military service. "However tedious it may be to the social worker," such a narration "may reveal how nervous or emotionally unstable their clients were as well as allow them relief from pent up emotions." Suggesting the popularity of such approaches, Helen Kempton, associate director of the American Association for Organizing Family Welfare, observed that by 1932 many social workers had a long tradition of "letting the client talk" (p. 111).

"Letting the client talk" also became a principle of sociologists during the 1920s, but for different reasons. In 1928, at a meeting of the American Sociological Society's Section on Sociology and Social Work, Ernest Burgess of the University of Chicago argued (1928, p. 526) that verbatim recording and first-person accounts would purge the "coloring, distortion, and personal equation or translations of the social worker" from case records. He also complained that characters in social work case records "do not move and act." They were "depersonalized, . . . robots, or mere cases undifferentiated except by the recurring problems of poverty." Ironically, Burgess's prototype, like Mary Richmond's, was the British model of the friendly visitor, Octavia Hill's approach to knowledge-building.

At the same event, Thomas Eliot (1928, p. 543) maintained that case records too often were mere "alibis" and that caseworkers' "subjective attitudes" could be thought of as "defense mechanisms." He suggested that it would be fruitful for social workers to model themselves after sociologists when recording a case, because a sociologist "keeps himself out of the picture as much as possible, to see what would happen if he wasn't there."[16]

Reaching a zenith during the 1920s, a rash of first-person, own stories, and life histories were written by sociologists in order to advance what Ross (1991) has described as knowledge of contextually based attitudes. Notable were Clifford Shaw's *The Jack Roller* (1930), Nel Anderson's *The Hobo* (1923), Frederick Thrasher's *The Gang* (1927), William I. Thomas's *The Unadjusted Girl* (1925), based in part on the case histories of social workers, and William I. Thomas and Florian Znaniecki's *The Polish Peasant in Europe and America* (1927), a mammoth work of more than 2,200 pages, including letters, diaries, and autobiographies. Sociologists not only regarded social workers' literary efforts in this area as defective, but they also claimed to be more proficient at producing the genre. Once again sociologists justified qualitative case study, own stories, and life histories as ways of providing remedial scientific instruction to social work.

The Jack Roller: A Delinquent Boy's Own Story

Sociologists often extolled *The Jack Roller* as an exemplar of case-recording. As Rodney Brandon, director of public welfare for the state of Illinois described its significance, "This book will teach social workers the importance of first studying the qualities of their subjects before they begin their ministrations" (1930, p. vii). Ernest Burgess, who had directed Clifford Shaw's work throughout its dissertation stage, loftily asserted in the preface to *The Jack Roller* that sociological life histories were kin to microscopes, enabling sociologists "to penetrate beneath the external surface of reality and to bring into clear relief hitherto hidden processes" (p. xi).

Shaw noted that although many illuminating and interesting autobiographies of delinquents had been published, their value was diminished by the absence of supplementary case material that "might serve as a check on authenticity of the story and afford a more reliable interpretation" (p. 2). He argued that own stories could not stand alone; they needed verifiable material such as family histories, psychiatric findings, and official records of offenses and commitments—the unacknowledged staples of a social work case record.

Both in the introduction and concluding discussion of *The Jack Roller,* modern readers can discern the conflicting allegiances of Shaw and Burgess. As they were engaged in type-casting, they also sought to reveal contextuality, that is, the unique inner life, attitudes, and the sociocultural world of "Stanley," the jackroller [thief]. In deference to his more quantitative critics in sociology, Shaw was quick to point out that life history data was indeed "scientific" because such data provided a basis for formulating hypotheses about causal factors that comparative study and statistics could later test.

To prepare Stanley to write his own story, Shaw first interviewed him. He then consulted official records to arrange Stanley's experiences in the order of their occurrence and presented them to Stanley to guide him in writing his own story. Stanley was instructed to give a detailed description of each event, the situation in which it occurred, and his reactions to the experiences. His first attempt proved unacceptable to Shaw, and he was asked to rewrite his story. From the first chapter on, Shaw made it clear that his role was that of executive producer, providing the preferred meanings of Stanley's experiences. Thus, in the first of his many annotations, Shaw wrote (1930, p. 47) that the "introductory paragraph is typical of Stanley's self-justificatory attitude towards his own problems and situations. Throughout the entire document, he makes a rather definite attempt to place the responsibility for his misconduct upon fate, circumstances and other persons, particularly his stepmother."

The Jack Roller reads like a pulp fiction confession. After six years of dress rehearsals and rewriting, Stanley's account finally became a performance of Shaw's preferred plot. Stanley, at long last, properly narrated his sins and crimes, his capture and punishments, as well as his repentance and redemption. Upon release from the House of Corrections, he was placed by Shaw in a foster home in a "nondelinquent community" where he received vocational guidance and a chance to develop relationships in "conventional" groups. Stanley's final words are just the kind of acknowledgement and praise that all professionals seek: "My reformation I attribute to the people I came into contact with after leaving the House of Correction and through whom I met today the woman who is my wife" (p. 183).

He was not to have the last word, however. In the last chapter of the *The Jack*

Roller, Burgess felt that more professional shearing of Stanley was needed and thus pronounced him a "known type, a member of the criminal species" (p. 85).[17] Classifying, annotating, and abstracting interventions were thus performed on Stanley's story throughout the entire account. The result was a precise set of study guides to aid readers in understanding Stanley, an authoritative interpretation that greatly circumscribed the supposedly unfettered textual space allocated to the man himself.

Despite the many professional operations that Shaw and Burgess performed on Stanley's supposed "own story," many suspicions were voiced from within the discipline about this kind of sociological research. Even adherents to such a research approach were worried about falsity and error due to subjects' tendencies to portray themselves in flattering ways. Bain (1925, p. 357), for example, argued that Stanley's "impersonal confession" did have a place in social research, even though it was an "art product, a species of sublimation, an elaborate self-justification" in which the confessant painted as "pretty a picture of himself" as he could. W. I. Thomas (1925) noted how often the plots for own stories and life histories were shaped by motion pictures, the newspapers, and "light" periodicals, which contain "a large and alluring element of sin over which virtue eventually triumphs" (pp. 83–84).[18]

Although unacknowledged by Shaw, Stanley had assimilated professional idioms and rhetorics, as long-term subjects of anthropology often do (Marcus and Fischer 1986). Florence Waite, a social worker, also noted (1926, p. 191) that such dynamics occurred in social work after a family had "experienced the pecks" of different visitors. Not all clients assimilated, however, and tailored their stories to suit professional preferences. And, unlike Shaw and Burgess's heavily orchestrated account of Stanley, social workers did not always impose such tidy captions, categories, and closures as were evident in *The Jack Roller.* Some clients were not only noncompliant but also actively sought to upset and resist their social workers' desires and preferred narrative resolutions.[19]

Given that sociologists sought to play a self-proclaimed role as methodological mentors to their scientifically immature colleagues in social work, it is ironic that social workers turned the tables. Directing attention to the contaminating role of sociologists in plotting own stories, social workers such as Frank Bruno (1928, pp. 532–33) were quick to point out that extraction and selection made sociological accounts hopelessly partial: "Selection of the significant statements introduces exactly the element of possible error which interpretation in a third person involves, namely the recorder is using judgement with respect to the material. . . . Admitting, however, that selection is necessary, most of the value of direct quotation disappears, saving only the element of apparent vividness

and direct reality which direct quotation carries as against narrative recital."
Thus, selectivity could not be avoided in any form of presenting client stories,
and therefore sociological own stories were vulnerable to the same critique as
social work case records.

Linton Swift (1928, p. 537) also criticized sociologists' verbatim interviewing
practices, observing that having a third person present at interviews as observer
and recorder was dangerous from a casework point of view because it resulted in
a "created situation" by introducing an "artificial element." With a background
in social work practice that emphasized intimate and ongoing contact with the lives
of clients, Virginia Robinson (1926, p. 300) attacked sociological methods of se-
curing life histories for their failure to consider the relational aspects of encounters. She argued that the methods of sociologist E. T. Krueger, for example, showed
little respect for the relationship that catharsis set up. For a social worker simply
to withdraw after an intimate history had been secured would be as "serious a
breach of responsibility as for a surgeon to abandon a case after inserting a knife."

Interest in such psychologically inspired problems as the establishment of therapeutic relationships, transference, and identification led many social workers to
begin to record interactive processes with clients, a precursor to the "process recording" format still used in social work education. Bristol (1936), for example,
argued that the part social workers played in encounters with clients should be
noted in case records, and many agency supervisors and teachers of casework required students and workers to record their thought processes (Colcord 1927; Jarrett 1919; Robinson 1926; Taft 1924). Gordon Hamilton (1936, p. 94) observed that
it was becoming common practice for the "stimulus remarks" (conversational
promptings) of social workers to be recorded in case records, much like the "asides
used in the drama of Eugene O'Neill." Rachel Childrey (1933) also recommended
extensive documentation of caseworkers' activity and process in all case records.
Attention to stimulus remarks and asides, however, was far from a self-critical
interrogation of the power of social workers as authors and of the narrative complications their professional and class-based privileges posed.

Finding the Right Words for Case Records

Social workers expressed a variety of responses to the unruly state of their field.
There still remained, however, additional professional tasks in what JoAnne Brown
(1986, p. 48) calls the "complex amalgam of social and epistemological activities
subsumed under what historians study as professionalization" as social workers
turned to justifying and devising a professional vocabulary. Brown notes that there
are "two contradictory tasks that lie at the heart of the project of professionalization, popularizing one's contribution to society so that it is comprehensive enough

to be appreciated and monopolizing one's knowledge, so that it is incomprehensible enough to be marketable" (p. 37). She also argues that monopoly in established professions tends to predominate, whereas in new professions popularity is emphasized. Social workers were extravagant when it came to popularizing their profession, yet they did not neglect the task of building a special vocabulary for displaying their distinctive skills and knowledge (chapter 6).

Some social workers applauded the lack of fixed words, conceptualizations, and taxonomies, boasting of the promise of fresh and youthful ways of thinking, seeing, and talking. As Gordon Hamilton (1923, p. 336) proclaimed, the nicest thing about social casework was that "we are all still young together." Virginia Robinson (1930, p. 64) also observed that social workers had not reached the capacity to "observe and record" clearly enough to be ready to "trust themselves in crystallizations of observation and interpretations." And in 1936 Gordon Hamilton admonished social workers that "records should be written to suit the case, not the case geared to a theoretical pattern. There are no canons of mass or coherence, no dramatic unities to which the living situation must be shaped" (p. 4).

Yet regardless of their comfort level with professional fluidity, many social work leaders struggled to bring order and meaning to their field by fashioning a professional vocabulary and formulating appropriate conceptual tools. Ada Sheffield (1937, p. 277) bemoaned the lack of "appropriate conceptual tools . . . and satisfactory guidance for shaping [social workers'] multifarious data into significant order—as it is evidenced by their case histories." They were to develop "word symbols representing complex conceptual groupings" (Bristol 1936, p. 50).

Sheffield (1922, p. 19) declared that the professional vocabulary of caseworkers was far from uniform and urged that "any advance in scientific standing of case work is conditioned upon the refinement of our descriptive vocabulary." In efforts to "refine" the vocabulary of the discipline, social work leaders recommended purging the nomenclature of words such as "worthy and unworthy," "helpable and unhelpable," "charity," and "slums" (Glenn 1913; Weller 1908). Mary Richmond (1917, p. 349) urged social workers to avoid vague meanings and never categorize something as "a tree if one may call it a spruce or a pine." Her "Index Expurgatorius" for social caseworkers ruled out such client descriptions as "refined," "dull," "shiftless," "bad," and "industrious." In the same spirit, the magazine *Charities and Commons* changed its name to *Survey* so "contributors to social progress will not be clouded or distorted by the meanings given to the concept charity" (1909, p. 1253).

Social workers did not confine themselves simply to banishing words, however. Many leaders understood that much more was at stake in refining vocabulary. In her study of how professions achieve monopolies of expertise, Magali Sarfatti Larson has shown that professional authority is dependent upon the appropriation of a "field of discursive expert power, . . . the right to speak in and about their domain" (Haskell 1984, p. 35). Sheffield (1922, pp. 19–20) anticipated this idea when she maintained that "undisciplined minds" must be replaced by "funded thought or a requisite set of expectations" and that even "vague terms" help infuse facts with meaning and content and increase the accuracy of thought, observation, and expression. In "funded thinking," a common terminology was thought to yield the benefits of guiding social workers to arrive at shared meanings, leading them to "observe with more discrimination" and supplying them with a "set of expectations as to the possibilities within a case."

Social workers were especially prone to borrowing interpretative concepts and vocabulary from better established fields such as psychology, medicine, and even engineering. William Healy's diagnostic terms were particularly popular. At the 1917 meeting of the National Conference of Social Work, Healy presented a scheme for classifying mental aberrations into a constellation of the "constitutionally inferior psychopathic personality," that is, individuals who exhibited a "strange lack of ability to adjust to the demands of society and who test neither mentally defective or insane" (p. 109). The diagnostic concept of the "constitutionally inferior psychopathic personality" subsequently appeared in numerous articles published in 1920, including Virginia Murray's "The Runaway Girl and the Stranded Girl," Margaret Powers's "The Industrial Cost of a Psychopathic Employee," and Jessie Hodder's "Disciplinary Measures in the Management of the Psychopathic Delinquent Woman." Jessie Taft (1922, p. 373) found psychiatric terminology such as "constitutional inferior," "moron," "defective delinquent," and "psychopathic personality" greatly preferable to popular social work descriptions such as "insane," "drug fiend," "sex pervert," and "moral imbecile." Once again, however, sociologists also found social work vocabulary wanting. Jane Clark (1926, p. 33), for example, argued that social workers had only a "vague sense" of the meaning of many concepts, and their propensity for words "culled hither and yon from the older professions" resulted in a professional terminology that was "adolescent."

Yet social workers did strive to develop their own vocabulary. In 1936 a *Social Worker's Dictionary* was published. Its authors stated, however, that the dictionary was not intended to provide authoritative definitions that would put to an end existing differences of opinion or settle current controversies. Such a task, they believed, was "hopeless." The Kansas City chapter of the American Association of Social Workers identified the pressing need for a terminology adequate to describe the technical aspects of interviewing in order to improve "process recording" and adopted a vernacular system of nomenclature in which terms such as "hostessing" and "cards on the table" were used to describe social work interview techniques. In discussing the committee's work, Joanna Colcord (1928–29, p. 519) justified the choice of such unpretentious terms by noting that "the scientists and medical men have had the advantage of sonorous Latin and Greek in which to couch their technical vocabulary but when their dignified terms are translated into plain English the names sound not unlike our own clumsy terms."

Frank Bruno (1936, pp. 232–33) likewise argued that psychology had also acquired "a lot of strange Greek sounding terms," and that the use of such terms often created the illusion that knowledge of them implied understanding. That illusion was created by "substitution of the symbol for the reality which is likely to happen to words which are associated with interesting but uncommon experiences." Because social workers could not possibly become expert psychiatrists, however, Bruno warned (p. 119) that they must "recognize the subtle danger involved in the acquisition of a large new vocabulary descriptive of human abnormalities in conceptual terms." Along the same lines, Hamilton (1936, p. 119) urged social workers to borrow words only if they have been thoroughly "naturalized" within social work, because "the foreign or imported word is all too frequently overworked which does not add to its charm. Sometimes lack of real knowledge of the subject leads to absurdities like: He never indulged in sex relations as he is conflicted over the sex act. There are indications of an Oedipus complex and schizophrenia. Fortunately, printing is his trade and in this he found sublimation."

Social workers, however, did go on to "naturalize" terms from other disciplines and circumscribe clients in a variety of words and concepts in their professional narrations. Many were frequently indifferent, however, to what was at stake in these professional interventions. Writing words, as Charles Stillman aptly noted in 1935, collapses and condenses clients into often demeaning categories and descriptions. Insufficient scrutiny of the politics of this professional act perpetuates a process whereby clients are situated in "problem-saturated discourses" produced through expert power-knowledge relationships (White and Epston 1990). Contemporary social workers continue to import diagnostic labels from psychology, and many are under pressure by third-party payers and agency funders to situate clients within the widely used nomenclature of pathology given in *The Diagnostic and Statistical Manual of Mental Disorders—III* (Hartman 1992; Kutchins and Kirk 1988). Pozatek (1994, p. 401) argues that using diagnostic labels and what Hoffman (1990) calls the "language of clinical blaming" is but "a socially acceptable way to speak pejoratively about people."

Such pressures heighten the contemporary urgency of questions about representation and interpretation and the disempowerment of clients as knowers and authors. Not only do many client characterizations and diagnoses abridge, abstract, and censure, but such descriptions are also often circulated to a wider audience, at times to the detriment of clients. Case records of rape crisis centers and abused women's shelters, for example, have been subpoenaed as evidence in custody battles and lawsuits. The debates of the 1920s suggest that although social workers must continue writing the stories of their clients, those narrations need to be intensively interrogated to ensure that they do not subvert clients' empowerment or stifle client self-expression and alternative forms of knowledge.

Conclusion

Too often social welfare historiography stops at this point, content with an analysis of what professional leaders said about a particular area or topic. There is more to the story of social work record-keeping and professionalization than that, however. Front-line social workers were engaged in the arduous process of translating the implications of such debates into practice. Their task was formidable because they could choose from a variety of approaches in writing descriptions of clients. Social work practitioners faced a loose, shifting, and paradoxical set of conventions for recording cases. They could use questionnaires to structure their compositions, or they could seek to capture the flair of novelists and dramatists. They could choose to share textual space and allow for the clients' voices and perspectives, or they could introduce themselves in the case record and assess the impact of their own presence. They could disappear by selecting a detached and scientific authorial pose, usually expressed in the third person. Alternatively, social workers could descend into the cavernous world of passions, sexuality, and personality that was opened by the mental hygiene movement or stay in the tried and true world of pauperism, heredity, feeblemindedness, and immorality. A plethora of words and concepts on which to ground case narratives was also available from fields such as psychology and sociology and from social work itself. Social workers, finally, were bombarded with paternalistic advice from their disciplinary colleagues in sociology and psychiatry, although such advice rarely was tailored to the convolutions of professional practice that distinguished social work.

In the fictional story of "Scattered-Brained Sally" a social worker is in despair: "Central office is yelling itself hoarse for slips, forms, face sheets, records. . . . And Sally, taking a breath, began a wild scramble through the heaps of paper on her desk, pulling a half-filled form from one pile, a face sheet from under *Social Diagnosis,* some illegible notes from a handbag . . . I resolve to be a model dictator and the first thing I know I am sitting in a stupor waiting for the right adjective or am sending out for a record or letter I forgot" (Dunham 1930, p. 363). Sally's dilemma is solved by her boyfriend from central office, who comes to her rescue by providing a way to systematize her records. Subsequently, she proudly proclaims that "best of all, her mind [was] no longer a big, buzzing, blooming confusion."

The plot resolutions in stories of Sally's real-life counterparts in social work, however, were both more complex and more untidy. The following chapters examine case records and textual practices from front-line social workers in order to trace how they translated debates over the construction of (and representation in) case records into the daily practice of early social work. The account begins by focusing on one child-placing and mental hygiene story: the case of Hazel.

3

The Rescue of "Juvenile Fragments": The Case of "Hazel"

On June 15, 1926, "Miss Sarah Champine," a caseworker in the Girls' Department of the Minneapolis Citizen's Aid Society (MCAS), accepted a dependent, delinquent child named Hazel for supervision and placement. In doing so, Miss Champine was heir to a long tradition of saving and protecting children, accomplished by such institutions as the Boston Children's Aid Society, founded in 1864; the Massachusetts Society for the Prevention of Cruelty to Children, founded in 1878; and the American Educational Aid Association, founded in 1883. Roughly ten years before she began her supervision of Hazel it had been estimated that more than two hundred organized agencies were finding homes for children in the United States (Slingerland 1919a).[1]

Miss Champine's inheritance, though, was a cumbersome one, because the task of saving children was thought to carry both divine and scientific responsibilities. Hastings H. Hart, a child-placing expert with the Russell Sage Foundation, evoked celestial metaphors: Child-placing "is a divine mission. . . . It is the mission of the Children's Aid Society to put itself in the place of God and to undertake to decide for an innocent and helpless child who shall be his father, who shall be his mother, where shall be his dwelling place, what shall be his religious training, what shall be his industrial training; in short what shall be his whole opening and opportunity in life; what shall be his destiny here and hereafter" (Slingerland 1919a, p. 82). Also in 1919, W. H. Slingerland, a special agent with the Department of Child-Helping of the Russell Sage Foundation, argued that "modern and systematic" child-saving demanded scientific expertise:

> [child-placing] no longer means the "home-finding" of past generations, the simple placing of a strange child in a foster home. It now implies law, method, organization, investigation, and social as well as individual betterment. . . . It is a technical branch of

social service, requiring expert agents and exact methods and should be done only by public officers duly trained for such work, or by trained representatives of public or private organizations that have been approved by a competent state authority. (1919a, pp. 40–41)

Like other fields of practice within social work, child-placing was redefined as the work of professionally trained experts. Among the "exact methods" it demanded of expert caseworkers such as Miss Champine were careful record-keeping and the professional accounting of contacts, interventions, and diagnoses of cases such as that of Hazel.

William Healy, a prominent psychologist and founder of the Judge Baker Foundation in Boston and before that a founder of the Chicago Juvenile Court, was emphatic about the importance of such records "since visitors come and go and memory is fallible, a record of events will have to be kept in some permanent form" (1929, p. 165). Healy insisted that the records be kept private and secure. He even discouraged social workers from having children report to the agency, because a child might be overwhelmed by the number of records, the number of people handling them, and the "extent of machinery of the agency which deals with the lives of others, including himself" (p. 165). Social workers were not to deny children's involvement with the agency or the fact that an objective record was being kept, but Healy clearly viewed records as the province of the profession rather than the client.

By 1926 record-keeping had become a canonical practice in child welfare work even though little consensus existed about what constituted good case records. In the fulfillment of her professional narrative obligation, Miss Champine's case-recording of work with Hazel generated a thirty-two-page, single-spaced account composed of more than 250 entries. She also filled out and attached a face sheet, the standardized form that preceded case narratives and, in this case, served as an abbreviated introduction to Hazel.

As was conventional by the 1920s, face sheets summarized family history and commented about disabilities and abilities, employers, institutional connections, results of mental testing, physical characteristics, habits, and other registrations with the confidential exchange (figs. 6–7). In addition, Miss Champine saved all correspondence concerning Hazel and kept scrupulous financial ledgers. What remains is an extensive paper trail of Hazel's life—her administrative record as seen, interpreted, and inscribed by the Minneapolis Citizen's Aid Society and related agencies.

In writing the life of Hazel, Miss Champine produced a professional text somewhat more in the mode of her scientifically inclined colleagues than of the local colorists. As Joseph Gusfield makes clear, however (1976, p. 31), even science necessarily has a literary dimension: "It is precisely in the acts of developing and presenting particular data as classified into general categories, the very nub of theorizing and/or conclusion making, that acts of selection, of nomenclature, artistic presentation and language emerge." But it was unlikely that Miss Champine thought of herself as an artist. To be sure, she did not expressly acknowledge that her case record-keeping involved artistic imagination or relied upon the elements a dramatist or story writer might bring to such materials. Her case record reveals no conscious efforts to present an aesthetically calculated or dramatically pleasing portrayal of Hazel, nor did she strive for literary appeal.

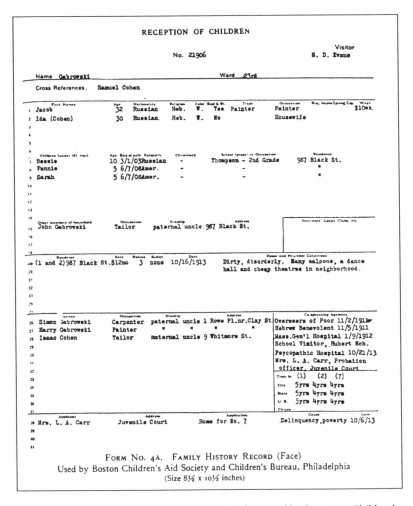

FORM No. 4A. FAMILY HISTORY RECORD (Face)
Used by Boston Children's Aid Society and Children's Bureau, Philadelphia
(Size 8½ x 10½ inches)

Figure 6. "Family History Record (Face)," 1915. This form used by the Boston Children's Aid Society and the Children's Bureau, Philadelphia was typical of face sheets used by a variety of agencies. Ralph (1915, p. 25)

Although some social workers of her era contended that the art of dramatic writing improved case narratives by highlighting the heroism, pathos, and tragedy of clients' lives, Miss Champine did not venture far into that camp. Instead, she sought to fashion a scientific and empirical document largely free of literary art and narrative design. Nonetheless, she constructed a story—interpretative in nature—based upon a rational accounting of her professional activities and her many

RECEPTION OF CHILDREN

APPLICATION NO. *L-9*   STORY SHEET   CASE NO. *204*

12-5-13.   Thomas H. Rogers, Mayor's Secretary, telephoned that Mr. D. Simms, Tea Merchant, 955 Franklin Ave., notified him that Mrs. May Brown, the applicant, with her four children, living at 900 Franklin Ave., was without food and clothing because the mother was unable to work, she having just returned from the City Hospital.

12-6-13.   Called on applicant; lives in one room in Rooming-house at 900 Franklin; prior to giving birth to Erwin (at City Hospital 11-15-13); she worked in the Kitchen of the Restaurant run by C.A.Appel, 800 Franklin; earned $6.50 per week and was allowed to take some of the unused food home to her children. Owing to mother's weakened condition she has not worked for three weeks and children are without food and clothing. The landlady, Mrs. Henry, and neighborhood merchants have given her assistance. The applicant states that her husband deserted her July 1912 at Dow Run, Mo.; that she did not see him or hear from him until April 1913 when she was with him one day. She stated that he frequently got into trouble through drinking and gambling; that he got all his money by gambling; that he sometimes abused and mistreated her, but that she loves him nevertheless. Applicant spoke feelingly of her love for her children and her desire to do well for them and cried at the thought of having to part with them. She gave the names and addresses of previous employers, Provident Association, Attendance Department, etc., as per History Sheet.

12-5-13.   Phoned Provident Association for emergency rations pending completion of investigation.

12-5-13.   Phoned Charity Registration Bureau; Case registered by Provident Association and Attendance Department, Board of Education.

12-5-13.   Called on C.A. Appel, Restaurant Prop., 800 Franklin, who stated that he had known applicant for about six months and that she was a hard working woman and a good woman, and seemed devoted to her children, and that he would heartily recommend her for assistance.

12-5-13.   Called on D. Simms, Tea Merchant, 955 Franklin, President, Franklin Avenue Improvement Association, who stated that he had helped the woman at the request of the Improvement Association, and so far as he knew she was very worthy and he would recommend her for relief.

12-5-13.   Called on Fred Inglish, 1000 Franklin, who stated he had helped the woman because requested to do so by Mr. Simms; knew very little about her but thought she was worthy of relief.

12-5-13.   Saw Mrs. Naunheim, Attendance Officer, Board of Education, who was surprised to learn that applicant was still in town. Stated that the children had failed to attend the Crow School during April 1913. On investigation she learned that the mother was working in the Grand Laundry, 3200 Lawton and was away from the children practically all day; that Loretta took care of Grace and Charles, but that she was a very forward and worldly-wise child and was fast developing into a delinquent. Mrs. Naunheim was amazed to learn that there was a son Erwin, three weeks old, because applicant had told her she was a widow. At time of her investigation applicant told her that she had just completed arrangements to return to her relatives in the country at Oates,Mo.; that the following week Mrs. Naunheim assisted her to the Iron Mountain Train and that she had received a postcard from the applicant, postmarked "Oates, Mo." stating she had arrived there safely.

12-5-13.   Phoned Mrs. Jones, Provident Association, who stated that they knew practically nothing of the applicant and that they had given relief to her at the request of Mrs. Naunheim of the Attendance Department.

FORM NO. 6C. (Story Sheet)

Figure 7. "Story Sheet," 1915. Early case narratives were typically organized as a series of dated, diarylike entries chronicling casework activities. Ralph (1915, p. 25)

interventions on Hazel's behalf. Her template for reporting that story can be seen as a professional diary of sequential actions taken to elicit Hazel's conversion and readjustment to the middle-class expectations of girlhood befitting her station in life. The result was thus inevitably partial. Miss Champine narrated professionally relevant fragments of Hazel's life—a life laid out sequentially in the case record matrix, telephone message by telephone message, interview by interview, visit by visit, shopping trip by shopping trip, and encounter by encounter.

The account was shaped throughout by narrativity because Hazel's story had movement, a beginning and an end, that involved change and development. It was a professionally guided construction of relevant facts, and it transformed Hazel's life into something else, a social work case. It imbued particular events and experiences with significance while suppressing professional irrelevancies, a reductive process akin to the literary act of metonymy. According to Kenneth Burke (1969, p. 507), metonymy, the selection of a part to represent a whole, and "reduction are substitutes for each other," both as much devices of "scientific realism" as of "poetic realism."

As the primary author of Hazel's story, which she recorded from June 15, 1926 through February 20, 1928, Miss Champine organized, selected, and ordered events; established a plot; and created a resolution with only a little help from Hazel herself.[2] Her professional construction of Hazel was not structured by a tightly ordered, conceptual frame; rather, like the case records I will describe in later chapters, it was enmeshed in a motley collection of impressions, events, and judgments. Occasionally, however, Hazel's undiluted sensibilities and perspectives were sometimes allowed to enter the story. Unlike Stanley the jackroller and the sociologists Shaw and Burgess, Hazel was not merely putty in the hands of Miss Champine; the case record reveals instances of defiance and resistance to some of her many agendas and interpretations.[3] If never completely erased, however, Hazel's subjectivity was professionally transmuted.

Meeting Hazel

According to her face sheet, Hazel, when Miss Champine encountered her, was a tall, slender seventeen-year-old who had straight, black, boyish bobbed hair, brown eyes, and a dark complexion. Her physical examination revealed no "history of self-abuse" or "immorality" (p. 91). She was a splendid student who had a Kulmann-Binet I.Q. of 140 and aspired to find work as a "stenographer or something to do with dramatics." Hazel's "disability" was "uncertainty of her station," and her single "dislike" was the "supervision of the Sauk School for Girls," a state industrial training school for delinquents.

Hazel was first referred to the Children's Aid Society by a visiting teacher (a forerunner of what now are called school social workers), "Esther Kingman," who became very "interested" in Hazel upon learning that the girl was on parole from the State Industrial Training School for girls at Sauk Center. Kingman had been told that Hazel was "unhappy" because she was required to be supervised by a parole officer. According to Miss Champine's recounting of Kingman's report, Hazel's unhappiness also stemmed from the fact that "every home that she [had] been placed in [had] received a letter from the State Training school giving instructions to the effect that she was a delinquent girl and, therefore, should not be allowed downtown unless accompanied by an older person. She was also not to receive any pay but would get the equivalent in clothing." One of the many passages that reveals Hazel's sense of things reported that she felt there was "little use in living if she were not allowed to have recreation, associate with girls of her own age, and have some personal freedom."

When Hazel was six, her mother left her father and shortly thereafter directed him to come for her, otherwise she would send Hazel to the state school because it cost too much to feed and clothe her. Soon thereafter, Hazel was committed to the Sauk Center school. School records show that she had been adjudicated not only as "neglected" but also—and more consequential to her case disposition—as "delinquent," despite the fact that she had committed "no acts of delinquency," according to Esther Kingman. Thus Hazel fell under state guardianship until age twenty-one.

In the year before the Citizen's Aid Society's intervention, Hazel's parole officer from the Sauk Center, "Mabel Campbell," had placed her in six different boarding homes. When the last adults in this series of boarding homes complained that she was "slow in doing the housework and wasn't interested in the baby," the parole officer became discouraged and decided to return Hazel to the Sauk Center. It was then that Esther Kingman, the visiting teacher, expressed her desire to see her "live a life free of the rigid supervision of the Sauk Center" and urged that she be placed out for boarding and supervision by Citizen's Aid Society.

Miss Champine learned directly from officials at the Sauk School that Hazel had been taken there because she had "no home, and insufficient clothing"; she was also "unmanageable at school." Her scholastic difficulties, however, were explained as the result of Hazel's failure to attend early Mass at the school because of her work responsibilities at the boarding homes. According to Miss Champine's notes, staff at the Sauk Center had characterized Hazel as being "extremely shy, apathetic, spiritless and not willing to go halfway in making friends." They reported her constant fear that people were aware that she was considered a delinquent and her three wishes: "to go on vacation as soon as school is out, get a good education, and that [her] sister Mary could get an education." They also reported two strong dislikes, housework and childcare, and that Hazel was "attractive, likeable, and *responds well to kindness*" (p. 3, emphasis added).

Hazel through the Eyes of the Child Guidance Clinic

When Miss Champine began supervising Hazel, she first took her to the Minneapolis Child Guidance Clinic for psychiatric evaluation and testing. The clinic, like others throughout the country, was an outgrowth of the child guidance movement. Spearheaded by the National Committee for Mental Hygiene, the organizational center of the mental hygiene movement, and financed during the 1920s by the Commonwealth Fund, the child guidance movement championed expansion of the visiting teacher concept, placement of social workers in public schools, and the development of child psychiatry (Cohen 1983; Horn 1989; Richardson 1989). The new science of child guidance, *The Survey* reported on May 1, 1930, sought "not to bend but to straighten children's personalities—to free them from the twists that may develop later into gnarled maturity" and it defined psychiatric service as one which "unbends minds and emotions, instead of waiting until the kink is actually a deformity" (p. 20).

Once under the interpretative jurisdiction of psychiatrists, psychologists, and psychiatric social workers at the Minneapolis Child Guidance Clinic, Hazel's life came to be retabulated and neatly enclosed within a mental hygiene framework. "Rose Leachman," author of the child guidance report on Hazel, noted:

> Hazel is a girl with superior intelligence and in most respects an agreeable disposition and favorable personality traits. In spite of her lack of childhood training, inadequate and temporary homes, she has apparently developed no anti-social tendencies. Her good record at the Sauk Center is indicative of her capacity to respond to a favorable environment. The chief complaint of her boarding homes that she was slow and not sufficiently interested was probably to be expected in view of the fact that Hazel feels she is doing work she dislikes, which is imposed upon her by others, and for which she has no incentive for doing well. Added to this is the frequent change of homes and the necessity for learning in each case to do the various tasks in the manner desired by each boarding mother as well as adjusting to different personalities and demands which would put a strain on an adult. Her physical condition [she was underweight] is a factor in her lassitude. Her resentment at being denied ordinary privileges and opportunities for recreational outlets is justifiable. Her feeling that she is discriminated against because of her Sauk record probably has some basis but is exaggerated. Part of Hazel's attitude is accountable to her father's influence. He is devoted in his way but has interfered with efforts of boarding homes and social readjustment.

Dr. Leachman concluded that in her professional opinion:

The patient is hypersensitive because of her Sauk Center record. Since she was sent there for a home and has no record of delinquency she resents being regarded and treated as a delinquent. *Her feeling of discrimination has some basis, but is exaggerated and is resulting in a withdrawal of herself from social contacts, an introversion, and a paranoid tendency which are unhealthy mentally and inimical to a satisfactory wholesome personality adjustment.* Her early childhood was not conducive to the formation of desirable habits. Her superior intelligence and generally favorable personality are hopeful of a satisfactory adjustment, in case the basis for her paranoid tendency can be removed, and definite motivation can be provided for her to exert her best effort. (emphasis added)

Dr. Leachman recommended that supervision of "the patient" be transferred from the parole officer to Miss Champine, who could "place [Hazel] as a dependent, help her to learn to handle her own money, and provide some social outlets." This change, it was presumed, "would remove the basis for patient's paranoid tendency." In addition, "personal work with the patient on her attitudes and personality difficulties" was also recommended. True to the conventions of psychological practice, after rendering a diagnosis based on only limited conversation and contact with Hazel, Rose Leachman departed from the scene, leaving Miss Champine to conduct her extensive "personal work."

Goodman notes (1981, p. 115) that some stories come to be so significantly reordered that they are no longer stories but "studies," the result of a rearrangement of incidents according to their significance as "symptoms." The reordering of Hazel's story by the guidance clinic staff resulted in such a study. It significantly reduced and realigned her life according to criteria of the mental hygiene movement. Specific features and attributes of Hazel's life were thus re-presented in what Kenneth Burke (1969) calls a "synecdochic form," that is, a reduction of the contours of her experiences and a representation of her within the limits of the mental hygiene conceptual paradigm. The diagnoses and prognoses made in Hazel's case were similar to what Roy Schafer terms "hermeneutically filled-in narrative structures" (1981, p. 49). Although "presented as the plain empirical data and techniques of psychoanalysis," such narrative structures have been shown to be "inseparable from investigators precritical and interrelated assumptions concerning the coherence, totality, and intelligibility of personal action."

The Hazel story produced by the child guidance clinic can also be understood in terms of what Dorothy Smith (1992) has described as the abstraction of individual experiences in professional narratives, that is, Hazel's actualities were transposed into professionally relevant conceptual currency. She was not allowed to be a speaking subject who had connectives, interpretations, and self-definitions, but was portrayed instead under a set of descriptions not of her own making. Staff at the child guidance clinic provided their own connectives to Hazel's story, disclosing only those events and feelings that fit their organizational ways of knowing and writing.

Professional practices of montage—the selection and extraction of the relevancies of Hazel's life—were thus deployed by clinical staff workers to transform her into a caricature shaped by their conceptions and preoccupations. Once Hazel's own connectives and self-interpretations had been suspended, her experiences could be refashioned as factors, allowing her to be molded into a professional type and category. As such, she became psychiatric data as well as a textual construct. As it emerged from the child guidance study, the narrative of Hazel became truncated, shaped and neatly encased within a conceptual meta-order. Her acts, utterances, and feelings were reconstructed as constituting syndromes, a "paranoid tendency" and "introversion" that resulted from professional actions that rendered Hazel's experiences professionally recognizable and thus actionable within the world of mental hygiene.

She thus entered the professional shuttle of presence and absence as the process of conversion to clinical categories and the conceptual grid of mental hygiene was enacted. The "study" of Hazel, as constructed by the staff of the Minneapolis Child Guidance Clinic, was incorporated into her case record, yet Miss Champine's rendition proceeded along an alternative narrative path.

Hazel through the Eyes of the Minneapolis Citizen's Aid Society

In 1928 Dr. Lawson Lowrey, a psychiatrist, acknowledged to participants at the National Conference of Social Work that psychiatric formulations were not always useful to social workers because diagnoses typically "present the total picture as seen in a patient in a single term":

> Such diagnostic statements as "not insane," "psychopathic personality," or "dementia praecox," represented diagnostic formulations of value to the psychiatrist and to some others, but they are not particularly helpful to the social worker since she must continue to deal with the individual to whom these and other terms might apply, that is, if the client is to remain in the community. One can well understand the impatience of the older group of social workers with formulations of this type which did not assist them to see the elements in the problem or give well defined leads concerning possible social readjustment. (1928, p. 362)

Miss Champine apparently had little use for such single-term formulations, nor did she assemble her narration of Hazel on the basis of a conceptual organizing frame such as "paranoid tendency."[4] Instead, her descriptions rested upon attributions of Hazel's "disagreeableness," "boldness," "ungratefulness," and "aloofness," that is, upon common-sense attributions that lacked the conceptual tidiness of psychiatry and were typical of the social work of that era. Although many social work leaders were already busy constructing what Ada Sheffield (1922, p. 50) termed a "requisite set of expectations" to anchor a professional vocabulary and guide observations of relevant "fact-items," that lexicon project was far from complete when Miss Champine initiated her relationship with Hazel.

For almost two years Miss Champine spent many hours building a relationship that was far more interactive than the time-limited, office-bound relationship that the staff at the child guidance clinic had with Hazel.[5] Jessie Taft, a social worker, recognized the unique quality of such social worker-client relationships when she observed (1922, pp. 371–72) that "it is not [the] innocent and remote experimentation of the lab in which the social worker is engaged. She experiments because she is forced to but her material is raw human behavior in a moving world. What the chemist, the physicist, the biologist, the physiologist, and the psychologist are attempting to understand in simplified, abstract, partial terms, the caseworker undertakes to influence or even control in all its concrete complications."

When social workers such as Miss Champine supervised their clients' "concrete complications," they produced case records that typically were far more dense and cluttered than the case histories written within more highly codified professions such as psychiatry. Yet just as prior clinical operations had created silences in the study of Hazel, Miss Champine's story—to a different degree—also suppressed, stripped, and stifled as it crafted a version of Hazel in accordance with the current conventions of the social work community. By no means were her representations innocent textual constructions devoid of professional ideology and contingency. They established authoritative definitions of Hazel's situation, needs, and feelings, even though such interpretations were based more on professionally informed common sense than on theoretically sophisticated etiologies and therapies, such as those of the child guidance and mental hygiene movements. Miss Champine did not produce a medley of dispassionate factual findings. Instead, her translations, tied to a professional community as well as to common sense, were the result of both professional knowledge and middle-class ideology.

Hazel: A Social Work Translation

Good usage, good grammar, good construction of sentences and paragraphs are the basis of all style, but the professional record can not quite follow B. Wendall's principles of unity, mass, and coherence. Life is too inconsistent and treatment usually too opportunistic for logical records. Yet the fact that each case is a sort of abstraction, a professionally conceived unit of elements which we feel relevant to us, does make for some unity.

∽Hamilton (1936)

In her search for a "professionally conceived unit of elements," Miss Champine devoted a considerable portion of Hazel's case record to an account of supervis-

ing Hazel's experiences in various boarding homes (fig. 8). An alternative to de-
tention in correctional and custodial institutions, boarding-out was based on the
notion that the "family circle" provided the "proper place" to "rescue the juvenile fragments of children from broken families" (Slingerland 1919, p. 25).[6]

While under Miss Champine's supervision, Hazel continued to be shuffled
around, ultimately to be placed in five different homes. In exchange for room,
board, and weekly wages amounting to between $1.50 and $2, Hazel was responsible for housework, child care, and meal preparation. Approximately $1.25 a week
was paid directly to Citizen's Aid Society, to be held for Hazel in a savings account.
Every expenditure such as a new brassiere, stockings, or a winter coat required Miss
Champine's approval and was duly noted in Hazel's record. Miss Champine furnished Hazel with a periodic accounting of her expenditures, but one can discern
Hazel's resentment to this arrangement from the case record. She "was quite opposed to the idea of having part of her earnings sent to this office even though they
were to be deposited in her own saving account."

Miss Champine included performance assessments by Hazel's boarding mothers in the case record, as well as Hazel's opinions about the homes where she was
placed. She regularly complained about her duties, the moods and idiosyncrasies
of her boarding mothers, the fact that frequent reassignments to new homes necessitated moving to new school districts and leaving behind old friends, and her
dislike of child care. Although regularly recorded, these complaints—especially in
contrast to the opinions of the boarding parents—were muted and often went
unheeded by Miss Champine, who must have taken to heart an adage recalled by
William Healy: "Evaluation of complaints made by the child is an important part
of the visitor's task. In this connection it should be strongly stated that the old
adage that children and fools tell the truth is disapproved repeatedly in placing
work" (1929, p. 170).

Although Hazel's perspectives on the trials and tribulations of boarding-home
life were allotted some textual space in Miss Champine's record, they were difficult
to hear above the clamor from a chorus of boarding mothers who complained of
Hazel's inefficiencies. Hazel, for example, was allowed the following story space
in one particular entry:

> One evening recently, the boarding parents went out for a short time. The children were
> in bed sleeping. Hazel decided that it would be all right for her to go out on the sidewalk
> and talk with a friend. They arrived home and found her there. Hazel said that the fos-
> ter mother had scolded her and for several days didn't speak to her. Hazel said she would
> just as soon remain in the home but for the fact that foster mom often gets spells of
> pouting when she will not speak to anyone and these spells last for days. Hazel said she
> did not mind being corrected but it was so unpleasant to be in a home when you were
> not spoken to. Hazel hoped that if a change was made she could remain in the neigh-

Typical Group at the Receiving Home   A Neglected Boy

Results After Eight Years in Good Family Homes
CHILDREN'S AID SOCIETY OF THE CITY OF NEW YORK

Figure 8. "Results after Eight Years in Good Family Homes," 1919a. Before and after photographs such as this one were used frequently in social work to endorse boarding children in private homes. Slingerland (1919a, p. 68b)

borhood. She had moved so much of her life that she wished she could get a home where she could stay. (pp. 6–7)

In commenting on this event, Miss Champine simply reported that Hazel had been "rather untidy in appearance," thereby minimizing the importance of the event and Hazel's response to it. In a similar move she flatly narrated a poignant incident that had brought Hazel to her office to complain:

Mrs. K. doesn't awaken her until 7:30. By the time, she has gotten herself dressed and the breakfast made for the family, there is little time for her to eat. The morning in question Hazel took the reminder of the breakfast made for the family and ate it thinking Mr. K. had eaten because he always eats before anyone else. When the Mrs. K. found the breakfast food was gone and that Hazel had eaten it she was very provoked. Said several things which hurt Hazel's feelings. Hazel never eats butter on her bread but the other night took butter for her potato. Mrs. K. said, "Well if you were home I bet you wouldn't eat butter that way." Hazel feels that she is begrudged the food she eats and now doesn't care whether she eats or not. (pp. 12–13)

Although Hazel was thus allowed some voice in the case record, the assessments and complaints of the boarding mothers were given greater space because Miss Champine recorded a plethora of their comments. One stated, "I will be very happy when Hazel leaves. If Hazel were a full-time maid it would be impossible to put up with her, however she is lovely with children." Another boarding mother was reported to have said that Hazel "has been of little service lately. She only does what is absolutely necessary. In fact, much of the time she is bored and disinterested. She is unhappy with Hazel for she has peculiar ideas and makes boarding mom nervous. Also, Hazel is brief in her answers when asked about her school work. Effort was made to have Hazel eat at the dinner table but they were able to do so for only a short time as her manner was such that the atmosphere seemed unpleasant." Another complained that Hazel "is impudent and doesn't want to keep early hours and takes one hour to dress. During Hazel's stay in her home, she has used the same tone of voice, facial expression, except lately, she has become sassy and talks back. She was also quite disturbed to learn from a neighbor that Hazel was once sent to the Sauk School as a delinquent."

The boarding mother of another Citizen's Aid case (Hazel's friend, "Edna") reported that Hazel complained about her boarding mother for going out every day to play bridge. She also reported that Hazel complained about being "too restricted under the supervision of a social agency." Miss Champine succinctly noted the real basis for this woman's concern: "this boarding mother felt that Hazel was making her Edna [who boarded in her home] dissatisfied."

In other entries, Hazel's additional domestic transgressions were duly recounted, including a charge that once she spent fifteen minutes in the bathroom and that she had allowed meat to burn. On a positive note, however, and soon after her assignment to a new boarding home, the boarding mother celebrated the fact that "no matter what she is asked to do, [Hazel] is always willing and good-natured and is splendid with children." This woman's child was also reported to have stated that "she wished Hazel was her mother all the time as she tells me stories when I go to bed."

Despite the amount of space Miss Champine made for the primarily negative assessments of Hazel by boarding mothers, Hazel's distinctive presence can be partially recovered. For example, she once complained that she could "not understand why, despite the fact that she tried so hard, that her boarding mother was so disagreeable and had not complimented her for anything she had done." After returning from two weeks at summer camp, Hazel was reported as saying that "the time passed much too quickly as every minute of the day was filled with fun. The idea of going back to work did not appeal to her. She had gotten tired of having to care for children." It was also reported that Hazel had stated emphatically that "no one could put her into another home to work. She was going to work downtown and have a room of her own."

In writings not wedded to the professional agenda of casework, such remarks as these might have been used to construct an altogether different plot, but Miss Champine chose to represent Hazel primarily as a site for organizational actions designed to protect the girl from a multitude of lurking dangers (fig. 9). Miss Champine was thus quick to admonish Hazel for improper conduct such as staying out late, going out with boys, or "wearing overalls, a red shirt, and a red bandanna," attire that would put her "in the way of receiving insults from men."

Miss Champine did not narrate her story in an anthropological mode, placing Hazel in the world of the culturally primitive, the unnatural, or the spectacular, and she did not signify Hazel with marks of otherness like the many "wayward" girls described in the following chapters. Nor did she employ Freudian concepts because she choose not to ferret out Hazel's deep memories or conditioning factors. Finally, and in contrast to the many tales of detection I recount in chapter 4, even though she did watch Hazel closely for signs of moral decline, Miss Champine was not a hard-boiled caseworker-as-detective, extracting information from employers, neighbors, and relatives and tailing Hazel to confirm prior assumptions. Instead, throughout the case record Miss Champine's two central themes concerned her parentlike struggles to have Hazel conform to her expectations in matters of appearance and act responsibly in how she spent her wages.

During the course of their relationship, Miss Champine and Hazel spent much time together shopping, and many such excursions were duly noted in the record. On April 13, 1927, for example, Miss Champine recorded: "Hazel at Daytons: purchased a black and grey all wool top coat, green slicker, blue regulation dress, pair

Figure 9. "At the Parting of the Ways: Ready to Develop Physical Degeneracy, Mental Retardation, and Moral Delinquency," 1910. *Psychological Clinic* 3(9): 265

of rubbers, grey wash gloves with Hazel. Hazel was simply delighted over her purchases." In a longer entry, written after a shopping spree gone awry, Miss Champine noted: "6/6/27—At 5:10, went to Daytons Department Store with both the visiting teacher and Hazel—had a terrible time getting anything that pleased the two of them. Hazel wanted to buy a blue dress trimmed with gold and black braid which the visiting teacher did not approve of. They finally settled on a yellow wash silk dress. As there was a balance of $1.25, the visiting teacher made up the difference and brought Hazel another dress costing $1.65" (p. 22).

Many of Miss Champine's descriptions focused on Hazel's appearance, an important signifier of morality. In one entry she noted with approval that "Hazel was wearing a green straw and silk combination hat which her sister had made for her. She looked neat and attractive in a short sleeved tan wool dress and had a very charming girlfriend with her." In another entry also given over to clothing, Miss Champine disdainfully noted that "Hazel was wearing a sleeveless black satin dress trimmed with a fancy lace collar. It was suggested that this dress was not suitable for school wear."

Under the rubric of Hazel's disposition, the young woman's "aloofness," "independent airs," and "disagreeableness" received a much attention, because such traits were believed to be signifiers of potential maladjustment. In two examples of entries organized around Hazel's tempestuous moods Miss Champine wrote:

> Hazel was rather disagreeable as of late and has shown a bold aggressive spirit; she has not been so willing to comply with suggestions.

> Hazel was quite stubborn, rather antagonistic, and in a disagreeable state of mind.

In a tone of deep frustration, Miss Champine also noted: "As usual, Hazel was in one of her discontented states of mind. Hazel has been unwilling to do her part; her attitude towards school and friends has been anything but agreeable and she has been most ungrateful for the interest people have taken in her. Hazel's disposition can't be counted upon for she is hasty and she can become disagreeable as quickly as she can become agreeable."

Hazel's visiting teacher, Esther Kingman, also had many complaints about Hazel, who, she stated, was only friendly and "confidential" with her when she had "a long tale of woe." The visiting teacher was especially offended by the following incident as it was duly recorded by Miss Champine:

> She [the visiting teacher] had interested a society of ladies in Hazel and, as a result, much more is being done for Hazel then should have been. Tickets to a concert had been given to Hazel and a dress and shoes had been purchased. The tickets, however, had to be practically forced upon Hazel. After the concert, Hazel had been invited to the home of one of the society's members and the visiting teacher had planned to take her but Hazel wouldn't go. The visiting teacher felt that Hazel was not at all deserving or appreciative of the society's assistance and the visiting teacher was going to try to interest them in "Mildred" instead. A few days later she learned that the women of the society were still interested in Hazel. They have talked constantly of what a wonderful girl Hazel is. How intelligent, how appreciative, etc. The visiting teacher thought that some day they would wake up and really know how ungrateful and undeserving of their interest Hazel had been. (pp. 31–32)

Throughout her supervision, Miss Champine narrated, deadpan, the various moments of pathos that befell Hazel. It is at such times that her silencing of Hazel becomes especially conspicuous. Attending high school, for example, was not an easy road for Hazel. Although she was elected captain of the volleyball team, won a first prize for folk dancing, and received good grades, Hazel's insistence on organizing a club for boarded-out girls created a disturbance. Miss Champine related the following story:

10/28/26—This morning Hazel and a girlfriend came to the visiting teacher's office asking permission to organize a girl's club at the school. For this club, they wanted only girls who attended school and who were working for their room and board. The matter was discussed with the principal who said that he was not at all in favor of that type of organization. Both girls tried to reason the matter out with him but his decision was definitely that he did not want anything of that sort in the school. Hazel was rather disagreeable and said she thought "his ideas were the berries and the school was a bum one." (p. 8)

In another school incident when Hazel's grades in biology had plummeted, Miss Champine noted:

2/15/27—Hazel was in the office this morning and her averages for the last semester were discussed. Biology mark would have been a B if she had handed in the paper required. Hazel didn't seem at all free to discuss the matter but when questioned said she had been required to write a paper on food values. Each student was required to figure out their average daily calorie intake. On a normal diet, one should eat 3600. In figuring her diet, Hazel found that she was only averaging 1800 so she did not want the teacher to get the impression that she was not well taken care of. (p. 9)

Although Miss Champine offered a somewhat tightly composed structure of meaning to potential readers, her reports on Hazel's reactions to life events were fuller and more frequent than many of the accounts I read in other case records, ensuring that Hazel's standpoint was never completely erased. To be sure, Miss Champine's custodial relationship with Hazel was hierarchical because she possessed the professional authority to select and redescribe those events and emotions in Hazel's life she judged to be relevant. Yet Hazel was never reduced to a constellation of symptoms nor to a problem type. Her words and interpretations were often allowed unexpurgated space in the record. Her expressions of hostility to supervision, for instance, were occasionally registered, such as when Hazel proclaimed that she "could see no difference between the supervision of this office and that of the Sauk Center. Both interfered with what she tried to do." In another entry, the following exchange was reported when Hazel came to the office with her friend Edna: "Hazel was quite excited as her sister Mary had told her that she was no longer under the care of the state. Hazel couldn't wait until she was eighteen and no longer under the supervision of Citizen's Aid Society. Hazel and Edna said that we had no idea how all the girls felt about being under our CAS. When they were told that the girls didn't seem to hesitate about coming to the office when they wanted help, Hazel replied, 'Oh, that is because their money is here.'"

Even though such reportage is a far cry from first-person, authorized contributions to the text, Hazel's spirit is conveyed throughout the case record. She does not appear to have been an acquiescent ward. It is possible to learn somewhat directly about Hazel as a person because Miss Champine did not claim highly professionalized and obscure knowledge of her as had the staff at the Child Guidance Clinic. In contrast to their clinical study, Miss Champine's story gives readers considerably less guidance on how to interpret Hazel and more room to appreciate her complexity.

Hazel's euphoria over turning eighteen was the subject of many entries. Miss Champine reported that "Hazel was quite delighted with the fact that she was eighteen today and was wondering if her money was going to be turned over to her now. She wanted to buy a coat immediately and wanted to pick it out herself." The story of Hazel ended abruptly when she had her way at last and was permitted to withdraw from agency supervision. Miss Champine's concluding entries on Hazel were:

1/12/28—A few days ago Hazel announced that she was now of age and was under the guardianship of no organization. Mary has started at the Barber College and she and Hazel planned to get work downtown and get an apartment of their own. Hazel has been going out quite a bit with boys and went to a party with Eldora who is by no means a good companion for Hazel.

2/1/28—Hazel's friend Edna at office: Hazel has certainly been having a wonderful time the last couple of weeks. She has gone to lots of parties. Edna expects to go to a sleigh ride that Hazel and her sister Mary were getting up.

2/6/28—Mrs. R. [the visiting teacher] phoned asking that a working home be found for Hazel and that assistance be given in supervising Hazel's recreation. She was to phone when Hazel could come to our office but nothing has been heard from Hazel.

2/20/28—Closing Entry: As Hazel has shown no desire to keep in touch with us now that she has become of age, nothing further for us to do. CASE CLOSED.

Miss Champine constructed Hazel to be a diamond in the rough, a juvenile in need of gentle supervision and character training to weather the dangers of girlhood. Unlike the stories of wayward girls and wily, immoral women (chapter 4), Hazel was not reduced to a conceptual archetype nor positioned as dangerous, opprobrious, or incoherent. According to Miss Champine, Hazel required only compassion, protection, and patience to navigate her stormy outbreaks of sauciness, disagreeableness, and independence.

Miss Champine's story was not encapsulated within a tightly ordered conceptual frame like the study of Hazel produced by the Child Guidance Clinic, but rather it rambled along through a patchwork of sometimes contradictory impressions, events, and judgments. In her narration, events often did not quite cohere or hang together to form tidy conclusions. Hazel was not reduced to an "introversion" or a "paranoid tendency" as in Rose Leachman's diagnostic typification. Instead of claiming authority by theory, Miss Champine's sprawling tale earned its authority by means of its copious descriptions of daily life, proving through its details that "she was there."

Although she revamped aspects of the professional protocol for realistic descriptions established by the more masculinized professions of sociology and psychiatry, Miss Champine still reproduced some key features of professional descriptions. She never appeared in her story as an author, nor did she display self-doubts or self-references. She omitted any mention of failure, pleasure, or puzzlement. She also used the figurative technique of past-tense narration that typically evokes the solidity of completed events to persuade readers that descriptions of events are true, and her voice was like the "Distant One" of ethnographic realism, which provides a "smooth voiceover in the bland style of a National Geographic special or a BBC documentary" (Van Maanen 1988, p. 67). In tone and posture, Miss Champine cultivated a detached, impersonal style as she narrated I-witnessed events in Hazel's life. Her starched writing style flattened everything to a single plane. In the same key, she described the facts of Hazel's birth, her grades, the lack of food at a boarding home, the refusal by school officials to let Hazel organize a club for boarded-out girls, and Hazel's final withdrawal from her supervision.

Although Miss Champine controlled the descriptions of Hazel's emotions and experiences just as she controlled the spending of her wages and her placement in working homes, she does not seem to have been the heavy-handed agent of social control so often portrayed in accounts of social workers. Her struggles with Hazel over appropriate clothing and exchanges of gifts bring to mind not the absolute power of a disciplining agent of the state acting on passive clients but rather a more complicated, cross-class relationship that featured somewhat maternal struggles with a recalcitrant daughter.[7]

Peggy Pascoe argues (1990, p. 103) that in mission homes "maternalism provided a form of female moral authority that softened the sharp edges of control in the homes," especially when there were significant age differences between matrons and residents. Undoubtedly, Hazel's version of her supervision by the Citizen's Aid Society would sound very different from Miss Champine's, but Hazel nonetheless emerges in Miss Champine's story as a spirited, complicated, and lively presence who talked back and resisted the agendas of her boarding mothers, visiting teacher, and Citizen's Aid Society caseworker. Unlike the child guidance study, with its orderly conceptual templates that neatly reduced Hazel to being representative of a diagnostic category, the protocol of social work practice propelled Miss Champine into a protracted, scrappy relationship as professional escort and friend throughout the girl's turbulent late-adolescent years. Her knowledge and description of daily things and events in Hazel's life—for example, the purchase of "two pairs of bloomers for thirty nine cents, one brassier at fifteen cents, and one white slip at forty nine cents for Hazel"—yielded a case report vastly different from the quickly drawn yet lofty caricatures of clients that characterized the narratives of mental hygiene and psychology.

Social workers' tales thus differed significantly from those told by psychiatrists and psychologists. Within social work itself, however, because the case record proved to be a pliable genre, considerable diversity existed in both the nature of relationships established with clients and in the narrations of those relationships. Some social workers embarked upon relationships and narrated their efforts as maternal, compassionate caretakers, whereas others positioned themselves as saviors of public morality from the threats posed by wily women and more willfully wayward girls than Hazel. To further complicate matters, many different professional models circulated, dictating how to compose social case stories. Some social workers insisted upon a tightly organized record of causal factors and judgments befitting the role of an expert scientific worker (chapter 2), whereas others demanded vivid coloration and bemoaned the fact that case stories lacked the sparkle and spice to ignite the general public's support of social work or its clients.

4

To Make a Case: Tales of Detection

The distinct ways in which the life of Hazel was or might have been narrated, as well as the rich debates among social work leaders about what constituted good case records, show that the case records of early social work practice cannot be viewed through a single lens. These records differed in a variety of ways, including motif, mood, and resolution, and reflected differences in the stance, tone, and activity of their social worker authors as well as the divergent missions of the various social work agencies that employed them. In this chapter and the next, I discuss two principal genres of case-recording that were representative of daily casework during the 1920s: tales of protection and tales of detection.[1]

Tales of protection and tales of detection were not two separate, free-floating discourses that dictated social work efforts, but rather two poles of narrative practice that marked the discursive boundaries within which casework occurred. This practice was influenced by many factors, including the kinds of evidence social workers gathered and the quality of relationships they established with clients. Agency missions and cultures, and the typical styles of practice they fostered, also influenced narration. The ups and downs of casework also affected case narratives, as relationships with individual clients soured or flowered, turning a tale of protection into a tale of detection or vice versa.

When social work authors narrated stories of grateful, favored, congenial clients who followed social work's preferred pathways out of maladjustment, these authors wrote what I describe as "tales of protection." These success stories (chapter 5) describe young women who bloomed with modesty rather than makeup and clients who successfully readjusted to meet professional expectations by abstaining from masturbation, arranging appropriate marriages, or scrubbing their homes and children according to standards of middle-class respectability.

In sharp contrast, caseworkers on the trail of wily, immoral women and wayward girls displayed a bent for writing tales of detection that narrated the sleuth-like methods of the profession. Written partly in response to specters of contagion and menace, these tales reveal the wary stances their social worker authors took toward clients who, in the language of such tales, did not "flower" but "coarsened." Written more like legal briefs of allegation and evidence than like success stories, case records of this genre typically featured an immense network of incriminating testimony and observations consisting of corroborative tales, reports, hearsay, rumors, and visual impressions assembled to document a vast range of unacceptable client behaviors. Tales of detection were mostly about literally "making a case" in the fullest judiciary sense of the term.

Although the stories early social workers narrated were wonderfully diverse, it is possible to distinguish among them. In tales of detection, clients were typically seen as strange, distant, or repugnant to caseworkers in the same way as criminal characters are demonized in detective fiction. Unlike tales of protection, which often read like etiquette manuals, these tales were composed like trial briefs for the prosecution. They were directed toward building a case and relied heavily on visual impressions and testimony about clients for empirical evidence. Clients' words recorded in such case records are treated with suspicion and skepticism, prefaced with words of reservation, and accompanied by disclaimers such as "client denied" or "client admitted" this charge or that.

Although tales of protection shared many commonalities with tales of detection, their narrative was more likely to resolve with the accomplishment of character reformation and readjustment or, at worst, to end in a stalemate between a social worker and a client. In tales of detection, however, endings tended to portray futile efforts with clients whom caseworkers judged to be incapable of rescue and salvation. Instead of being measured by the client's rehabilitation, professional success rested upon social workers' efforts to save the community from contaminating influences. In fact, rather than being reformed, clients often found themselves in court, institutionalized, or denied material aid—reminders of the material consequences for social work's "beneficiaries" in everyday life as well as in the pages of case-recordings. In either genre, however, professional authority and class power saturated not only how social workers crafted narratives to represent their versions of reality but also shaped the grounds on which they established relationships with clients and exercised the ability to control emotional and material resources, recommend commitment to institutions, and assume guardianship over children.

Naturally, considerable overlap existed between these two poles of narration because the record-keeping methods common to the emerging practice of casework anchored both kinds of accounts. Differences were often merely matters of degree and intensity. In tales of protection, for instance, especially those describing long-term relationships between social workers and clients, affairs might sour over the course of time, changing the narrative stance of the social work author.[2] When such shifts occurred, potential tales of protection became tales of detection as caseworkers sought to justify their lack of professional success in attempted acts of redemption. Consequently, the genres I discuss here are by no means intended to fix the narrative fluidity of case records but rather to point to significant poles in casework practice and writing during a critical phase in the growth of social work as a profession.

It is also important to point out from the outset that tales of detection were most likely to originate from agencies devoted to child protective services, for example, the Massachusetts Society for the Prevention of Cruelty to Children and the Minneapolis Child's Protective Society (MCPS). Although family welfare and child-placing agencies shared a variety of casework techniques with child protective agencies, the latter accentuated specific casework techniques for gathering evidence and embarking upon distinctive treatment resolutions that relied on the courts.[3] Agencies such as the MSPCC also reflected distinct staffing patterns because they employed much higher proportions of men at all levels, often people with law enforcement backgrounds and interests.[4] In 1908 all male MSPCC agents carried police badges and by special appointment of the governor of Massachusetts were empowered with limited police powers. One staff member observed, "If the occasion demanded it, they [the agents] showed their badge and then they reported that 'all was clear sailing'" (Blake 1947, p. 12).

Caseworkers employed by child protection agencies were not the only ones to write such accounts. Many examples of tales of detection were written by caseworkers from child-placing agencies as well, such as the Boston Children's Aid Society and the Minneapolis Citizen's Aid Society. Social workers in child-placing agencies, however, and also those in family welfare agencies were more likely to write tales of protection because they resolved their cases not with the legal system but with individualized diagnosis and therapeutic relationships.

Finally, it is important to note that although agency missions and approaches to casework informed patterns of social work narration and service and the kinds of relationships established with clients, it was nonetheless true that agency workers had a great deal of freedom to pursue distinctive, individualized relationships with clients. Their tales of detection and protection convey the diversity of casework approaches.

Casework and the Quest for Social Evidence and Testimony

Before social workers could write their tales of detection or protection, they had to gather evidence about clients' needs. Casework emphasized the uniqueness of individual clients' problems and situations. Mary Richmond asserted that an effective caseworker was one who had learned to "examine deeply," so she or he could find "every case unusual and interesting" (1930a, p. 395). Consequently, Richmond pointed out that "one of the tests to apply to a caseworker's records is to seek, in comparing them, for signs of this power to develop an individual and colorful picture." Clients and the troubling situations in which they found themselves were to be individualized instead of being treated as generic cases of neglect. Although the vigorous style of investigation pioneered by the charity organization society movement remained central to emerging forms of casework, the accumulation of evidence was reconceptualized during the 1920s as part of a rational diagnostic process, leading casework ideally to tailor treatments to individual needs and resources.

Casework cut across the boundaries of many agencies and was used to address a variety of problems in child protective and placing societies and in family casework and relief work. At the Boston Children's Aid Society and the Minneapolis Citizen's Aid Society it was applied to presenting problems such as an unsupervised, rash girl wandering at the bus station, girls impregnated by foster fathers, girls posing as college students, harried fathers wanting to place children after the death or disability of the fathers' wives, and single or widowed mothers who wanted to board children so they could work. One case was opened at the request of a twenty-one-year-old young woman who had primary responsibility for her ten siblings and was attempting to attend nursing school; another was opened when grandparents felt that their sixteen-year-old charge should be self-supporting. The Minneapolis Family Welfare Association was called to intervene in a wide array of family disturbances caused by alcohol, immoral behavior, or parents who were lazy, nervous, rundown, or lacking household necessities. In one case, a mother's drinking was so pronounced that her milk was supposedly bad; in another, a women feared for her daughter's safety because her husband was misbehaving with young girls in the neighborhood. The agencies not only saw different kinds of problems, but they also had different histories and missions that helped shape how they handled casework.

Despite these distinctive agency mandates, caseworkers exercised a great deal of autonomy in the relationships and services they provided to clients.[5] Nor was the practice of casework static over the early decades of the twentieth century; notable changes occurred, especially during the 1920s, that helped reshape every aspect, including the nature and perception of presenting problems, investigation, the nature of evidence, the kinds of clients seen, and the relationships established with them.[6] Not all agencies, however, remained equally sensitive to the changing currents of mainstream casework practice.

Mary Richmond's *Social Diagnosis* provided an analytic framework for refining older practices of the charity organization society movement, advancing a claim for specialized scientific knowledge and tying together many of the approaches practiced by disparate social work agencies and specialties. Borrowing rhetorics and processes from physicians and attorneys, investigation was revised as the science of gathering evidence and making diagnosis, and friendly visiting came to be seen as a skilled relationship.[7] Interviewing techniques, personal influence, and the collection of what Richmond termed "social evidence" were added to long-standing charity organization society methods for investigation and documentation. Negative perceptions of the movement's investigation techniques as amateurish and invasive were muted as the new rational scientific framework of skilled methods came to dominate practice, a precursor to what Wenocur and Reisch (1989, p. 96) call the still popular "study-diagnosis-treatment trilogy."

According to Richmond (1917, p. 50), an essential step in casework was the gathering and interpretation of social evidence, which she defined as "consisting of all facts as to personal and family history which, taken together, indicate the nature of a given client's social difficulties and the means to their solution. Social evidence often consists of a series of facts any one of which would have slight probative value, but which added together have a cumulative effect. Social evidence differs from legal evidence in that it is more inclusive and that the questions at issue are more complex." Richmond noted that because the kinds of evidence available for social diagnosis were largely testimonial in character, they were never likely to be "equal to the facts in the exact sciences. All that is possible for us is to obtain proof of reasonable certainty" (p. 55). Thus, despite social workers' use of scientific investigative methods, "social evidence" could never achieve the status of scientific fact. The speculative nature of social evidence had a variety of implications for the profession, for case narratives, and especially for clients subjected to the speculations, insinuations, and verdicts of an array of witnesses.

Family welfare and child protective and placing societies each had a long history of compiling social evidence. They collected extensive information on family and personal history, worked with confidential exchanges, and interviewed an array of witnesses about each client's character and behavior. Over time, however, agency callings and responsiveness to scientific influences within the field helped shape the relative emphasis put upon this aspect of casework, the earnestness with which evidence was pursued, the timing of the move to new forms of medical and psychological evidence, and the character of case-recordings.

Although the methods of child protective societies such as the MSPCC overlapped with those of child-placing and family welfare casework, the application and intensity of those methods departed greatly from the latter. Child protective societies tended to be forceful in implementing adversarial methods of evidence collection and thus advance the successful prosecution of cases on behalf of children believed to be endangered by cruelty, neglect, and "moral contamination and ruin" (Massachusetts Society for the Prevention of Cruelty to Children 1909).

Adversarial and unrelenting investigation, however, was not unique to child protective societies. In 1912, for example, the Boston Children's Aid Society, a child-placing agency, boasted in its annual report of the practice of sending confidential letters requesting the "rugged truth," both to references given by applicants and to others not given by them. By 1914 the society still acknowledged the importance of detection and investigation under the guise of "thorough study of child's history, family, and surroundings" but added the caveat of doing so "without unnecessary intrusion on [the clients'] self-respecting privacy and reserve" (Annual Report 1914, p. 37). Even more significant was that instead of focusing primarily on making a case for court, the society aimed for "friendship" and "liking," declaring that BCAS visitors sought to "maintain the "position of a friend to all seeking advice" and that the agency's aim in boarding-out work was "to have the visitors know and like their children and families, and to have these children and families know, like, and trust the visitors" (Annual Report 1912, p. 39). Detection thus took on a gentler aspect than it did at many child protection agencies.

By 1921 the MSPCC's rhetoric had also begun to move closer to the less severe methods and "friendlier" approach of child-placing agencies. The agency's annual report that year noted (p. 17) that "when conditions endangering the physical or moral welfare of a child are reported, our agents investigate the facts, and with a friendly approach, seek first the correction and rehabilitation of the family itself. This Society is not merely a prosecuting agency. Only when persuasion and all other expedients fail, does this Society take a case into court." By 1929 the society boasted (p. 19) that "as it works out, about four out of five of these family problems are handled without resorting to court action. Friendly advice and persuasion, coupled with good social casework, as it is called, succeed. In the fifth case, legal action, of one kind or another is called for." The same annual report, however, noted that child protection work required contacts with parents who were often "vicious," and that workers needed "understanding, tolerance, sympathy, patience, skill, tact, judgement, perseverance, and *often, aggressiveness*" (p. 23, emphasis added). Based on the cases I sampled from the society from throughout the 1920s, however, aggressiveness rather than the friendlier methods of child-placing better describes the casework methods of MSPCC social workers.

As result of their missions and dependence on the courts, agencies such as the MSPCC viewed case narratives as a tool of making a successful legal case, and to that end they encouraged workers to be fluent authors of tales of detection. The workers organized client stories using legal, police, and detective motifs designed to produce "reasonable certainty" of wrongdoing. Consequently, the gathering and displaying of what Richmond called "probative" testimony were the foremost elements governing this genre of the case story. Except in rare instances, caseworkers who wrote these tales did not work for the defense. Instead, they typically assumed the role of prosecutors as they embarked upon the relentless search for social evidence of wrongdoing by talking endlessly to landlords, grocers, tailors, neighbors, relatives, teachers, and nurses. By doing so, they functioned as professional rumormongers. Gossip and innuendo, formulated into patterns of "reasonable certainty," were thus rationalized as professional knowledge.

Frequently, such knowledge was brought into courtrooms by social workers who served as expert witnesses and offered professional judgments such as "proof" of "neglect," "incorrigibility," and "feeblemindedness," to name but a few judicially recognized areas of social work authority. For example a neighborhood tailor and an Italian grocer proved indispensable fountains of information in a case referred to the MSPCC by the Associated Charities of Boston in 1916 and continued until 1925. The social worker reported that "mother is a hard drinking woman who has become a nuisance in the neighborhood on account of her frequent drinking and the bad language she uses when under the influence. In consequence, she neglects her child. In the tailor's shop, there happened to be a Mr. R, an Italian grocer, who upheld the statements of the tailor adding further that it seemed like the mother conducted herself most improperly with men on the street when she was under the influence." Another neighbor was quoted as saying, "Mother had a fight with the iceman and her shrieks bothered the whole neighborhood." In a case that remained open from 1915 until 1931, the forceful accusations of informants eventually helped make a case of immorality against a women who had reputedly transgressed neighborhood norms: "The Jewish storekeeper and two Jewish women with whom the agent talked denounced mother as a bad woman and absolutely neglectful of her children. Told graphically how she entertained several different men each night and allowed the children to run around half clothed and sometimes naked. She was not fit to have them and the family was a disgrace to the neighborhood." The gossip of child's play could also contribute to professional knowledge. The worker wrote in a later entry for the same case: "Even the children on the street say that the mother was out of her mind."[8]

Often the absence of physical facts did nothing to discount the presence of discursive rumors. In an MSPCC example from the late 1920s, a police officer offered tidbits to a male agent who, using the impersonal third-person pronoun to refer to himself and so objectify his perspective (a common practice in case records), wrote that he "visited the home because of a complaint of drunkenness but he found everything in perfect order. Although he has no evidence, he has a feeling from the mother's appearance and the things he heard that she is a drinking woman."[9] Finally, in a Minneapolis case, an agent who found herself faced with an angry client shifted plans for how to make her case. She narrated instead the following account, which evoked the collective power of "we" to report rumors in the face of client resistance: "The mother was very indignant that a complaint had come in. She said there was absolutely no grounds for it. Agent said that maybe there was no grounds for physical neglect but possibility moral neglect as *we* had numerous reports that she drank and had men in all hours of the night." As these cases show, social evidence was often nothing more than gossip.

Social evidence was open to manipulation by community standard-bearers. Disgruntled neighbors often collaborated with social workers in assembling evidence to settle neighborhood disputes. In many cases, the social workers sided with neighborhood informants and the community standards they evoked against clients suspected of deviance and immorality. As the agent wrote in one MSPCC case, "The Dr. and his wife were very glad to tell agent what they knew of the family as they were greatly annoyed by them and would be glad to rid the neighborhood of them. He had seen mother several times during the summer laying outside in an intoxicated condition and indecently dressed." In the MSPCC case of "Lizzie," which was open from 1911 to 1913, a worker wrote that "Lizzie with her companions 'Edna' and 'Ruth' were the source of considerable annoyance in the neighborhood because of the misconduct of herself and friends. Investigation showed that some boys claimed to have been infected by gonorrhea from Lizzie."

Even as "professional friends" rather than adversaries, social workers embarked upon a quest for evidence, although they were likely to do so with a kinder manner. They were even apt to interview school-aged children. In the case of "Bessie," open from 1906 to 1920, an MSPCC agent interviewed "James," a sixth-grader who stated that "Bessie and her friend 'Cecila' were both known as rough girls. Bessie swore badly. He knew older boys went with these girls and knew they were on the street very late at night. They both had considerable money. He would get the names of the older boys for the agent." In the Minneapolis Citizen's Aid Society's case of "Opal," a visitor interviewed "two of the nicest girls in the school who happened to be in Opal's classes. They told of the freedom with which Opal discussed sex matters, the parties that she had been at with her boyfriends. Furthermore, they said that she has smoked a great deal."[10]

At the same time that caseworkers of all philosophies were engaged in fashioning rumor into professional knowledge and collecting extensive information for family and personal histories, some also patrolled and stalked clients in order to make "cases" from firsthand observation. The presence of "flashy women," bottles of liquor, and anonymous men were always portentous signifiers that could justify policelike methods. In a Minneapolis Family Welfare Association case, for example, the visitor "called at the address and a man was out back cutting wood. Don't know if he lives upstairs or downstairs. He volunteered no information. Possibly this is the man mentioned as being around the house a great deal." Much time was spent in determining the man's identity. In the Minneapolis Child's Protective Society case of "Ethel," a school social worker found indications of not only men but also moonshining at Ethel's home: "when [the visitor] entered the kitchen there were several men around and before she left two or three more came in. All of them entered without rapping and seemed thoroughly familiar with the home. When leaving talked to a neighbor who has seen three sacks of sugar go into the house." Ethel remained under the oversight of this protective society for many years, and agents were constantly on the lookout for suspicious sacks.

Because of the speculative nature of social evidence and a willingness to employ intrusive methods, social work was vulnerable to becoming an instrument of social discipline. In varying degrees, some child protective agencies adopted a mission of social control and exercised policelike enforcement methods. Many social workers relied upon police escorts during their surveillances. For example, in a Minneapolis Family Welfare Association case that involved an obese moonshiner, the agent reported that "the mother claims that her husband is about 38 and weighs over 250 pounds. He has always been implicated in liquor for he claims that is all he can do for no one wants to hire a fat man." The agent then "stopped in a presumed soft drink parlor that father is a proprietor of. However, as there was a number of men intoxicated in the place she left and got an officer to go into the place with her as she was under the impression that the man at the bar was the father." In another case the Associated Charities of Boston reported to an MSPCC agent that a certain woman could probably be found drunk on any given Saturday evening. It was agreed that the agent would call on her home at that time with a police escort. The raid, however, proved that the mother "was perfectly sober" and "everything was in good order."

The typical process of making a case and building a narrative, a text of moral neglect for court action, was exemplified in an MSPCC case opened in 1911 and narrated by a male agent. The case began when the assistant clerk of the court reported to the agency that three children were being left unsupervised while their mother worked in a Greek restaurant. The clerk judged the mother to be "immoral." Consequently, an MSPCC agent called at the home and talked with the "landlady who stated that she has been suspicious of mother for a long time but knows nothing positively of any wrongdoing. She goes out every evening. Has no gentlemen callers. Children are well clothed and seem well cared for. Father seems to let mother do as she pleases. He comes home from work directly and usually is in the home all evening. Has never seen mother or father drink but she imagines that both of them drink some." Then the agent met with the mother in question, whereupon he was confronted by a client who violated the norms of drinking and sexuality. "She admits drinking and states that her husband will not let her bring alcohol into the house. Consequently, she goes out to get it. She spends her evening with a gentleman friend whom she has known for years. She likes him a good deal better than she does father who will not let her have any company in the home. She confessed frankly to having improper relations with this man. Agent found the tenement of four rooms reasonably clean. Children were likewise clean and well dressed."

The agent's next step was to seek out the wife of a police officer who lived in a tenement that bordered the same yard as that of the family under investigation: "She stated mother appears to be a hard working little woman. Is always ironing or washing or cleaning about the house. Knows nothing about her however other than what she can see from her back window. Has never observed anything questionable and knows nothing at all about her possible relations to men." At loose ends, the agent returned to the clerk, who stated that he had seen the woman with sailors in cheap cafes in the square. That comment led the agent to embark upon a series of evening stalkings until he "found them in Clark's Cafe. They stayed at the table until 11:00. Then they stopped at a liquor concern and bought a quart of liquor. Agent lost them in the crowd at North Station. The next night the agent went to the cafe at 9:00. Mother was not there." Like minor characters in a novel, each friend, neighbor, and acquaintance had a say about the shadowy main character, the client.

Despite the particularly energetic efforts of the agent, this MSPCC case did not end up on a court docket for neglect, fornication, drunkenness, or cohabitation like so many other cases did. Even by social work's standards of that time, the social evidence the agent collected was, in his own words, "slender." Instead, the woman was stricken by a hemorrhage, her children were placed with a friend across the street, and the father obtained employment cutting ice in another town. According to a final entry, "Mother's chief enthusiasm now seems to be getting a divorce so she can marry her friend of whom she speaks with astonishing frankness." The agent did manage, however, to have the last word when he "warned mother that on his first bit of evidence that her atmosphere touched the children he would take them where she would not get them."

Social work agents often bemoaned the fact that so many of their attempts to secure evidence were unsuccessful. On a mournful note, one wrote: "Mother came into the house. There were indications that she had been drinking but agent would not swear to it. We are trying to secure evidence to bring the case into court. So far have no definite proof except for something that transpired a long time ago." "Slender" evidence was especially problematic when social work agents faced attorneys hired to defend clients in court, a fact that helps challenge the myth of client acquiescence. In one MSPCC case, for instance, an agent was accompanied by a police officer to serve a warrant on a mother thought to be leading an immoral life of fornication and child neglect. When they entered her home, they found a man half dressed and although he and mother both denied that he spent the night there, one of the children told officer that he had slept with mother. Mother evidently feeble-minded. She was also half dressed. Got the children ready and came to juvenile court with them. In court, the case against the children heard and the officer, a shopkeeper and agent testified. A doctor pronounced mother feebleminded and said she was a committable case. Children adjudicated neglected, custody pending the result of mother's mental exam. Mother was represented by an attorney who was very opposed to any commitment by the court. He thought mother unfortunate and ignorant.

This same mother later appealed her three-month sentence to the house of corrections and was released on bail. Through the appeal she raised enough questions about the evidence against her to gain her freedom; she did not, however, recover her children from custody.

Many social workers' verdicts, although often based on scanty evidence, resulted in severe consequences for clients, including the legal policing of their homes, court-ordered commitments to institutions, and the removal of children from parents. Pauline Leader likely voiced the sentiments of many social work clients such as herself when she asserted that her social worker had condemned her on "circumstantial evidence" (1932, p. 243).

In addition to investigative and inquisitorial skills, agents also brandished other powerful tools such as the withdrawal of material relief to discipline working-class wards and build arsenals of probative evidence. In an early MSPCC case (from 1906 to 1921) the agent described a situation in which the withdrawal of aid was used to further professional goals of breaking up a family on relief: "The visiting nurse is attempting to get various relief agencies to withdraw aid with a view to breaking them up permanently. The nurse feels that the parents are FM. Talked with the principle who said that Gertrude was in his school and was an absolutely hopeless case, filthy in her habits and quite unteachable. Mother had often been to see him and he considers her FM. Talked with Miss P., teacher of special classes, who said she examined all the kids for the school and would be willing to testify that they are all FM."

The manipulative practice of denying aid persisted throughout the 1920s at the MSPCC. In a case opened in 1926, an agent wrote a letter to the Overseers of the Poor, stating, "I have never had a good opinion of her or her husband. They are much the same as a number of other colored people who want to live as they please supported by the city or state. Before taking up this case, *I despair of getting any evidence against her.* I would therefore suggest as a preliminary step that all aid be discontinued so the children may be taken as dependents. *In cases where the evidence is weak or lacking, it is hard for us to accomplish anything.* However I am willing to try" (emphasis added). Faced with the lack of compelling evidence for removing children from homes, some workers simply forced families apart by driving them deeper in need.

Social workers also battled other professional speculations that were often at odds with their position, which illustrates the contested status of social evidence. Protective societies whose workers were in strongly court-identified agencies sometimes found themselves feuding with other caseworkers. An MSPCC case opened in the late 1920s, for example, reveals dissension between a protective social worker and a child guidance worker:

> Agent testified to the facts observed on her two visits to the home. One police officer had strong testimony of the fact that there was a lodger in the home posing as a paternal uncle. He had also seen drunkenness. Two other officers had the same testimony. The judge was just about to make an issue of neglect when a representative of DCG [an agency] said he thought mother should be given another chance. He did not think the children should be taken away at the present time. Judge said he would continue the case with agent supervising the home.

Social evidence gathered by caseworkers was ripe for differing interpretations and challenge. In one instance, for example, a hospital social worker refused to testify against another MSPCC worker's client, stating that "although she has seen the house and children dirty, she did not think it worse than many of the families she visited. The children were apparently defective but she had no proof of this and because of her relations to the families in the neighborhood did not feel she should testify against the family."

The case demonstrates that a social worker's embeddedness in a set of neighborhood relationships made her hesitant to testify against a resident and suggests that investigations in poor and working-class neighborhoods depended on local cooperation. Dependence characterized the relationships between some social workers and neighborhood residents and also within communities, where the potential existed to resist professional intrusions. Sherri Broder (1988) has argued that residents in poor and working-class neighborhoods during the early decades of the twentieth century were by no means united in their views on family life, alcohol, and sexual behavior and that these differences of opinions resulted in various meanings of evaluative terms such as *respectable* and *rough*. "Both the norm of the respectable laboring family and its antithesis, the abusive or neglectful one, were constructed through a process of negotiation within the working class and between laboring families and child welfare reformers" (p. 34).

Neighbors contributed to caseworkers' pools of social evidence as well as subverted them. In many instances social workers were stymied by uncooperative witnesses and recalcitrant informants and thus obtained no evidence. Neighbors could be assets or obstacles in the pursuit of evidence, providing glowing testimonials to the stellar character of otherwise suspicious characters or shielding them by refusing to testify against them. In one case, a Minneapolis protective agent "found the house in fair condition, lace curtains on the parlor windows and a piano which was new to the house since agent last called. Looked under the sink and found twelve ale bottles, some empty and some fresh. Agent warned mother that if she drank we would take the children away from her once again." Talking with the neighbors, however, failed to tighten the agent's case. She reported that she "later interviewed several of the families in the yard—very unsatisfactory people of the same class. All claimed to know nothing." Similarly, in another MSPCC case, the agent interviewed a neighborhood junkman who was also leery of his role as informant. He "feared the child will develop criminal instincts as he got older. He was interested in the idea of the children going to a FM institution. He agreed to keep an eye on them although he evidently objects to the 'idea of being a stool pigeon.'"

Although much social work practice narrated in the detective genre was spent pursing probative evidence that would make compelling cases against clients, social workers should not be seen simply as agents of social control who barged into the homes on reconnaissance or search-and-seizure missions. Because responses to their authority within poor communities varied considerably, social workers' actions were alternatively perceived as helpful or intrusively authoritarian. The complicated processes of discovery, investigation, arbitration, and negotiation that took place once they successfully gained entry into clients' lives will be examined subsequently.

The Main Quarry: Wayward Girls and Immoral Women

There are unadjusted girls in your community that need you now. . . .
Don't wait until their nerves are shattered by debauch, their brains
pulsating centers of obscenity, and their bodies maimed by disease.
∽Smith (1920)

The early twentieth century witnessed an escalation of concern about female sexuality and mothering that helps explain why woman and girls were overwhelmingly the protagonists in case records. Regina Kunzel, along with many other feminist scholars, has argued (1993, pp. 51, 57) that the period was characterized by widespread apprehension over the "state of moral life in an urban industrial society," "the future of the family," and what one social worker termed problems associated with the "sexual experimentation and freedom, which characterizes our present era."[11] The proliferation of dance halls, movie theaters, and amusement parks was said to promote "unnatural excitement" (Fowler 1922, p. 82), and the presence of wage-earning women on city streets and the idea of single women living apart from the moral purview of their families led social workers to focus attention on what one termed the "girl problem" (Kunzel 1993, p. 57).

Escalating apprehensions about the declining morality of women and girls led professionals to preoccupy themselves with the constellation of dangers thought to be associated with female sexuality and independence. As a result, social workers devoted great attention in narrations to ever-growing categories of women's wrongdoing, especially sexual indiscretion. In doing so, they revised traditional religious understandings of women's sexual vulnerability to accommodate emergent notions of sexual aggressiveness. Wayward girls, like immoral women, were thought to be capable of "aggressive self-direction" and therefore to pose a menace to moral society. Sex delinquents of all kinds were overwhelmingly female because, as Vida Hunt Francis asked, "Who has ever heard of a fallen boy?" (1906, p. 142).

As social workers' professional gaze became increasingly riveted upon sexual and moral transgressions, they constructed a lengthy array of signifers that denoted immoral and sexual disorder in their tales of detection. Case records were thus replete with visual and behavioral signs of women's and girls' breaches of conduct. Among the most important were keeping company with unwholesome associates and entertaining men, using profane language, riding in automobiles, haunting dance halls and cheap cafes, and transgressing gendered spatial boundaries by loitering in train stations, on neighborhood doorsteps, and in other public places. In the relentless search for such signs, social workers sexualized the physical appearance of impoverished clients. Women with vermilion lips and rouged cheeks, gaudy jewelry, and tattered or flashy clothing became ominous physical signifiers, and ruptured hymens, venereal disease, and personal habits such as masturbation, poor housekeeping practices, and drinking were likewise telltale behavioral signs of waywardness and immorality. Interpreting these signifiers to indicate underlying moral qualities, social work could easily attribute many problems that impoverished and immigrant clients experienced to the wrongdoing of women and girls rather than to the inequities of gender, class, race, and ethnicity. Women's transgressions were also typically treated more harshly then men's because of the serious consequences thought to ensue when women neglected what were perceived as their primary obligations: scrubbing their homes and shielding their children.

The tenacity social workers displayed toward foregrounding women and girls in case narratives, regardless of the nature of the presenting problems, is illustrated in a Minneapolis Family Welfare Association case. Although the worker noted on the record's face sheet that "George," the nominal client, "drinks to excess—irregularly employed—wants children to support him—complains of kidney trouble," she nonetheless imputed blame to "Martha," George's wife. Her character flaw was conceptualized as being "too easygoing." The bulk of the case story thereafter revolved around "easygoing Martha," who was relentlessly chastised for fourteen years for not charging George with drunkenness and nonsupport. George's drinking and sporadic employment were thus relegated to subplot status as Martha's defect became the predominant focus of the case record.

Even in the few cases in which women were not given star billing, interviewing women was a precondition for any type of aid or service. For example, in another Minneapolis Family Welfare Association case, a man looking for work was told that no aid would be given until "the visitor saw his wife," who thereafter provided all information on the trials and tribulations of the unemployed man.

First Visits and First Impressions

Visit: (1) to go or come to see for social pleasure, business, or sightseeing; ... (3) to go ... for official inspection; (4) to assail or inflict.

∾ *The Random House Dictionary*

Social workers gained initial entry into the worlds of clients in a variety of ways. In some cases, neighbors, interested agencies, landlords, churches, teachers, relatives, and family members themselves sought the help of social workers. Before donations of shoes or school clothing, for example, were given by Public School Child Welfare, or before a mother's pension was awarded, the Minneapolis Family Welfare Association was asked to investigate. Anonymous letter-writers also sought out social workers to initiate complaints against clients. For example, the Massachusetts Society for the Prevention of Cruelty to Children received the following unsigned letter that served as the basis for opening a case against a woman named "Mabel": "I am writing to you about a family that I have reason to believe is a menace to the laws of this country. The daughter Mabel had an affair with a married man. I know for a positive fact that she danced nude with a party of men and woman looking on. She is out every night drinking and carousing. She is simply no fit mother. I have proof."

Such letters were red flags to professional social workers and often prompted first visits. In addition, letters of "introduction" or slices of other case records were frequently sent from one charitable agency to another, providing impetus for opening contacts between social workers and clients as well as a template for guiding first impressions. Occasionally, agents received "invitations" for visits from clients themselves, although that was far more likely to occur at child-placing and family welfare agencies than at child-protective societies.[12] The high numbers of self-referrals, however, debunks simple social control explanations of harsh caseworkers administering to placid clients and suggests that a more kaleidoscopic understanding is needed to account for the mutuality and accommodation between clients and caseworkers.

Caseworkers referred to themselves in case records as "agents or visitors," who either "called" on or "visited" a variety of locales, including homes, schools, and work places. The longest single entry in each case narrative was typically a recording of the social worker's impressions of the first visit. These reports included a wide range of reactions from clients, who were sometimes described as "ignorant but agreeable." Others, happily for the visitors, were found to be "cordial, refined, and tastefully dressed." Some rolled out the welcome mat and gave social workers the pleasant experience of being "cordially received." Occasionally, caseworkers even wrote of being ushered into "pretentiously furnished parlors" or, in one case, being greeted by an apologetic client who "seemed sensitive to the fact that she had no parlor to receive guests in." Not all visitors, however, were politely received. Upon being piqued by a breach of etiquette proper to the middle-class world of receiving visitors, an agent in the case of Ethel noted that she had "called on mom Friday evening. Two men walked into the house in the most informal manner. The mother did not introduce them although the visitor asked to be presented."

Often social workers were limited to seeing clients for the first time on doorsteps, in hallways, or through half-opened doors and thus were frustrated in initial attempts to see the interiors of clients' lives firsthand. An example reported by a Minneapolis Family Welfare Association worker suggests the resistance some visiting caseworkers encountered: "The man led ESG [the social worker] into the house rather reluctantly and as ESG entered, someone who was laying in bed in the room they entered rolled over grabbing the comforter. As she did so she wrapped it securely around herself. There was nothing visible except for one foot sticking out of the comforter. It was a woman's foot." Other social workers wrote of clients who answered them only in "monosyllables," and one described a client who threw the cover of a lard pail against the door during her first visit.

Social workers were often forced to become avid snoopers who left no stones unturned when it came to visiting. Even when clients were not at home, some social workers "visited" nonetheless in search of social evidence. In one Massachusetts Society for the Prevention of Cruelty to Children case, the agent "called and found no one at home. The door was open and the kitchen and bedroom were untidy. One of the beds was in great disorder, looking as though several people slept in it. Clothing, food, and one or two beer bottles and also some rubbish were scattered all over the floor." In the case of "Wilma," a Boston Children's Aid Society social worker visited and searched Wilma's rooms when she was not at home, discovering that the young women had received three letters from three different boys.

Reading them without hesitation, the social worker concluded that although the letters were "filled with cheap sentimentality," she found "nothing to indicate wrongdoing."

Snooping was not without risk, however. In a particularly lengthy Minneapolis Child's Protective Society case (running from 1919 to 1932), however, it was the client who had the last laugh. A visiting teacher had warned the worker that "in all her years experience this is the only house in which she is afraid to go in without an officer because of the dog and the reports of what goes on inside of the house. She is anxious to get something on the mother for she has heard that the girls are running wild. Mother is a very sly women and it is hard to get any definite charge against her." Taking up the challenge posed by investigating this particular case, the agent recited the ensuing episode: "No one answered the bell. The door was open so agent started up the stairs. One of mother's cross dogs bounded out after agent. Agent just got the door closed as he got a hold of her stockings. Agent had to hold the screen door shut so the dog couldn't get out. After agent had been there for about a half hour with the dog barking furiously a well dressed man came down and said that he was sorry this happened. Agent told him to have mom call office as soon as possible. Later mother called, laughing about the incident of the dog."

Much space in case records was also devoted to first impressions based on visual cues gained through the observation of the kitchens, bedrooms, faces, and apparel of clients. This form of social evidence would remain the cornerstone of agency narratives throughout the 1920s and can be found in the tales of all the agencies I studied. In their efforts to respond to the perceived menace of wayward girls, immoral women, and incompetent mothers, caseworkers wove tales around the raw material of empirical "facts" they believed themselves to have discovered through visual observation and clues.

Scholars who have investigated the origins of psychoanalysis point out that Freud's youthful writings reveal the same naive empiricism, as when he asserted that his method was "to follow the unforgotten advice of my master, Charcot: to look at the same things again and again until they themselves begin to speak" (quoted in Bernheimer and Kahane, eds. 1990, p. 315). Along with listening to rumors and allegations, seeing, looking, and watching "again and again" were likewise among the primary methods social workers used in their search for social evidence. In this insistence they had much in common with the diagnostic methods of Jean-Martin Charcot, a pioneer psychiatrist who relied heavily on visual impressions during clinical examinations. According to one of Charcot's students, his examination practices proceeded as follows: "The patient then was completely undressed. The intern would read a clinical summary of the case while the master listened attentively. Then there was a long silence during which Charcot looked, kept looking at patient while tapping his hands on the table. . . . After awhile he would request the patient to make a movement . . . and then again the silence, the mysterious silence of Charcot" (de Marneffe 1991, p. 78).

Whether their stories ultimately stressed detection or protection, caseworkers typically surmised certain realities about clients' lives from observations far more deeply contextualized than those of medical colleagues in psychiatry or psychologists in child guidance clinics. Not limited to office rooms, hospital wards, or mental hygiene clinics for short interviews, social workers cast their gaze over a remarkably large group of witnesses as they ventured beyond the confines of professional office spaces. The female provinces of homes and neighborhoods in particular became the primary sites for observations and descriptions. Devoting pages and pages of narrative to descriptions of clients' homes and furnishings, especially kitchens and bedrooms, caseworkers were no strangers to the domestic arrangements of the poor.

By invading clients' most private concerns, including observations of sleeping arrangements and the quality of bedding and bed clothes, even social workers who related to clients through the most minimalist means gained intimate knowledge of the lives of the poor. As professional friends, caseworkers visited and lunched in clients' kitchens or at restaurants; as detectives, they patrolled clients' streets and haunts, ferreting out clues. In either mode, they acquired extensive knowledge of the everyday worlds of poor and immigrant women and their children. They witnessed the ups and downs of family fortunes and the daily struggles of coping with winter cold and unpaid bills. In one instance, a social worker reported that she had "talked [with her client] at considerable length about the differences between the outlying stores and the downtown market," comparing notes on the price and quality of the merchandise. Such caseworkers knew what their clients ate and how they spent much of their days and evenings. They saw and heard of those who took in lodgers, shared space with relatives, made moonshine, altered clothes, took in washing, and did day-work to stay afloat, and they witnessed, sought, and probed the seamy realities of prostitution, alcoholism, and child neglect.

A social worker's encounter with "Ethel," thought to be a moonshiner, provides a good example of the close-up view of domestic arrangements that social workers typically reported in tales of detection:

> The children were all nice looking. Mother wore a red and white apron and cap but had brown torn stockings. Said they had an eight room house including three bedrooms for which they pay $28.00 a month. Mother is quite worried about how she will pay the rent. Would like very much to have two Finnish boarders. She prefers men because girls use so much gas and electricity. The children were going to have pancakes for lunch and something to drink. Mother gave agent a glass of the "concoction" which tasted somewhat like beer. Mother said it was much better for the children than milk and they like it very much. It is made out of a extract of malt and hops and mixed with water and sugar

and one-third cake of yeast. The only place to get the extract in Minneapolis is from Anderson's on North Street.

It is hard to imagine the psychiatrists of Ethel's era leaving their offices or wards to sit around a kitchen table with her tasting her "concoction" and later, back at the office, painstakingly recording the recipe. The matter-of-fact narration of such daily events and the ramblings of client conversations probably caused apoplexy among social work's counterparts in psychiatry and sociology. One can only guess how a sociologist might have reacted to reading the report of a visitor who wrote that Mildred, plagued with a bad complexion, was "taking a new remedy called Dr. Reynolds' Russian Remedy and it seemed to be helping her greatly. They used it once a week but improvement had been noted. She showed visitor the bottle on which it was stated that it was a double strength laxative compounded from herbs. An old man from Northern Minnesota had come to see Mildred and told her of this wonderful remedy."

Regardless of the nature and setting of first encounters, most descriptions of first impressions in case records are heavily visual in their reconstruction. Ironically, social workers' deeply probing professional gaze thus began with the recital of observations derived from little more than a glance. That glance, however, was an important point of departure, because such visual impressions often anchored subsequent interactions with clients, directed interpretations, and led to far-reaching judgments about clients' essences, needs, and appropriate professional actions.

Precise details and judgments about clients' faces—thought to be among their most telling characteristics—were an integral part of assembling social evidence and making the case narrative. Visages—painted, powdered, tired, joyless, or in need of washing—were thought to provide clues of character and morality.[13] For many adolescent girls seen by the placing-out agencies, the face offered the first tell-tale clues of "sex weakness," "sex saturations," "prostitutes in the making," or "incorrigibility." "Opal," for example, was described in MCAS records as "very attractive with the exception that she was very rouged, lips scarlet with lipstick. She is a large girl of light complexion. Her boarding mother stated that 'she was sure that she wouldn't continue to use makeup for Helen was the same type but after she had been there awhile was quite modest in her appearance.'" "Evelyn" also had "been using lots of makeup and looks like a girl of the streets for her cheeks are rouged and her lips painted." In a Boston Children's Aid Society case, a visitor wrote of "a girl with regular features, attractive face and manner. Gives the impression of being open and frank. Expression of the mouth is slightly sophisticated. She tends towards an appearance older than thirteen." Such superficial visual clues lead this caseworker to conclude that the girl "probably plays with boys more than girls." In another case, a social worker made an even quicker judgment, writing with an air of finality, "She was very painted up and looked as though she needed custodial care."

Not only did sexually precocious girls fall within the purview of social workers but such ambiguous groupings as "hard" and "unhygienic" mothers did also. With them as well, the visages of women and mothers, like the faces of wayward girls, provided clues to character and morality, enabling social workers to imagine that they were ferreting out sinister women from otherwise simply poor and tired women. In a letter referring a case to the Massachusetts Society for the Prevention of Cruelty to Children, the Associated Charities of Boston described its client as follows: "The mother is away all day and the child runs wild. We were told that the mother drinks and she looks capable of anything. Her face is covered with a repulsive eruption." An entry that immediately followed the first visit reads: "Called at the home. Saw the woman who had a bad appearance and an eruption on her face. She did not like this investigation and would not let me see the bed where the child slept." Elsewhere, a visitor wrote, "The woman was neatly dressed and was not a hard woman. Her hair was a little curled and her face not made up to any extent." Although it appeared that the client had passed her initial litmus test of appearance, the next sentence reports that the visitor "noticed that she [the client] had a violent temper because she flew off the handle at any mention of moral neglect." Other reports on visuals impressions were particularly graphic. "The house was neat but gave the appearance of being unhygienic. The woman hobbled to the davenport where she sat down. Her feet were bare and dirty. Her clothes were filthy. A bit of flesh resembling an ulcer hung from her upper lip. Several of her teeth were gone. The baby appeared defective; had a lopsided smile, and a strange abnormal look in her eyes."

Not surprisingly, given large families, inadequate jobs, hard labor, and other harsh realities of poverty, social workers saw many women who had tired faces. Reflecting their middle-class moorings, however, the social workers typically interpreted the appearance of these tired women as indicative of moral disorder and neglect. Diagnoses of feeblemindedness and other mental defects were also made on the basis of little more than appearance, including tiredness. In a Boston Children's Aid Society case, a mother was described as "a short, thin young woman neatly and simply dressed. She has bright red hair and green eyes which have a far-off dreamy look, indicating a tired mental condition. Seemed very listless." In another case, the social worker "called and found mother at home—She is a young looking woman with a dissipated face. Appeared to be somewhat dopey and talked in a dazed and peculiar manner. Agent was greatly surprised at the frankness with which she told of her life, giving the impression she was not mentally strong." Still another social worker, although conceding that her behavioral evidence was vague, wrote that "with very little evidence beyond signs of repression, apprehension, and a defensive attitude, visitor felt suspicious of the woman's sanity." A mother in a Family Welfare case was described upon first meeting as being a "colorless languid middle-aged woman who seemed overcome by their difficulties. She was on the verge of tears several times and then would relax. They had received an eviction notice." Despite the contextual situation, that initial impression formed the basis for a case tale of feeblemindedness.

For many visitors, an orderly house meant an orderly moral family life, and assessments of tidiness formed the plot of many case narratives. Social workers also noted instances of poor personal hygiene, often based upon the state of clients' laundry or dishes or the type of food they ate. One social worker noted disdainfully that her clients had "crumbs on their table and they did not have a tablecloth of any sort." An agent in another case, however, made allowances for a particular mother, perhaps because she had ten children, and reported the home to be a "little tumbled shack in a small Italian community. The home was extremely untidy but did not appear particularly dirty. The family has five rooms but they have ten children so it would be impossible to keep them in good order. The mother was rather sloppy in her appearance. She seemed to have the interests of her children at heart and be looking to the future of the family." In another MSPCC case, however, the social worker made no such allowances after a morning visit: "The father had just finished his breakfast and was smoking a cigarette. House was in great disorder and dirty. Mother apparently has no ambition and is very slack in her person. The children were only partially dressed. Agent endeavored to show them that the house must be kept cleaner and the children better cared for or else action would be taken."

Despite the ridicule social workers often received for their own matronly style of dress, records show that they were preoccupied with the dress of clients as potent signifiers of morality. They went to great lengths to describe clients' fashions. In one case, it was observed that a client "was dressed in a brocade plush coat with a fur collar. She had a silk orange dress trimmed with fur and satin slippers. Also, a hat with raccoon and flowers. She looked a bit overdressed but very attractive." Sometimes social workers were pleased to find clients express virtuous qualities such as thrift and gratefulness in attire. A BCAS caseworker, for example, pointed out that in remodeling a hand-me-down suit, "Gertrude shows considerable ability in what she makes for herself. Another quality which she has is her cheerfulness in accepting an old suit and making the best out it. This is her second cast off suit."

In addition to the attention social workers showered on the appearances of clients, a variety of behavioral signifiers in the records are also noteworthy. In the case record of identical twins "Martha" and "Myrtle," for example, the caseworker's ongoing anxiety over any hints of budding female sexuality was extensively recorded. In one instance she reported that "the foster parents realize that the girls are the type who are likely to lose their heads over boys and as they know something of the family history they are especially anxious that the girls' minds should be kept free of sex interests." In the case of Julia, a worker noted that Julia "is eleven and is only in the fourth grade. She is backward and indifferent to her studies. The teacher showed agent a vulgar note that had been taken from her today." Especially repulsive to the visitor was the discovery that Julia was a "self abuser," a potent signifier of sexual disorder for most social workers. Although noting that "Julia admits to having bad personal habits but she said she is alone with her vice and it has nothing to do with the other children," the social worker remained critical of Julia throughout the narrative. In another case, a worker reported that she had "talked with the Overseer of the Poor in regards to Harriet. It was their opinion that she was going with bad girls and needed a word of warning."

Coarsening was a fashionable term used especially by caseworkers from child-placing societies in tales of detection. It represented the progression of negative behaviors among wayward wards and documented a downward spiral of behavior. In one such account, for example, a Boston Childen's Aid Society worker noted that her client's actions were "coarse and vulgar, and show evidence of unwholesome home environment." In another BCAS case the visitor wrote that the client "had picked up a man of the most undesirable character. About this time the girl's whole personality seemed to change. This sweet demure country girl suddenly coarsened. She began to dress conspicuously and far too scantily. She seemed to lose her self-respect."

Contamination fears, emanating especially from improper behavior on the part of young girls, was also an overriding concern in tales of detection. In one case a social worker reported that a "teacher kept the child by herself in one part of the classroom as she was so dirty." In another, a visiting teacher was quoted as saying that "Georgia was definitely FM and should not even be in an ungraded classroom."

In many cases, clients, especially those perceived as feebleminded and or too weak to resist temptation, necessitated special attention in order to shield the community from harm.[14] In the case of Myrtle and Martha, for example, the social worker reported that "the girls still have the habit of self abuse and largely on this count, it seems desirable to separate them for the sake of combatting this vice in each girl separately." C. C. Carstens, general secretary of the MSPCC, wrote that he considered one of his cases, "Nellie," to be "a bad influence on the community" and "a hopeless case of FM." He noted, however, that "it seems unwise to force a commitment because family insisted that she is more carefully watched than ever before. We are planning to keep the situation under our eyes from our New Bedford office. If any information reaches us that supervision is lacking we shall be ready to proceed and bring the matter directly before probate court." Professional success depended as much on protecting the community from disorder as from rehabilitation of the client.

Social workers as a whole were realists. They shared a passion for recounting in detail all facets of clients' lives, suggesting the intimate, if not always welcome, quality of the social work relationship. Professional claims to authority and verisimilitude were thus based on presence, long-term association, and a plethora of detail rather than on the effects of a theoretically organizing schema. Throughout casework tales, social workers were frequently unable to pinpoint a single problem to be apprehended in their clients or to apply a unifying theoretical and diagnostic frame such as the one psychologists at the Minneapolis Child Guidance Clinic used to structure their account of Hazel. Social workers displayed little uneasiness with gaps and ruptures in case histories and thus were less likely than professionals in other fields to achieve narrative closure by the insertion of theory and a sharp diagnosis. Filled with splinters and fragments and lacking grand theory, casework tales typically rambled, yet they were ultimately moored in paradigmatic procedures of investigation and discourse. The practice of examining clients physically provided one such unifying procedure.

The Signifying Hymen

> On the top floor I was taken into a room where there was a woman doctor. She beckoned me to undress and then I got on the operating table. Then she explored me, as I had seen my mother explore the inside of a chicken with a finger. I was shocked and revolted . . . I began to be afraid.
>
> ∾Leader (1932)

In their determined pursuit of evidence, social workers moved beyond relying upon initial glances to exercising more penetrating gazes intended to probe even hidden recesses of the body. As Jennifer Terry's study of "lesbians under a medical gaze" of the Committee for the Study of Sex Variants shows, along with psychiatric interviews came a "scopic regime which searched for markings of deviance on the body" by x-rays of skeletons and inspections of genitalia (1990, p. 337). Likewise, in social work the inspection of genitalia had long been considered a routine and essential part of the social investigation of young girls. All girls seen by the Massachusetts Society for the Prevention of Cruelty to Children and the Boston Children's Aid Society were required to have a physical examination before being placed in boarding homes or temporary shelters. Each agency had required physical examinations from as early as 1905. The MSPCC employed physicians on its staff throughout the 1910s and 1920s, while the BCAS engaged a medical staff, including a medical social worker shared jointly with the Boston

Dispensary and Church Home Society, where medical services as well as instruction in sexual hygiene were available.

Thus social work's search for definitive evidence lead to an all-important physical examination. Such examinations were perceived as essential for exposing masturbation, venereal disease, and promiscuity, and social workers diligently recorded the results of the examinations. For example, "Opal was given a physical exam. Hymen ruptured. Opal admitted having been promiscuous. She was, however, not diseased." Lizzie's examination "confirmed our suspicions in regards to her immorality." "Mona's" examination likewise revealed a ruptured hymen even though "the girl persistently denied immorality. The Dr. said that there must be a history of immorality to bring about the condition which she had found." Another caseworker wrote that "Alice's" examination revealed a "general condition indicative of a sex experience" and necessitated a visit to a doctor, who "thought her condition highly suspicious and she must make weekly visits to be observed. He expressed a rather hard attitude about girls who contracted disease. Thought of her as a girl not worth much consideration." Not only was such evidence highlighted in case records, but it also played a vital role in determining subsequent interventions.

Even physical examinations could not always provide the profession with completely unequivocal evidence, however. Because the evidence from physical examinations was often nebulous and contradictory, social workers floundered in attempts to frame bodily evidence based on the condition of clients' hymens. "Helen," for example, was examined twice. A physician reported after the first examination that "the condition of the labia suggests habits of masturbation. According to Helen, for a long time she practiced bad habits two or three times daily. She never had talked about it with anybody and asked 'Is it a sin to do it?'" Helen was then taken to another physician, who "gave as her opinion that the hymen showed some interference, probably sexual intercourse as the membrane was so torn that the girl could not in all probability have done this by any ordinary means of self abuse." Helen's social worker decided that "the exams were contradictory so it was only fair to assume that the girl was not misbehaving." But the matter was not allowed to fade away. In her self-analysis of the case, the social worker wrote, "It will be noted that Dr. S's report is directly contradicted by Dr. L. As girl frankly admitted the fact of earlier masturbation and had always denied with horror and indignation the suggestion that there had been any interference from the foster father, I felt that when the Drs. disagreed I was justified in giving her the benefit of the doubt."

Many girls described in the case records had been sexually assaulted by lodgers, neighbors, fathers, and brothers. Although at times social workers aided in the prosecution of such men, in the case of "Eve" the ultimate responsibility for moral behavior—hers as well as her assailant's—was assigned to Eve. She was the adopted daughter of a "miserly apple farmer." According to Eve's mother, her stepfather was "annoyed that [Eve was] not his child and vent[ed] his disposition on her." Eve's mother wanted to place her in a summer camp. Upon meeting Eve, the Minneapolis Child's Protective Society social worker was favorably impressed, noting that she was a "tall for her age, wholesome, good hearted child with a very sweet expression and smile." Up to this point, the social worker's tale rejoiced about the rosy future that awaited Eve, who was safely ensconced under her protective wing.

Once the nefarious physical examination was given, however, and it was revealed that Eve had had sexual relations, the tale turned somber, revolving solely around questions of evidence and Eve's rebuttal of the charge of immorality. Instead of a sprawling tale of the ups and downs of navigating a ward through the pitfalls of adolescence, the social work tale narrowed to a singular obsession with Eve's misconduct. When confronted with the accusation of immorality, the social worker reported that Eve had burst out, "I hate it. I hate it." The social worker then reported Eve's mother's feeling that "Eve ha[d] taken the matter of her sex delinquencies very hard." Next, Eve gave her side of the story, reporting that "she never had relations with Clarence [an older neighbor and brother of Eve's friend] without the presence of his sister Ann. She has been with him in back of the schoolhouse and twice in his home where she had gone to spend the night with Ann because her mother had to go to the grange and would not be home until late. On these occasions she slept in the bed with Ann and Clarence came in and got in bed with them. She said that she was frightened of Clarence." A physician at the Psychopathic Hospital, disputing that "each succeeding sex experience" could be explained by Eve's "claimed fears," concluded that "the continued act signifies a weakness which may become very real and certainty should be watched." According to the caseworker, the physician placed "considerable emphasis on [Eve's] sex weakness and would be interested in seeing her in a year's time."

The taint on Eve's character proved to be indelible, because the social work visitor later decided that "it seemed necessary to inform Mrs. S [a boarding mother] of Eve's former relationships with a boy in her hometown and asked that she keep a special watch on this side of Eve's nature and inform the social worker the minute she felt faced with any situation that seemed to be serious." In a long talk with Eve, the "visitor tried to show her the importance of a clean life and instructed her in the right way of living. The weakness in her character was laid before her and it was thought that the child must face the conditions fairly and honestly in order to become the master." From the visitor's perspective, however, Eve's tale ended tragically. After a series of placements in the Boston Children's Aid Society's boarding home, Eve was returned to her mother, where it was reported that "Eve [was] riding in automobiles promiscuously. Undoubtedly living an immoral life. Mother knows and does nothing. Feels there is nothing for BCAS to do." Eve's case was, therefore, closed.

Uncertainties about the causes of venereal disease during the early decades of the twentieth century left a void all too easily filled by fear of clients perceived to be infectious. Such fears could dictate the course of subsequent actions that social workers pursued. Despite the discovery of the Wassermann blood test, social workers were haunted by confusion and trepidation about venereal disease and uncertain about the sources of contraction, sounding many alarms about contagion. In the case of one client's examination that did not conform to expectations, the visitor "raised the question with the Dr. whether it's possible for the girl to be sufficiently sophisticated to have used some kind of disinfecting douche before coming in." In the case of "Ruth's" suspicious smear, the social worker felt hopeful because she felt that the client had contracted it in an "innocent way" and that the necessary precautions, such as giving Ruth her own dishes, were implemented. In another case revealing the uncertainty and confusion about the sources of contraction, the social worker struck a speculative note when she wrote that she had taken "Barbara to the doctor who says that Barbara's trouble is gonorrhea. The child must have caught it at school for children are very suspectable to this trouble."

Even after all initial signifiers of face, appearance, family history, housekeeping, and physical examinations had been investigated and documented, many caseworkers were not through with the assembly of social evidence. Beginning in the second decade of the twentieth century, the Minneapolis Family Welfare Association, the Massachusetts Society for the Prevention of Cruelty to Children, and the Boston Children's Aid Society all became alert to the problem of feeblemindedness. The BCAS's annual report of 1914 was the first to include statistics on mental conditions, and it noted the frequency of "extremely eccentric, neurotic, insane, and feeble-minded" among its clients (p. 36). Despite their different missions and orientations to practice, the BCAS and the MSPCC collaborated in 1913 in the preparation and distribution of a bulletin entitled *The Menace of the Feeble-Minded*.

Although the BCAS mentioned the use of mental examinations in its 1912 annual report, the specifics of such examinations were not given. In ensuing years the society, always responsive to new trends in casework, would refer many clients to the Judge Baker Foundation for mental testing because of the belief that "really scientific principles of conduct, diagnosis, and treatment" were available in this type of social inquiry (Annual Report 1918, p. 10). The MFWA reported a substantial increase in instances of recognizing mental defects between 1917 and 1926 because "methods of diagnosis" had become "more expert" by 1926.[15] The MSPCC, on the other hand, did not require mental testing until 1929, an indication of a lack of responsiveness to shifting parameters of casework practice and evidence-gathering.[16]

Once social evidence was in, caseworkers would then turn to the arduous task of disciplining their clients and enmeshing them in Foucaultian webs of watching, supervising, and safeguarding. They artfully practiced the disciplinary gaze as they pursued a professionally ordained quest to shield the community from contagion and contamination and, if possible, to reform their wards. Clients, naturally, were ever mindful of this watchful phase of the social work relationship. "Clara," a ward of the BCAS, was reported as having said, "Sometimes I feel suspicious that people are watching me and trying to put me away." "Billie," a dormitory waitress at Wellesley College, "explained her attitude in not wanting the society to supervise her. It was due to some statements made by the other girls who warned her against this course, saying she would be followed from place to place and her work carefully watched."

Final Judgments

In addition to her call for social workers to become experts in the accumulation of social evidence, Mary Richmond also reminded them that it was "more important to make a judgement than to suspend it" (1917, p. 355). The fact that social workers read evidence they gathered in a variety of ways naturally lead them to a write a wide and variable range of narrative resolutions and judgments into case records, which resulted in variable consequences for their clients. The story of two wayward sisters placed under the agency guardianship of the BCAS from 1908 to 1925 illustrates the different fates that befell "Winifred" and "Bertha" despite both having been identified initially as traveling on wayward tracks.

Although Winifred ultimately succumbed to sexual excess and misconduct, Bertha overcame temptation and triumphed over her past. More than simply about two separate fates and final judgments, however, the stories of Bertha and Winifred also represent distinct literary efforts. Winifred's narrative, a detailed apologia, was tailored to exonerate the social worker from responsibility for failing to prevent the coarsening and decline that eventually necessitated Winifred's commitment to custodial care. Consequently, the caseworker painstakingly noted, in much greater detail then she gave to Bertha, all the overwhelming forces that seemed to make a deplorable outcome inevitable. Bertha's story, in contrast, demanded much less attention and fewer justifications because she was saved and eventually married.

"Amanda Smith," the social worker in both cases, noted that Winifred initially manifested a variety of troublesome behaviors: "Winifred is doing fairly well in school but is not well behaved in general. Thinks nothing of saluting boys on the street, is loud in her manner and does not seem to appreciate the difference between modest and common behavior. She does not do anything which is decidedly wrong but the whole atmosphere of the girl is common." Not only was Winifred's "atmosphere common," but she was also growing "bold" and "unladylike." Subsequently, the social worker discovered that Winifred had begun "visiting the rear entrance of a straw factory with two other girls and behaving in an unladylike manner." A brief flicker of hope, however, presented itself soon thereafter when Winifred promised "to stay away from the red-headed girl whose home is so bad and whose influence is so disastrous." But Winifred's resolve was short-lived. When Smith "approached the house she found Winifred walking along just in front of her. There were some small boys up a tree. They called to Winifred in a very familiar, cheap way, showing that she had made herself rather common." In order to prevent the contamination of other children by Winifred's "commonness" as well as to protect her charge, the social worker advised Winifred's boarding mother to forbid her to go to the playground and or leave the house after dinner.

Meanwhile, Smith continued to accumulate a wide assortment of damning testimony about Winifred, which she dutifully and carefully inscribed in the case record. She recorded the boarding mother's report, for instance, that not only was Winifred "ill-bred at the table" but also that the room she was supposed to have cleaned one particular morning was "covered with clothes and peanut shells and old scraps of paper on top of the bureau." Smith further recorded the fact that Winifred's teacher had "observed Winifred's behavior with some of the boys in the school and she could see that the sex problem was beginning to be very active." In keeping with the protocols for making a case that dictated that no stones be left unturned or potential informants ignored, Smith even recorded a milkman's report to the boarding mother. He "had seen Winifred on the street after school with some boys near the cemetery and although he makes no definite charge he says she was not behaving as she should."

Following the accumulation of such evidence, Miss Smith next took Winifred to a psychologist for mental testing and consultation so "that treatments with him might correct some of her rude habits and extreme liking for boys. This latter trait is so marked that it seemed to AS [the worker] that there will be trouble later on." This trait, indeed, proved to be the proverbial final nail in Winifred's coffin. Her psychologist concluded that she "could never be called feebleminded but that there was something peculiar about her makeup. Would not be surprised if sometime she might go insane." Mere mention of the possibility of future insanity—based merely upon the psychological intuition that there was something "peculiar about her makeup"—caused the social worker to forsake her previous ministrations.

Closure on the case was achieved when Smith formalized a complaint against Winifred as a "stubborn child," an action that lead to her commitment to the Lancaster Industrial School for Girls in Massachusetts.

During the same period, Winifred's sister Bertha was also being watched. Amanda Smith described her as "unintelligent, oversuggestable, and easily led into foolish and even wrong behavior." A teacher reported that Bertha had been heard "talking dirty" at school, an ominous signifier of trouble. In response, Miss Smith "impressed upon Bertha that she was starting on the same road Winifred had taken by talking vulgar with other girls." She warned her that "she would certainly end up in reform school, too, unless she picked out good girl companions and made herself a clean girl morally." The social worker also reported that "one of the most serious things about [Bertha] is that it seems impossible to raise her interest in anything which is high or good." Nonetheless, Smith eventually believed that she had succeeded in arousing Bertha's interest in things both high and good, because Bertha was first placed out at housework and then successfully moved on to work in a candy store. The social worker described a "pleasant walk she took with her which left Bertha much cheered" and reported that she herself "came away feeling that the girl had a sweet disposition and with the right influence should grow into a good woman." Bertha's story did, in fact, end sweetly with her becoming "adjusted" through a proper marriage.

Clients who caught the accusatory eyes of caseworkers were sometimes mercilessly subjected to years of policing, court appearances, institutionalization, and loss of material relief and their children. Concurrently, they were also entrapped in sinister archives of case-recordings whereby the encapsulated tales of portentous signifiers of immortality, deviance, and waywardness had both immediate and long-term repercussions. In one case, a protective agent noted that "Miss P. of Legal Aid said father came to her for help in getting the children back. After reading our record she of course decided to do nothing about it." In addition, a majority of case files included records kept by other agencies and caseworkers. Not only were records regularly shared among agencies during the duration of a case, but many were also read by other "interested" agencies and persons after no longer being considered active in the originating agencies. They had the power to haunt clients for a long time. One case record, opened in 1910 and involving a woman suspected of running a disorderly house, was requested and read by an agency in 1965, more than a half-century later.

Not all caseworkers were in antagonistic relationships with clients, however, and many fought for the clients' interests. In one case record, "Madeline," whose widowed mother ran a manure business and had lodgers, was graphically described as a victim of sexual assault. The social worker's avowed goal was to punish the offender and keep Madeline safe, a responsibility social workers took seriously.[17]

"Wilma," a pregnant waitress who had been betrayed by a showman, was given assistance in the form of material aid by her social worker. The case of "Mary" involved a girl who was "hated" by her "sour" stepmother and banished to sleeping in a room "that was cold and had a musty odor," was "cluttered with broken toys," and had "hooks for clothes placed over the bed in such a manner that they hung over Mary's face." Such conditions led the social worker to fight on Mary's behalf. Even after it emerged that Mary was pregnant, the social worker continued to battle for her by reprimanding the mother, finding Mary clothes for her wedding, and buying her a "pretty nightgown" as a wedding present, suggesting a commitment to helping resolve Mary's plight.

Despite the harsh and often unfair judgments made by protective workers, social workers should not be caricatured as heartless detectives of a therapeutic state, driven to trample on the lives of poor and working-class clients in search of evidence that would confirm existing middle-class assumptions of deviance and transgression. They did much trampling to be sure, but they were also invited to intervene in situations by clients themselves; in some cases they provided genuine relief from desperate material and emotional circumstances. Although the case records described as tales of detection tended to invoke a world infested with sexual excess, feeblemindedness, drunkenness, and contagious immorality, not all case narratives were saturated with menace and suspicion. Rather than being merely restricted to evidence-gathering and the positioning of clients as wily, loathsome, and incorrigible, social workers also built cases upon deeper levels of relatedness, some of which were permeated with optimism for reaching pleasant outcomes.

Occasionally, even respect and affection for special clients became the main story, but, as Maurice J. Karpf's examination of published case records (1931, p. 266) suggests, this situation was relatively rare. According to Karpf's survey of "methods used by family case workers in their attempts to influence the behavior of their clients," attempts by social workers at "ordering and threatening" clients were as common as attempts at "discussion and persuasion" (26.7 and 25.2 percent, respectively). Giving "advice," friendly or otherwise, was employed only 9.7 percent of the time.

Throughout the 1920s, casework moved toward emphasizing less adversarial relationships with clients than had characterized the work of such child protective societies as the MSPCC and Minneapolis Child's Protective Society as well as earlier family welfare and relief work. In 1916 Mary Richmond wrote a chapter in *Social Diagnosis* on caseworker and client relationships, not included in the book but published in an edited volume of Richmond's writings (Colcord 1930). In it, she accurately predicted that casework would move from ruthless detection to root out fraud, immorality, neglect, and contamination and toward more congenial therapeutic relationships. Caseworkers had "a tendency to ignore the rights of the

individual immediately before them in order to save the community from impo-
sition, or a child from neglect, or a family from moral contagion," and the this
tendency was in need of correction (p. 389). Social workers, Richmond urged,
should avoid "unfair methods of inquiry" and also redress the "scolding habit"
of the untrained, "older type of relief agent who lost his temper and bullied clients." Caseworkers' irritation at "being balked by the stupidity or the stubbornness of a client may really be due to inability to take the steps which will reveal his
point of view and his actual situation" (p. 394).

By 1927 C. C. Carstens had also noted this shift in casework practice. He asserted that children's societies assuming a legalistic or policelike attitude toward social work were suffering from "dry rot" and were in an "eddy rather than in the
stream of progressive social work at this time" (p. 128). Carstens applauded new
trends of protective work that were gentler and less judicial in nature, especially
the protective work increasingly integrated into the work of family welfare and
children's aid societies. In 1924 Mary Brisley, district secretary of the Minneapolis Family Welfare Association, attempting to articulate systematic procedures for
her staff's casework, argued for a new set of tactics that deemphasized detection
and policing. Casework, according to the MFWA staff, should revise many of its
former processes and implement new ones designed to increase clients' self-
respect. Among the recommendations was: "When you come to a stone wall, recognize that fact, and do not try to break through by main force; Do not put him
on the defensive; *Do not use detective methods nor take advantage of your own position of authority; Do not allow the client to feel that you are inevitable,* that he has
to put up with you and do as you suggest until the need for relief is past" (p. 159,
emphasis added). The more sympathetically portrayed, deeply nuanced narratives
of gentler versions of investigation, evidence-gathering, and protection that characterized casework practice in relief and family welfare agencies and child-placing work in the 1920s will be described in chapter 5.

Tales of Protection:
Personal Appeals and Professional Friendship

Social workers were capable of responding ruthlessly to perceived menaces to middle-class ways of life posed by the presence of immigrants and the living conditions of working-class and impoverished people. They shadowed clients judged to be in danger of falling into depravity and ferreted out social evidence to make cases against them, spinning Foucaultian webs of scrutiny as they gathered and displayed probative testimony.

But not all case records were constructed around the motif of detection. Certainly, painted women, ruptured hymens, masturbation, filthy homes, mental defectiveness, venereal disease, sexual excess, and drunkenness provided potent signifiers of a nightmarish world of social disorder that required taming by threats of withdrawal of material aid, court-mandated supervision, and institutionalization. Yet some caseworkers' tales depicted far more docile, and occasionally even cordial, encounters with less frightening clients. Around such cases social workers spun affirmative narratives that described protracted, convoluted, contradictory, cross-class relationships with clients whom they perceived to be worthy and promising. These clients' problems were attributed to external circumstances, a "lack of sunshine and roses." Tales of detection, in contrast, rarely imputed problems to the environment but rather traced them to defective heredity or characterological deficiencies. Instead of the sleuthlike methods and evidentiary accounts found in tales of detection, social workers in tales of protection narrated sympathetic stories about those special clients they sensed to be more congenial to their professional ambitions.

Mary Dewson, superintendent of probationers at the Massachusetts Industrial School for Girls, argued that there were two forms of delinquency, one rooted in mental defect and thus incurable and another that could "be uprooted by training, the right environment, and a strong personal appeal" (1911, p. 355). In addition to "strong personal appeal[s]," Dewson thought that "there was [also] a need for a friend—not a casual friend, but the kind of friend that we should want ourselves if we were to go as a stranger among people who lived and thought in unaccustomed ways" (p. 357). The Boston Society for the Care of Girls (1922) urged its social workers to think of themselves as such "best friends" to clients.

In tales of protection, clients were not likely to be judged as incurable, deranged, or uncontrollable. Instead, social workers narrated stories of attempts to protect and instruct in "unaccustomed ways" those clients thought to be worthy and promising. Personal appeals and friendly relations, not primarily the marshaling of negative evidence and testimony, formed the core of casework as it increasingly came to be practiced during the 1920s.

In the protection genre of case narratives, social workers described clients as "modest," "refined," "mannerly," "wholesome minded," and "cordial." Consequently, they tended to describe their first impressions of such clients in glowing terms. In the case of "Helen," for example, a social worker wrote of being "particularly impressed with the bright attractive little girl who came in and greeted her with smiling cordiality. She is a short, well developed girl for her age. She has an intelligent face, sparkling black eyes, beautiful black shining hair, and a clear olive complexion. Agent is convinced that there is excellent material here waiting for someone to make the best of it." "Alice" was also described as "tall with light hair, blue eyes and pink cheeks. She is very polite in her manner." Marie's social worker wrote, "She is so sweet and modest in her manners that everyone falls in love with her." Polite manners and cordiality were often enough on first encounters to open the door to a "professional friendship" with a social worker, although as in the case of Eve (chapter 4), subsequent revelations of wrongdoing could quickly transform the guiding motif of a social work relationship and narrative from friendship to detection.

Suspicion, accusation, and the hot pursuit of damning evidence were far less apparent in tales of protection than in tales of detection. Instead, social workers' records in the protective mode did not rely predominantly on a network of informants and the pursuit of incriminating testimony but rather on talking to clients and attempting to establish genuine relationships with them. Such case narratives were relatively devoid of the extreme skepticism toward clients' words shown in detective-oriented case records, expressing instead hope that personal appeals would bring about preferred outcomes. Rather than being structured like legal briefs that built court cases for attributions of moral neglect, feeblemindedness, intemperance, or incorrigibility, these narrations recounted the convolutions of long-term relationships between social workers and clients and recorded long conversations about the ordinary trials and tribulations of everyday life, including loneliness, dating, marriage, and memories of life in the old country.

Even more than tales of detection, tales of protection highlighted the nature of professional proximity and the quality of client relationships that distinguished social work's approach from the methods and relationships of professions such as psychology and psychiatry. Social workers listened to clients not only on weekends but also while accompanying them to department stores, to "delightful little tea rooms," to "Filenes to buy a trousseau," and to "pretty spots down by the Charles river" (Boston Children's Aid Society case files). In one such example, a social worker noted, "The visitor had the most trying time with the girl while shopping. For some reason or another she was unwilling to accept anything that visitor picked out. She tried on probably forty hats some of which looked exceeding well on her but no sooner would she put one on her hat than she would dash it off and put another one on. The girl was quite aware that she was not behaving well but at the same time seemed to be possessed with an impish perversity." It is hard to imagine either Sigmund Freud or Jean-Martin Charcot at the hat counter of Filene's Basement in Boston, listening to and watching patients during shopping excursions.

Caseworkers not only socialized with clients, but they also devoted many pages of their records to describing such contacts. They regularly accompanied worthy clients to edifying entertainments, for example, including performances of *Little Women, Snow White,* "an illustrated travel talk on the war with Germany," and a "mystery play at the Copley." "Ruth" was taken to the Boston Art Museum, because, as her visitor explained, "this [excursion] was suggested by Ruth's story of a dream she had of going into a beautiful house, 'the most beautiful house she could ever imagine.' As this dream seems to indicate an appreciation of beauty, visitor believes it is time to form her ideals by showing her the many beautiful things the art museum contains."[1] Providing such uplifting experiences was a natural expression of social work's proximity to clients.

Social work's lack of theoretical rigidity was its distinctive feature as a discipline and as a textual field. Social workers established sustained cross-class and cross-cultural relationships outside the boundaries of an office or hospital ward and produced accounts that reflected the relative openness of their professional expertise. As previously discussed in the case of Hazel's "disagreeableness" and "impish perversity," social workers were not as theory-driven or as given to neatly ordering their accounts in terms of sonorous diagnostic closures as were the better established scientific professions. Social work leaders simultaneously celebrated and bemoaned the lack of highly crystalized observations, expectations, and interpretations to govern their field. Psychiatry, by contrast, was vastly different. D. P. Spence (quoted in de Marneffe 1991, p. 103) notes the prevalence in psychiatric narration of the assumption that every case has a single possible solution or interpretation. That tendency has left an unfortunate legacy to contemporary psychoanalysts, "whose clinical reports tend to present case material geared to confirming or disconfirming existing theory, rather than revealing the actual interchanges and inferences that take place in therapeutic sessions."

In a similar vein, Oliver Sacks (1986, p. 17) has pointed out that the "first act of medicine is to listen to a person's story, extract or abstract from it a (symptomatic and etiological) 'case,' and exclaim "Migraine!', and 'Parkinsonism' with all that this implies." Both medicine and psychiatry have been intensely uneasy with gaps and fragments in case histories. Consequently, both disciplines have striven for narrative closure, which is most often accomplished by the insertion of theory. The tendency to fill gaps in order to present cases in a tightly interconnected, completed form was especially apparent in a case history written by Freud, *Dora: A Fragment of an Analysis of a Case of Hysteria* (1905). Because Dora broke off her treatment with Freud prematurely, he was forced to achieve narrative closure by applying theory as grout. As he described his operations, "In the face of my incompleteness of my analytic results, I have no choice but to follow the example of those discoveries whose good fortune it is to bring to the light of day after their long burial the priceless though mutilated relics of antiquity. I have restored what is missing, taking the best models known to me from other analyses" (quoted in Moi 1990, p. 186). In narrative operations such as these, patients' biographies and own stories are tided up by the insertion of prototypes. As aptly noted by W. H. Auden in "Lines to Dr. Walter Birk," "The specialist has a function, but, to him, we are merely banal examples of what he knows all about" (Sacks 1986, p. 17).

Freud insisted on a complete elucidation of Dora despite his willingness to point out the fragmentary nature of the material on her case. Toril Moi (1990, p. 194) argues that a "desire for total, absolute knowledge exposes a fundamental assumption in Freud's epistemology. Knowledge for Freud is a finished, closed, whole." By contrast, the records I have read suggest that social workers had a far greater tolerance for ambiguity and leaving accounts inconclusive. Despite the importance awarded by many social work leaders such as Ada Sheffield to "funded thought" and "definiteness of expectation," caseworkers in actual practice were much less likely to fill gaps in their accounts with theory as Freud did in the case analysis of Dora. Their case stories, consequently, were less diagnostically ordered and coherent than those of psychoanalysis and far more scattered and enigmatic. Unlike Freud, who conjured up a complete work from analytic fragments, social workers lacked the professional theoretical agendas and diagnostic schemes to tightly organize their accounts.[2]

Social work descriptions were thus far less conceptually ordered than those of psychoanalysis, and social workers navigated the crosscurrents of inter-class relationships without a governing professional compass other than their middle-class judgments and proclivities. Although professional crafting undeniably influenced social work tales, the accounts were far less systematic than their psychological counterparts. Social workers' claims to narrative authority rested not so much on theory as on close association with the daily lives of clients, on fanatical devotion to recording details of personal and family history, on impressions of behaviors and appearances, and on extensive investigations and conversations that suggested presence, eyewitness authority, and sometimes even intimacy.

Operating without the firm theoretical earplugs and blinders characterizing better established professional communities, social workers were able to learn more about the details of the everyday lives of working-class clients. There were noteworthy examples of social workers' fetish for detail and proclivity for "getting down, deeper down" into clients' daily lives.[3] After attending the wedding of a client, one, for example, provided a specific description of the decorations and food: "The back of the pulpit was gorgeously decorated with crepe paper and flowers banked on a green background. These decorations were left over from Easter on purpose for this wedding. There was about fifty people present. Gertrude looked very attractive in her little wedding gown and the groom was of the yokel type, obviously honest and very shining, but very embarrassed. After the ceremony, there was a very nice spread, ice cream, cake, sandwiches, etc. The living room was attractively decorated with early spring flowers."

Social workers were far less likely than other professionals to frame accounts of clients' behavior theoretically in terms of professionally significant syndromes. They were especially less likely to pass judgment and convert clients into professional types. That lack affords those who read early case records the opportunity to hear the echoes of clients' sometimes strident challenges and to view attempts to negotiate with those clients—interactions not afforded the readers of medical case histories.

Clients did indeed circumvent and openly challenge professional advice, and generally social workers reported these challenges without much interpretation. The language of clients who were angry as well as those more cordial was characteristically incorporated into the narrations, especially in tales of protection. One woman was reported to have asserted to her social worker that "your idea of pleasure is completely different than mine." A Minneapolis Family Welfare Association case described a single mother who made a living by selling milk and was behind on her rent. When told to sell the cow, the client forcefully proclaimed that "she got her living by selling two quarts of milk a day. She will under no circumstances give up the cow. Said she would sit in the road with the cow first." Another client was reported to have renamed the Minneapolis Family Welfare Association the "Family Wrecking Association." Still another worker wrote that a client "informed agent that if she ever called again, she would attempt to use an ax on her. She showed the agent the ax she would use." In yet another instance, a mother with a sick baby and an unemployed husband was told to obtain day-work to buy needed food. The visitor reported that the client then "became very angry and threw the cover of the lard pail at the wall. Said if that was the case she would beg or steal food. Went out to the kitchen where the visitor heard her swearing at such red tape. She refused to come back until the visitor left."

The case records, relatively unedited, did not exclude distractions such as client obstinacies, which in medical or psychiatric records would have been edited out as extraneous. Doing so would prevent readers from apprehending a particular interpretation or problem. Without a high degree of orchestration, social workers allowed clients' voices to creep into case records and allowed them to be especially garrulous if perceived as mannerly and receptive to professional advice.

A Chaste and Grateful Girl: The Case of "Marie"

> The relationship between the visitor and her girl should be genuine and helpful and too valuable to be broken by a change of the girl's locality. It is not wise to swap horses when crossing a stream. The girl cannot have much respect for a relationship if it is lightly cast aside. A regular siege has to be laid to capture the girl's better nature and to defeat her faults, and she suffers from a change of generals.
>
> ∼Dewson (1911)

The twenty-two-year siege of Marie provides a rich example of the kinds of child-saving work carried out during the 1920s. Her case illustrates the differences and commonalities between the casework practiced by the Boston Children's Aid Society and that of the Massachusetts Society for the Prevention of Cruelty to Children or the Minneapolis Child's Protective Society. It also helps show how individual caseworkers translated their agencies' missions. Unlike Hazel's caseworker, who worked for a child-placing organization similar to the BCAS, Marie's worker, "Miss Constance Church," went well beyond shopping trips in her efforts to build a successful casework relationship with her promising ward.

Marie first became known to the BCAS in 1917 through a referral from the Associated Charities of Boston, which had been investigating Marie's family since 1911. Associated Charities reported that Marie's father, a widower, employed his children in playing an unlicensed hurdy-gurdy on the streets of Boston. The agency had received complaints from a worried neighbor who stated that there might be a "question of immoral relations between the father and Josephine" and feared that the same would happen to Marie. Marie's father was said to want to place out all of his children and to be indifferent to their care.

In contrast to descriptions of wayward girls on a downward spiral, the entry following the first visit with Marie began a lengthy tale of protection wherein Marie was described as bravely waging an uphill battle against poverty and a brutish father. Miss Church reported that Marie had "appeared glad to see agent and to talk over plans for herself and the children." At age fifteen, Marie was

apparently mothering the whole family. Ever since her mother's death she has been trying to run the house on 50 cents a day. Would not have minded this, even though she did want to return to school, had it not been for the fact that her father nagged at her continually and finally ended up beating her unconscious a month ago. The father's one idea is to get rid of the children and the first thing he says every night when he comes home and sees the children is "For God's sake, haven't you gone yet?" All of the children are practically in rags and Anna can barely walk because of rickets. The twins cannot go out at all because they have no clothing to wear. While agent was there, Marie gave the children lunch. This consisted of about six small slices of pressed ham as thin as tissue paper which looked as though they were picked out of a scrap heap in some meat shop. Marie was rather shy about preparing lunch at first but finally brought it out and said that was the best she could do. It had cost 15 cents and that was all she could afford.

After that visit, Marie was removed from her home in the North End of Boston, an Italian section of that city, and placed under the guardianship and supervision of the Boston Children's Aid Society. In accordance with casework conventions, her family's background was investigated extensively, and the lengthy record that resulted became part of her file.

Instead of an antagonistic approach, Miss Church employed gentle and supportive tactics with Marie, whom she constituted as an exemplary and promising client. Early on, the worker proclaimed that she had a unique plan for helping Marie, asserting that the right road to take with her would involve "long talks under favorable circumstances [which] are absolutely necessary if one is to keep in close touch with the girl's inner life." Marie did not remain mute. Rather then being subjected to a litany of threats, she was treated to an extended course of instructive interactions that might better be compared to the curriculum at a finishing school. Thus, "favorable circumstances" and attention to Marie's "inner life" prompted a social work strategy based apparently on affection and optimism.

Throughout the twenty-two-year relationship that ensued, Miss Church showered Marie with gifts, including a coral necklace, "a very pretty wisteria colored dress which just fit her," "a copy of Tennyson's poems as a special Easter gift as Marie had wanted them for a long time," and a "second hand mandolin which filled her with joy." She gave Marie special attention in other ways as well, as when she wrote a "long friendly letter to the girl endeavoring to cheer her and encourage her" and, later, "a funny letter enclosing silly jokes." The visitor continuously reported the lengthy conversations she and Marie had. For example, while they waited at a physician's office, Marie told Miss Church "about the wonderful things she was learning about clams and oysters in biology, . . . the girl's eyes are being opened to the wonders of the universe and a whole new world is being revealed to her."

On several occasions Marie's visitor went so far as to invite her to stay overnight with her. During one such event Miss Church reporting having a "long heart to heart talk with the girl about the many interests and problems that come into an eighteen year old high school girl's life. As the girl is very pretty and has a peculiarly sweet manner, she has many admirers and was anxious to talk to the visitor about these matters." On another occasion Miss Church wrote that she "had a happy visit with her. The girl is very interested in visitor's souvenirs and pictures of Italy. Had a nice talk with her about the natural beauty of Italy. Visitor had noticed that the girl had been a little sensitive at times about being Italian and hoped that she might get a new viewpoint." Under Miss Church's protective gaze and gentle supervision it was hoped that Marie would blossom.

A recurring theme for many visitors was the importance of clients' appreciation of their efforts. Miss Church was no exception, regularly recording expressions of Marie's gratitude. In one such entry she reported giving some "very pretty clothes which she thought would fit Marie. She was exceedingly pleased with them and they proved to be just what she needed. There was a rose colored suit which delighted the girl. There also was a nice petticoat, camisole, and a nightgown. Marie could hardly express her pleasure and appreciation." In another entry she noted that Marie "is learning the value of money and to appreciate her opportunities." Marie scored many points on one occasion when she invited the visitor to supper. "She brought a written invitation from the foster mom for visitor to come to supper. Marie was very anxious for visitor to come saying that they could have a nice walk by the river after supper. Marie had been anxious to get out the best dishes and do everything possible to honor visitor. After supper it turned out that she had a surprise for the visitor which turned out to be a new song, Dutch Dolls, which she sang with foster mother providing the accompaniment." The success of the visitor's protective gaze must have been measured by Marie's admiring, reciprocating gaze.

Throughout their relationship, Marie continuously confirmed her visitor's first impressions. In one entry, Miss Church boasted that Marie had told her that "some of the girls at school would not associate with her because she would not use rouge and powder and put black beauty patches on her face as many of them do. Marie said the girls would 'fix themselves all up and then parade up and down before the boys to attract attention.' They think she is odd because she will not do so. Visitor spent some time telling Marie how the girls at the seminary dressed." Later, after going shopping together, Marie was again praised for her decorum. She had "developed surprising high ideals and self control. Had a pleasant shopping trip with her and she showed good judgement, thrift, and taste in selecting her clothes."

Miss Church's intensive instruction in the genteel ways of living did not preclude trespasses into Marie's love life. She routinely met Marie's suitors, for example. After meeting one, "Mario," at the agency office, Miss Church wrote: "Evidently he liked Marie and hoped that the visitor might allow him to pay some attention to her. He suggested that he would like to take her to a band concert or show now and then as well as take her, along with her brother, for a walk in the park." After Mario left the office, Miss Church—using the inter-agency case file exchange—looked up his record and found that he had been arrested for nonsupport and was probably a "gambler, immoral, and diseased." She noted that "it is quite evident that he believes in free love and Bolshevik doctrines." Consequently, she "took the girl aside and had a long heart-to-heart with her. Visitor very frankly told her the bare facts concerning Mario's past history and his present views but tried to do it in a sympathetic way so as to not antagonize the girl speaking always as if the visitor was most sorry for any man who had done what Mario had done and who believed as he did." Another suitor, "Henry," had more success. Miss Church wrote that she "quite fell in love with Henry who is wholesome, frank, apparently clean minded, with pleasant manners and high ideals."

The freedom accorded Marie was not often afforded to those under the otherwise watchful and suspicious eyes of social workers. In one entry, Miss Church wrote with sympathy of Marie's need for "good times"; at the same time she was quick to steer Marie in the direction of wholesome recreations. "As is natural, the girl longs for recreation and good times and the girls are urging her to go to a cheap public dance tonight in Gloucester. While sympathizing with Marie's desire for a good time, visitor talked with her about the necessity of making wise choices and above all preserving her self respect trying to make her see that was more important than what other people thought of her." In another entry, the social worker had a scare when she found that "Marie has been staying out later than she should on three or four different occasions. Her last offense was Monday night when she went to the movies with three other girls but did not come home with them. Was accompanied by a sailor whom she evidently picked up." Marie's sympathetic social worker, however, did not use the incident with the unidentified sailor as an opening to embark on building a case for Marie's waywardness. Instead, she excused Marie by concluding that "it was a piece of girlish folly walking home with the sailor but nothing more." Wayward girls such as Winifred (chapter 4) were convicted on much thinner evidence.

Instead of threatening institutionalization, Marie's visitor used kid gloves in handling disputes. One suitor, for example, had wanted Marie to spend the summer with him and his mother on a farm. Miss Church responded to the request by using gentle methods of persuasion. "Visitor did not encourage this plan but did not say very much against it thinking that it would be better to help the girl think it from all points of view and then let her decide herself. Visitor made one or two suggestions which doubtless influenced the girl against going unconsciously." As usual, being a dutiful and praiseworthy client, Marie complied with her worker's recommendation.

Although Miss Church's tale of protection appears loftier than the tales of detection, the relationship it describes is nonetheless hierarchical and problematic. The amicable relationship she charted with Marie was contingent upon Marie's adopting her social worker's middle-class sensibilities and accepting her instructions about proper suitors, recreation, clothing, and demeanor. In addition, the case record displays the flagrant disparities of power between clients and workers, regardless of the tone of their relationship. For example, Miss Church did not allow Marie to be placed in an Italian home, despite Marie's strong preference to be "with her own people." On numerous occasions she had asked to be placed with a family in Revere who were "dear old friends of her mother." Although the family was anxious to have Marie, Miss Church concluded that both parents impressed her as "very ignorant but kindhearted people." She "doubted their ability, however, to supervise a girl of Marie's age and disposition." Consequently, Marie was told that the visitor had been unable to find a suitable Italian home for her.

From the social worker's perspective, the case of Marie was a professional success story. Miss Church concluded that she "feels the girl has especially high ideals and good habits and is now fixed in them so that she is in no danger of doing anything wrong." Even after the case was closed, Constance Church kept in touch with Marie, and they corresponded regularly. In a later summary on the case, another worker reiterated the tone of approval and support that Marie had received from her primary social worker:

> Marie was attractive, capable, and well worth the supervision of CAS. Girl improved greatly in behavior and personality characteristics. Was most appreciative of what was done for her. She married "Tony" in 1925 and has written frequently to her former visitor about her martial difficulties. Tony has deserted her many times and she has yielded to his pleas for forgiveness and has taken him back though advised against this by our Miss C. We consider her on the whole one of our best girls. I would strongly advise that every help be given her in this divorce proceeding.

The case of Marie was not an isolated example. Other social workers also documented their "intimate" conversations, the exchange of presents, shopping trips, plays and movies, lunches, and the expressions of gratitude they received from clients. For example, twelve-year-old Ruth, while out shopping with her visitor, won the social worker's good graces after revealing that she was deciding whether to become a social worker or to buy clothes:

Ruth says she intends to be a social worker when she grows up but she does not know whether she would rather buy clothes or save souls. Visitor is each time impressed with the fine feeling Ruth shows in all matters. Visitor tells Ruth very seriously how many girls try to get all they can out of the society. Ruth is disgusted with this attitude and says that she believes in being thankful. She thanks the visitor for the book she sent for Christmas and said it must be quite a lot of work to send a gift to every child. It is quite remarkable for a child of twelve to have any perception of the labor expended by older people at Christmas.

As in Marie's case, the child was praised for valuing the work of the visitor and the profession itself.

As the case-recordings show, caseworkers in child-placing and family welfare societies, especially during the 1920s, were preoccupied with struggles to establish what they defined as genuine, congenial relationships with clients. "Clara," for example, had been transferred to a new social worker from one she had liked and was indifferent to the charms of the new visitor. Frustrated, the worker reported:

The girl spoke of Mrs. S [her former visitor] and asked when she would return. She said the present visitor was alright but she liked going around with girls of Mrs. S's age. The visitor then invited Clara to lunch and an auto ride where girl talked rapidly for about forty minutes from the moment she stepped into the car until they reached Framingham. Her attention was then diverted from her own affairs by the friendly visits made to various foster homes. This experiment appeared to be successful in alleviating some of the girl's suspicions of the visitor and CAS. Of course, the visitor made her stories of the visits as glowing as possible and the general bent was to counteract the stories told by delinquent girls in the psychopathic hospital with whom the girl had free intercourse throughout that long period.

Even when relationships were frustrating, tales of protection reveal social workers' proximal care and sympathetic tone. Ruth, a client of the Boston Children's Aid Society, was also transferred to another visitor, who reported her frustration over the inability to settle into a satisfying relationship with the girl. She reported that Ruth was "as usual inexpressive though cordial in her attitude. Ruth's former visitor expressed surprise that Ruth who had always been spontaneous and outspoken should develop repression" and bemoaned the fact that she had "failed to secure confidence of the girl which the first visitor had."

Worthy Wives and Dutiful Mothers

Cordial relationships were not only reserved for chaste, grateful, young clients such as Marie who were supervised by child-placing societies. Increasingly, relief work as the charity organization society movement had defined it gave way to casework premised on emerging sensibilities of the importance of congenial relationships and to expanding notions that each case of economic dependency had unique origins, often emotional, and thus was treatable by individualized means. As a result, family welfare workers found worthy women who needed a receptive audience more than the traditional heavy hand. Yet their relationships with women were more paradoxical and prescriptive than those established with young girls, because women brought to the surface many of the more perplexing gender role issues, including day work, motherhood, marriage, family life, and the problems associated with relief.[4] As the diversity of responses and activities in case records reveals, however, social workers by no means adhered to a professional party line on such matters. Furthermore, family welfare caseworkers, like their counterparts in children's work, defined casework activities broadly and after investigation pursued eclectic and often unpredictable relationships with individual cases.

Women brought complex pasts to their cases that complicated the client-social worker relationship. In a Minnesota Family Welfare case, for example, the social worker introduced a client who was "by no means the ordinary run of women who come in for work. She had been married three times including once to an elderly man worth $25,000. She divorced him but did not want any of his property. She had no children of her own so she adopted a child 'out of the gutter.'" This client, referred to as "Ina," had character references from a police matron and a juvenile court judge, both of whom had known her when she worked as a home mission worker among Finnish immigrants in Minneapolis. With little trouble, the social worker arranged for her to receive coal and groceries from the Family Welfare Association. On February 5, 1913, a moment of reckoning occurred, however, when the agent learned that Ina was a woman with a past. Possibly because of the influence exerted by her character references, documentation of that past was inscribed as "confidential and cannot be recorded." The worker, consequently, provided only an unusually vague synopsis: "Ina has lifted herself out of unfortunate surroundings; has met and overcome much trouble and temptation. Her one ambition is to bring up her child in a wholesome environment. Ina lives an upright, clean, and hardworking life." Despite this rare bow to confidentiality, the social worker's fanatical devotion to documentation ultimately won out. At the end of the record, a "confidential memo" recounted the whole suppressed story: "The woman, an inmate of a resort, later reformed and married. Adopted a child of another resort inmate. Later found that the man she married had a wife and child in the old country. She then secured a divorce and worked to support herself and adopted child. She is a woman of strength, of will power, and has met and overcome untold temptations since she left the old life."

Despite Ina's checkered past, aid was generously given throughout the six-year span of the case.[5] In one entry, for example, it was noted that "Ina is making out well but is worrying because she has not paid the loan of $5.00. Agent says we will not ask for it because it helped to establish her." Such generosity may have been due, in part, to the client's references as well as the fact that Ina often spoke very much like a social worker herself. On one occasion, she came to the agency and reported that "'Frances,' who is living in the same house in which Ina lives, is not a proper person to have near her daughter. A sister of Frances was reported as being immoral and was sent to a school for the feebleminded. Frances has been requested to have nothing to do with her daughter but insists on forcing her way into the family. Ina wished AC to do something. Thinks there is some law which might be used to restrain her." Just as Marie's appreciation of Miss Church's work gained her praise, Ina may have profited from her inside knowledge of the language and worldview of social work.

Even without references from reputable sources, however, social workers embarked on amicable relationships with clients less cordial than Marie or Ina. In another Minneapolis Family Welfare Association case, that of "Hilda" (1919–25), a "nervous, possibly neurotic" Dutch woman whose "mental illness seems to be lack of ambition to get well," the visitor devoted a large portion of her record to inscribing not only conversations with Hilda but also their disagreements over budgeting.[6] She wrote long passages on Hilda's girlhood in the Netherlands, her courtship and wedding, her loneliness in the United States, her perceptions of the eating habits of Americans, her problems in American schools, her social life in the Netherlands, and the "lack of sunshine and roses in her married life." During one of many home visits, Hilda played Dutch folk songs for the visitor, who, touched by this expression, subsequently went to the Dutch consulate to see if they could provide transportation so Hilda and her three children could visit the Netherlands.

Yet as Hilda's case proceeded, marital conflicts arose over her husband's philandering ways, the origins of his venereal infection, and later his physical abusiveness. Things became especially raucous when the visitor tried to mediate in the family dramas that ensued. For example, Hilda's husband complained that Hilda spent money recklessly. She complained that he was thoughtless and reported that "one day she had been cleaning all day and he came home and sat on the porch while she prepared dinner without help." In response, the social worker noted that Hilda "was very reasonable in her conversations, yet in telling of her troubles that she and her husband had, she used a very dictatorial manner of speaking to the man. This was pointed out to her and it was suggested that perhaps if she used different methods she might be more successful." The client's physician at the general hospital then added fuel to the fire by telling the Family Welfare agent that they were "bumping their heads against a stone wall with this woman. As far as her husband's interest in other women, he said he did not blame the man if he did most anything for he could not live with that woman a day and hated to see her come into the office." Later, however, when things had deteriorated to the point of abuse by the husband, the caseworker took up for Hilda and threatened him with court action.

Subsequently, the social worker continued her pilgrimages to bring the relief allowance and the husband's wages, which was paid to the Family Welfare Agency and thus under its control. As she described one exchange, "[Hilda] came to the door holding her side and groaning. Her hair was in strings and her voice was weak and hardly audible. She told how she was suffering and the agent insisted that nothing was the matter. She became angry and as always insisted that her allowance should be larger."

Unlike the appreciative Marie, the relationship with Hilda began to spoil as time went on, yet the social worker conscientiously reported the nosedives it took. An exchange of insults began, for example, over the amount of Hilda's allowance: "She could not get more money for food when the children needed it. The agent explained that she was getting more than a regular budget and she must simply learn to buy more simply. The woman became angry and said it was no use to try to explain anything to a person with no brains." The next time Hilda called, the agent made clear her displeasure about being described as a "person with no brains," noting that she had told Hilda "there would be no use talking over the phone for she would say things like she said before. She wanted to know what she said and the agent told her and she said she would never say such rude things and the agent must have misunderstood her." This particular volley continued until "the woman said the trouble with the social worker was that she did not realize how much it took to clothe children and the agent said she realized it was very expensive when a mother did not fix up clothing and take care of the things they had. The woman said that there was not a woman in Minneapolis that worked harder for her children. Told her no sense arguing over the phone. She said the agent had insulted her and wished that she would never set foot in her house again."

The rocky relationship continued for many years, and in later case entries the social worker persisted and did indeed set foot in Hilda's house on many more occasions. In contrast to revelations of wrongdoing and immorality, which often radically transformed the narrations of social workers and drastically altered relationships with clients, Hilda's social worker remained wedded to maintaining a somewhat amicable relationship characterized by heart-to-heart talks, advice, and frequent disputes.

As shown by the cases of Hilda and Marie, social workers embarked upon protracted and often contradictory cross-class relationships with clients judged as worthy and promising. Unlike the cases described as tales of detection, they established relationships that permitted them to realize their mission of making personal appeals for conformity and respectability. They were thus able to minimize the harshly disciplinary entanglements that all too often characterized routine turn-of-the-century child protective and relief work, a mission that hinted at yearnings for an alternative type of cross-class relationship.

Many studies of women's reform and religious activism in the nineteenth century argue that middle-class women were guided by the hope of bonding with chaste women and girls in sisterly and motherly relationships that would transcend class (Berg 1978; Bordin 1981; Epstein 1981; Ginzberg 1990; Ryan 1981; Stansell 1987). Such faith did not vanish with the dawning of the twentieth century and the emergence of expert models of professionalism (chapter 1). Many professional social workers continued to cling to the belief that "benevolent femininity" would purify the unchaste and ill-bred and thereupon unite all women—at least all white women—in universal sisterhood. The numerous shopping trips that Miss Champine took with Hazel and the "long talks under favorable circumstances" that Marie's social worker relished were manifestations of that hope. In case-recordings describing such occasions it is possible to sense hints of wistfulness for affable relationships and womanly bonding, although such bonds were always premised on clients assimilating social workers' middle-class values. Too, notions of benevolent femininity always camouflaged class power and privilege, social workers' professional authority, and notions of racial superiority.[7]

Professional social workers thus continued to display many vestiges of the class and gender contradictions that had previously characterized the long traditions of middle-class and religious women's involvement in the work of benevolence. One of the most insidious of these vestiges was racism. The case records I read were conspicuously silent about racial matters; only four involved African American clients, and three were seen by material relief agencies that had few black workers.[8] The silence in the records was a sign of the exclusive practices of early social work.[9] In addition, white reformers often ignored or ridiculed African American efforts to create a child-placing system that relied on kinship and to establish unique settlements, clubs, and benevolent institutions within the black community.[10]

Focusing almost exclusively on the white population, professional social workers, like the volunteer friendly visitors who preceded them, practiced a paradoxical program that targeted impoverished, immigrant, and working-class clients. On the one hand, they were committed to class discipline and the moral policing of unruly clients. On the other hand, many embraced egalitarian notions that included faith in the power of a united and wholesome sisterhood in the form of professional friendships and therapeutic relationships to improve the public order. Attempts by middle-class female reformers to bond with their working-class sisters were thus contradictory. The promise of sisterhood was contingent on the adoption of middle-class conventions and ideologies, and the pledge of sisterhood was further compromised by the vulnerability of working-class women with regard to their social workers. Even so, the relationship was not a simple story of class domination, although surely class privilege was exercised. The complexities of professional expertise and personal relationships also came into play in a field composed primarily of women and one that needed to navigate between "friendship" and power. The result was not only class domination but also uniquely gendered webs of power relations and sensibilities.

Although it is important not to lose sight of class and professional domination in the practice of early social work, it is also important to acknowledge that professional social workers were no strangers to the harshness and desperation of clients' lives. They routinely wrote about clients who valiantly made over clothing, moved to smaller tenements to save on rent, canned fruit and vegetables, and took in boarders, laundry, or sewing. They met tired women who had "dark circles under their eyes," women in "desperate circumstances," and women without food, fuel, or enough clothing to send their children to school. A Minneapolis Family Welfare Association worker received the following letter from a client in 1924:

> I just wanted to say hello and I hope you are fine. I am not very well for I have a bad cold and so do all my children. I am a bit unhappy for there is not enough money to pay the rent and buy food and we can only have a fire once a day. There are not enough clothes, "Olive" needs shoes, and I have no underwear nor do the children. Would you please help me out as it is awful hard to be in this shape. I am sure worried. Please come and see me as I never can come into town. Let me hear from you if you can do anything for my need. If I did not need these things I would not say so.

Yet social workers' knowledge of the pathos described in such letters was neither pristine nor undefiled. Because they could either withhold or grant resources to alleviate distress, their knowledge was always entangled with gatekeeping privileges.

Some social workers failed to alleviate distress—and some created it. The power to regulate and intervene in family life often lead to the removal of children. When that happened, social workers could not easily elude the pain and loneliness of clients subjected to professional interventions. Thus, one social worker filed a series of letters that a client, "Bessie," had written to her mother and school chums after being placed in a shelter operated by the Massachusetts Society for the Prevention of Cruelty to Children in 1912. Bessie, whose mother had been sent to the House of Corrections for two months on charges of fornication, was a thirteen-year-old who, after having been reported to the MSPCC for "running wild," was adjudicated "wayward." In her first letter to her mother, Bessie wrote:

Just a few lines to let you know that I am well and hoping you are the same. I have been a long time waiting and thinking that you might write but I suppose you do not know where I am. I could not keep the house after you were gone. Sometimes, I feel so lonesome I do nothing but cry. I am in the house on Mount Vernon street. Say, Mom when you answer this letter, tell me how long you will be gone and how to address the letter to you. Oh Mom, even though it is nice here I am so lonesome for you. I hope when you come back you will turn over a new leaf and go back to work like you did last summer. I will be able to go to work next year because I am thirteen and that will be something off your hands. We have to show all the letters we write and receive so please write a nice one. I hope you have enough money to answer my letter as it would cheer me. Your Loving Daughter.

In a subsequent letter, Bessie wrote:

Well, Mom it is raining today and I feel so dreary. I feel like having a good cry. I hope you have enough money to answer my letter for it would cheer me. We have to show all the letters we write and receive so be sure to write a good one. "Cecila" [her best friend] does not know where I am and I am afraid to tell her for she might tell the kids and I would rather give up the world then let them know where I am. The other day the matron took me to get shoes and they are awful nice. If your shoes are not good when you leave, they will let you take a pair. I am wearing my hair in curls. If you were near enough to get my kisses I would not mind. Your loving daughter—Bessie.

Manifest in the entanglements of power and control in this case are the contradictions that plagued relationships between social workers and clients. Bessie's loneliness was produced by the actions of a social worker who had separated her from her mother. As well as monitoring all of Bessie's letters, the social worker does not appear to have facilitated any communication between the child and her mother, because the letters were apparently never delivered.

Social workers may indeed have yearned for, and in some cases achieved, forms of intimacy unparalleled in male-dominated professions, yet relationships with clients were never innocent of the forms of privilege embedded in class standing and in the power that issued social workers' their professional authority as gatekeepers and mediators between middle-class order and institutions and the worlds "beneath" them. They could withhold not only letters but also services and relief in their attempts to control perceived or potential transgressions.

In their diverse methods for constructing knowledge as well as in their approaches to clients, social workers' professional relationships were always power-laden and class-stratified. Professional power was expressed through judging (judgments based less on the application of scientific or theoretical schema than on professionally articulated and legitimated intuitions presented as knowledge) which clients provided "excellent material" and which situations constituted "favorable circumstances" for intervention. Such professional judgments were ideological and grounded in the values of white, nativist, middle-class women who had the impulse to reform and uplift. But to end the story with that statement would be reductive. Social workers' practice and narrativity, by virtue of the intimate relationships they idealized, also inscribed the dreams, ambitions, voices, and viewpoints of clients, who, as junior partners, helped construct the diverse worlds of social work.

Dreams, Ambitions, and "Feasible Substitutes"

Social workers' narratives, as illustrated by Bessie's poignant letters to her mother, document clients' despair and loneliness. At the same time, however, to the extent that workers got to know the lives of specific clients, they also recorded dreams and aspirations: going to college, wanting more time with children, working less, or simply of having enough money for food, clothing, and housing. Mary Dewson (1911, p. 357) urged the importance of heeding such dreams, arguing that a client needs "someone to inspire and encourage her, someone who cares about her success or failure. She needs someone to guide her and to show her what is practicable for her. Every young girl has day dreams, or she should have them. She needs someone to set her on the road towards realizing her dreams or toward realizing some more feasible substitute. She needs someone to arrange for her to have the right sort of pleasure and suitable companions."

Clients sometimes clung to their dreams with ferocious tenacity in the face of overwhelming obstacles. In some cases, professional social workers were among the most formidable of these obstacles, because they had the power to override, undermine, reduce to subtext, or "substitute a more feasible alternative" to clients' dreams and ambitions. But clients were not the only ones with hopes and desires. Social workers also had their own hopes and dreams for clients, dreams that were sometimes at cross-purposes with those individuals' own. Social workers were variously driven to "make clients more modest," "arouse their ambitions," "build them up from their bad habits," "control their independence," and "cure their liking for boys."

Although I have described an idealized, middle-class social worker, it is important to remember that caseworkers differed in the extent to which they were aware of their class-based power and privilege and in the degree to which they imposed class-specific values and solutions on clients. Attributions of waywardness, immorality, refinement, and worthiness had variant meanings to middle-class women in social work, who as a result spawned not only inconsistent translations but also divergent responses to the dreams of clients.

Social workers were especially divided on the issue of working mothers. Some caseworkers demanded that mothers with husbands out of work obtain employment to survive rather than seek relief. In one case, a mother with a sick baby was told to find day work despite her distress over the child's illness. But not all social workers saw paid work for women as a suitable way of surviving the ups and downs of family fortunes. The case of "Rosa," a client of the Family Welfare Association of Minneapolis from 1905 to 1928, vividly illustrates how the class-based judgments of one caseworker in regard to the wage work of her client created not only many oppositional encounters over what constituted good mothering and a well-kept home but also a tale that revolved around a social worker's perception of Rosa's maternal deficiencies rather than her fortitude.

The case was opened in 1905, when Rosa, an African American, came to the Minneapolis Family Welfare Association to seek work. Upon stating that her husband was "not ambitious," she was advised either to obtain an attorney in order to take action against him or else seek employment on a farm. The next recording occurred nine years later, in 1914, when Rosa's husband, William, then seventy and unemployed, sought food, fuel, and employment from the Family Welfare Association. Six months lapsed before a worker visited William and Rosa. After that one visit, the worker concluded that "it seemed impossible to make any headway with the family as they seemed quite contented to live in their dirt and filth. The man did not seem responsible enough mentally to talk intelligently and the woman seemed quite willing to work and support the family. Felt that it was not worth the time and effort to obtain a visiting housekeeper." Revealing her racial bias, she added, "Because of the sentiment against colored people in that community, the visitor did not call again."

Seven years went by, and then, in 1922, the case was reopened when a teacher informed the association that Rosa's children would not be allowed to attend school with their present supply of clothing. Subsequently, a different caseworker visited Rosa and judged her to be cordial and hardworking but neglectful of her domestic duties. The social worker wrote the following impressions of Rosa's plight:

> Rosa is a small neat negress. She was very cordial to visitor. She explained that she was not dressed very neatly because she was very tired and resting. She was working very hard. Visitor tried to make her realize that she was working too hard and that she should rest at least a half a day during the week if not a whole day. The visitor impressed upon her the needs of her family that she should take care of them even if she should not earn as much money. The women said they had gotten along well until lately since they needed coal and warm clothing. Last month was rather hard on account of taxes. The woman said she never wanted to accept charity as she could work and support the family. She thought that there was so many others who needed aid that she hated to accept any. She wished FWA would help her with the court proceedings for her husband's accident. If they could realize money from this source they could get along.

Meanwhile, Rosa's elderly husband was losing his vision, and the social worker procured aid from the Society for the Blind. This aid was sent to the FWA and was to be given conditionally once Rosa discontinued working four days a week so that "she could take better care of the family and keep the house in better shape." That opened the door for supervision of Rosa's home and mothering as well as a six-year battle to reform her of her working ways.

Interspersed with giving gifts such as a radio to Rosa, the social worker had numerous conversations with her and harped upon the theme of Rosa's neglect of her family, which stemmed from the fact that she worked. In a particularly poignant exchange that occurred after Rosa's daughter had died from tuberculosis and on the occasion of school truancy by her eldest son, Rosa was reported to have

> agreed that the children needed her at home and also that it was very hard for her to continue to working as hard as she was, but that she could see no way out of it. She had indebted herself to the plumbers. She explained that although it might appear to the average person coming into her home that she did not care how she lived, she really had a dream about how she wanted to live and hoped that someday she might obtain it. She was employed doing day-work everyday of the week, except Sunday, and right after work would rush home, get the evening meals, make a fresh fire, put the children to bed, and rush to a dressmaking establishment where she worked every night. She admitted that it was beginning to wear on her and did not know how long she would last. She also agreed that Edward [her eldest son] was delinquent on account of the lack of care but she could not see a way out of the situation.

Rosa's caseworker, however, was not moved by Rosa's dream, nor was she impressed with Rosa's efforts to provide for her family. Instead, she continued through subsequent interactions to impose middle-class standards of motherhood upon Rosa while failing to acknowledge Rosa's enormous efforts to care for her family.[11]

Throughout later contacts the social worker never gave up her ambition to impose middle-class ideals of domesticity upon Rosa and thus narrated a story that stressed dirt, squalor, stale food, and shabby clothing. At the same time, Rosa never accepted her caseworker's interpretations, nor did she stop working. In one subsequent contact the caseworker explained to Rosa that "her first duty was with her family and the second duty was to go out to work." Rosa asserted that "she did not see it that way and she did not think the house was in such deplorable situation as she thought the visitor had different ideas as to what a dirty house was." The case was closed in 1928 because of staff layoffs at the Minneapolis Family Welfare Association. A chance encounter in the streets between Rosa and the caseworker was noted in Rosa's record—"she was going to work and getting along nicely."

Home-Training

> The fact that no one was interested in getting Wilma started in the right things has resulted in her being an industrial as well as a social misfit.
>
> ∾From the Case of "Wilma," Boston Children's Aid Society

> If her boarding mother does not conquer her, some other woman will have to do so.
>
> ∾From the case of "Alice," Boston Children's Aid Society

Despite the antipathy that Rosa's social worker showed to paid employment, social workers usually devoted considerable efforts to preparing wayward charges for "practical study," "proper" employment, and the "serious business of becoming responsible." Planning suitable employment and education for working-class clients was not a simple matter, however, because class and gender tensions also arose in such matters. The lack of middle-class domesticity, as in the case of Rosa, was not only the problem social workers battled, but proper domesticity was a goal for those more promising girls who were not sexually infectious, vicious, or defective enough for custodial care—those given starring roles in tales of protection.

Numerous children were boarded in the homes of middle-class private families as placing-out increasingly became the preferred solution for reforming and protecting girls and for instructing them in the arts of homemaking and child-rearing, activities that would "build up character, good sense, self-reliance, and industrial efficiency" (Boston Children's Aid Society 1914, p. 39). Placing-out was perceived as critical because of the growing numbers of vulnerable children who were unable to "grow in character and body in their own homes" (p. 39). Officials of the Massachusetts Society for the Prevention of Cruelty to Children noted that placing-out allowed social workers to "rescue children from immoral surroundings and shield them from contamination" (MSPCC 1926). The Boston Children's Aid Society pointed out that the success of placing-out was contingent upon a variety of factors, including the fact that visitors had to conduct searching investigations of boarding homes "to avoid mistakes and transfers," to "make the child a full member of the family," and to build trust and liking between the visitor and boarded-out children (1914, p. 39). Case records describing this process teemed with details on social workers' cross-class navigations of knowing, liking, and trusting in these highly volatile, servile, and involuntary home-training relationships.

Placed girls voiced many complaints over their servile status. Some complained about being segregated for meals, having no recreation and little free time for study or play, and being subjected to a range of indignities and sometimes outright abuse, including sexual assault by boarding fathers. Strains in boarding-home arrangements often began before an actual placement over such issues as the necessity of wearing uniforms, which many boarding parents expected. In the case of "Mildred," a client with the Minneapolis Citizen's Aid Society from 1926 to 1930, the social worker reported that Mildred was "getting cold feet about the move to a boarding home. She had heard that they would make her wear a uniform. The visiting teacher told Mildred that the final arrangements had already been made so they had to be carried out, but she would bring up the issue of uniforms. The boarding mother said that she did not intend to have Mildred wear a uniform to the extent that she would be considered a maid, just white for baby care and lavender-blue for serving." Mildred was later reported to have been "unhappy because a dinner party for 16 had been scheduled and she had to wash dishes until 11:00 and get up and wash some more and she couldn't finish her schoolwork."

Mildred was not the only one with complaints. Her boarding mother complained as well that "Mildred was abrupt and reads everything and she doesn't do the dishes the way she wants them done. Mildred puts them in hot water and then goes to the bathroom for forty-five minutes and then the water is cold. She also finds the candy she hides and she hasn't washed her bra."

Unlike Mildred, who failed moral testing when she found and ate candy purposely hidden by her boarding mother, "Eugenia" was praised by her boarding mother, who boasted that Eugenia was "clean-minded, truthful, and has not stolen anything although she leaves pennies purposely around the house."

Social workers narrated many complaints about girls who did not abide by their proper place and position within boarding homes. Indeed, complaints about inefficient, irritating, slow, or saucy girls filled the pages of case records, and caseworkers typically took the side of the boarding mother and admonished their charges. For example, Alice, under the supervision of the Boston Children's Aid Society from 1923 to 1928, was the subject of many complaints about her lack of domestic talent. Early on, her boarding mother had complained that when it came to housework Alice was a "typical Bolshevik." Subsequently, the boarding mother reported that Alice "doesn't throw her dirty clothes all about the floor any longer, and does not sweep the dirt under her bed. She is still very careless and [the boarding mother] has to watch that she gets into bed properly instead of simply rolling herself up in the blankets on top of the bedclothes. She can dust and has learned to iron quite well but she argues about everything and tosses her head in a manner that is scornful and irritating. Has no intention of being obedient."

At times, however, the demands of boarding mothers for servitude were so extreme that social workers were offended. Thirteen-year-old "Eleanor's" boarding mother had gone away for a vacation and left Eleanor in the care of a housekeeper. The social worker was chagrined, however, to learn that "the housekeeper is working away from the home and Eleanor is taking full responsibility. There are three children in the home. The visitor feels that this is not a satisfactory arrangement." Many girls such as Eleanor moved from one boarding home to another, like tumbleweeds. Because tempers inevitably flared, reassignments were frequently necessary. Girls complained regularly to their social workers, not only of the hardships of their enforced labors but also of the anguish that constant reassignments and being uprooted caused.

The girls' performance of household and childcare duties, as assessed by middle-class boarding mothers and social workers, played a key role in evaluating their "industrial efficiency" and planning their vocations. A boarding mother's interpretations of a client's domestic skills and attitudes had severe consequences for the client's vocational opportunities, especially if the boarding mother reported disobedience, inefficiency, or irritation. After a complaint that Martha "took no responsibility about getting breakfast" and had "shown little interest in housework," the girl was whisked off to Dr. William Healy of the Judge Baker Foundation for psychological evaluation. Healy reportedly threw "up his hands for he could not recommend anything further except work as a chocolate dipper. He feels that factory work, even if a little unpleasant, might be a good thing for her."

In a similar tale, Alice had long expressed a desire to become a teacher, yet in a visit with the foster mother to talk about the "problem of the girl's vocation" Alice's caseworker learned that the boarding mother "was in agreement with the principal who does not think she is college material. Probably doesn't concentrate very well. It is hard to explain but we all feel some lack in Alice." Alice's dreams were opposed not only by her boarding mother but also by her social worker, who concluded that "her desire to go to Simmons to be a teacher is higher than she can achieve." Yet the opinions of boarding mothers were not the only tools social workers had available for vocational guidance. The results of mental testing, commonly unreliable and contradictory, often eclipsed the dreams of many social work clients as well.

IQ Roulette

The Washburn shelter should be asked to take "Cecila" on as a problem child. It was pointed out that her IQ had increased from 79 to 81. Also, they should take Ann. The woman from Washburn felt that they would consider Cecila first. Ann had too low of an IQ to be interesting to them.

∽Case conference at the Minneapolis Children's Bureau-Institutional Placement Division (April 1929)

Beginning around 1909 with the introduction of Binet intelligence tests and psychologist William Healy's tests designed to measure reasoning ability, mental testing began to enjoy enormous popularity within social work (Lubove 1973). It was conducted on social work clients; on inmates of child guidance clinics, prisons, and psychopathic hospitals; and on children thought to be difficult, defective, or delinquent.[12] The use of testing spread rapidly after World War I because mental examinations were viewed as increasingly valuable to child-placing organizations, schools for vocational planning, and home placement of dependent or delinquent children (Brown 1991). Mental examinations, like physical examinations, however, often left indelible stains upon the lives of clients. Like the discovery of ruptured hymens, low IQ scores were portentous signs that tended to dampen the relationship between social workers and clients, potentially fracturing narratives of protection and frequently leading to severe alterations of vocational plans. Together, ruptured hymens and low IQs signaled a potential community menace. Visitors rarely treated girls perceived to have overdeveloped bodies and underdeveloped minds to a course of personal appeals and friendship in the context of boarding homes. Instead, they were more likely to be committed to custodial care.[13]

Although mental testing was popular with those who placed children, it was not highly regarded by some clients. "Maud's" social worker described her efforts to take Maud to a psychopathic hospital for mental testing: "Just before entering the building the girl realized what type of institution it is and refused to enter. Says her teacher in high school said only crazy people go there. It was only after half an hour of persuasion that the girl decided to follow the wishes of the society and have an exam there." Maud was also taken to the Judge Baker Foundation for psychological study and vocational advice. According to her social worker, she "was very nice there and gave her best attention to the tests. Dr. Bronner talked with her a little on this date and arranged a second interview." After that interview Maud was reported to have said, "I had another talk with the same doctor I saw last time and she isn't old but she forgot everything we had talked of before. We went over all the same things."[14]

The case of Mildred vividly demonstrates the loose yet nooselike quality that characterized IQ testing. Mildred's mother had died in 1917, and Mildred had been abandoned by her father, a baker, who had left the city and whose whereabouts were unknown. She was referred to the Minneapolis Citizen's Aid Society in 1926 by her grandparents, who could no longer afford to keep her. Mildred's ambition was to teach in a small town. She was placed as a boarder in a series of working homes while pursuing her high school studies. Numerous entries document Mildred's unhappiness with these living arrangements. One entry, for example, reported that Mildred told her social worker, "Miss Wood," that she wanted to join the Girl Scouts but was afraid to ask off for the afternoons of the troop meetings. Her school social worker also reported that Mildred was upset by a teacher who had kept the class after school on her only day off.

Mildred found herself subject to the vagaries of IQ roulette after her visiting teacher reported that even though Mildred did not "chase around" she was staying up too late and, therefore, experiencing grade problems. But the worst was yet to come. The visiting teacher confronted the social worker about "why there was the idea that Mildred would go to the university as her IQ showed her to be slightly retarded. Miss Lewis, a counselor at school, had looked up her record and found that on March 1927, when in grade 9a, she had a Terman test that gave her an IQ of 96 and a C group reading level. The visiting teacher recalled that the child guidance clinic gave her 141. However, Miss Lewis said that 'she has not acted like a person with an IQ of 141.' "

Mildred was subsequently subjected to a "complete clinical study," including a retesting of her IQ by Dr. Chamberlain, a psychologist, at the child guidance clinic. Before tackling the issue of Mildred's IQ and her ability to pursue a university education, Dr. Chamberlain gratuitously noted that Mildred was "quite particular about her looks although her face is oily and blemished which at times detracts from her looks." He acknowledged, however, that the girl showed a great deal of poise. Mildred scored more than 200 on the Kulman-Binet test. Although impressed with such results, Dr. Chamberlain was nonetheless prudent in his "outlook" assessment, concluding that "her intellect is such that she should be encouraged in academic lines as her position allows."

Miss Wood remained dubious, however, and reported that she intended to call Dr. Chamberlain because she did not agree with the diagnosis or his recommendations. The record on Mildred ends abruptly at that point because the child-placing division of the Citizen's Aid Society was closed in April 1930. Because Mildred was nineteen she was not referred to another agency, and the social worker never made a final determination of her fate at the IQ wheel of fortune.[15]

Helen's Abiding Ambition

The problematics of class, IQ, and home-training converge in the story of Helen. Beginning in January 1925 and spanning the next four years, Helen, an Italian girl of fourteen, was an active case with the Boston Children's Aid Society. She had been adopted by an Italian family in 1905. After the death of her adoptive mother, her adoptive father remarried a woman described by Children's Aid as a "half crazy Italian widow with three children of her own," whereupon Helen was said to have become a "willing, loyal, unselfish little drudge in this wretched household."

Helen made a favorable impression on many levels, however, and was seen as a promising case. The principal at her school considered her a "bright girl who promised well for the future if she could only have proper training." One of Helen's teachers reported that "Helen seemed ladylike in her deportment and he enjoyed her in his class." The visitor, too, "was particularly impressed with this bright attractive little girl who came in and greeted her with smiling cordiality." She reported that "in talking about her past life, the child told her, in a casual way, of the many times she had taken her school books to bed with her so that she might study in the early morning. Often, her adoptive father's wife would catch her and bang her over the head for doing so." The agent concluded that "there is excellent material here waiting for someone to make the best of it." She vowed that the Boston Children's Aid Society would "use every means to send her to school and develop her into a self-supporting young woman." Indeed, at this point Helen's future appeared rosy, and she dedicated herself to her studies with the social worker's blessing. Typical of case records narrated in the protective genre, the social worker's tone was compassionate. No whispers of an impending parting of the ways were yet in evidence.

By this point in the story, Helen had won the wholehearted approval of her social worker, who went so far as to pardon her for past masturbation because "in spite of this habit she was quite normal and wholesome minded. The trouble seemed to come from a nervous temperament and the combination of circumstances that have kept all the sunshine out of her life." Early in their relationship Helen's visitor took her to a factory, thereby providing a hint of her more elevated aspirations for Helen's vocational training. After the trip the visitor proudly reported that Helen "thought that all the girls looked cheap and shabby and indeed they did." Helen received a great deal of support for her superior academic performance and commitments. The social worker reported that Helen had told her "with great pride that she had the best standing of any girl in the class. There was only one boy who stood higher and she aimed to stand higher."

This idyllic state of affairs, however, was interrupted when Helen was boarded out in the home of a Wellesley College professor. Although she liked the stimulation of the home very much, Helen complained from the beginning of the stay about her required servitude, thus indicating a strong sense of self-worth. Helen felt that she was "looked down upon as a servant and she does not like that. In particular, she dislikes having to wait on the table." The caseworker tried to minimize this tension by pointing out that "this was just a point of service that made things easier for other people and that it was nothing to be ashamed of."

Helen's boarding parents soon complained of her "inability to steer herself" and her "lack of common sense," although they praised her "conscientious loyalty." Although Helen was described as lacking self-direction, the social worker noted that she was reading a biography of Alice Freeman Palmer, a president of Wellesley College famous for saying that, as a youth, she was determined to get a college degree, even if it took fifty years. According to the case-recording, the book made

Helen think that she, too, would like to go to Wellesley. Her ever-practical visitor, however, retorted that it would be good if the book "also made her see the importance of doing everyday things well such as darning her socks and wearing her glasses." She also told Helen that "it was definitely becoming a question at CAS whether she would ever make good," to which Helen replied defiantly, "Well, I am going to college anyway." The visitor then attempted to "make her see that going to college in and of itself would not help her learn self-direction and self-control." As if trying to convince herself, the caseworker added, "Even supposing she managed to get through high school and college, if she had no more ability to manage her affairs then as now and with no greater degree of efficiency, then her education would be valueless."

Helen's inability to "steer herself" (at least in preferred directions), as well as her quick mind, began increasingly to vex the social worker. She observed, for instance, that Helen "detects a great deal of inconsistencies in the attitudes and requirements of the Catholic Church" and worried that such attitudes would make trouble for herself and the agency. Soon thereafter, the foster mother reported that Helen was doing poorly in school and under the threat of suspension for "disobedience," stemming, in part, from her refusal to attend chapel. Such willfulness and defiance began to reshape the tone of social workers' narrations and the course of their relationship with Helen. Increasingly, as her defiance became more frequent and public, the case record shifted in emphasis from the protection of Helen from an inadequate home life to the protection of the social worker's professional identity and class status. After a visit to Helen's school, it was reported that her English teacher felt that Helen "showed a marked inability to follow any prearranged plan. If given books to read, would come up and ask for others. Felt that she might be a genius however." Such testimony provided further confirmation of Helen's growing recalcitrance to her social worker's desires for a compliant client.

Helen was then taken to Dr. Healy at the Judge Baker Foundation, where her destiny was drastically altered. Although she was reported to possess "good general ability," her IQ tested at only 100. Her "outlook," according to Healy, was that "this girl has been regarded by almost everyone who has some contact with her as having exceptionally good ability; even as being brilliant but we see no signs of this on tests. The point now is whether with all her ambition it is worth the effort to help her realize her ambitions. It would seem as though this girl has reached the limits of her educability along the line she is following now in spite of her expressed ambitions." The prediction was duly noted in the case record and did much to influence the social worker in subsequent encounters.

Helen's domestic situation also began to be troublesome. Following Healy's examination, the social worker noted that Helen was doing poorly on the domestic front and also proving to be "profoundly irritating to [the boarding parents'] well-poised conventional temperaments." At the same time, though, the visitor had some reservations about Helen's treatment in the boarding home:

> She [the social worker] could not help but feel that for a long time the girl has not gotten what she needed. The boarding mother has many outside interests and activities and there seems to be very little home life. The girl is just thrown back on her own undisciplined wayward self to sink or swim. The boarding mother feels she has been very interested in her and has done much for her. The fact that she gave the girl no presents of any kind for Christmas shows that there is a certain lack of personal element in her attitude towards the girl.

Despite her qualms about the placement, the visitor concluded that Helen had not "really adapted to any home and things might be better in an institution under group discipline." Fortunately, however, Helen was given another chance and placed in another home that was "less stimulating" but where she would experience "more like that of a normal home life," because "Helen's struggle to fit in at Wellesley was in part due to her suppressed desire to fit into the social background and, at the same time, she was conscious of her limitations. Therefore she could not make the adjustments she would have liked to make."

Subsequently, and by her own volition, Helen returned to her immigrant relatives in the North End and obtained a job in a candy factory. She "looked like a typical factory girl with a torn dirty gingham dress and no hat." Helen was reported to have "vividly described the contrast between her surroundings now and formerly" in a "bemused tone."

After a short stint in the candy factory, Helen next decided to attend nursing school, although she was quick to point out that nursing was merely an alternative to working in the factory, not a replacement for her hopes for college. Soon, however, Helen was expelled for a variety for reasons, including poor grades and inattentiveness in class. She was indebted to the Children's Aid Society for $56, the cost of uniforms.

After Helen's expulsion from nursing school, the visitor was at wit's end. She consulted with her supervisor and then made the bold decision to let Helen read her case record, feeling that doing so "would give the girl comprehension of the degree of her irresponsibility and stubbornness and just how her almost insane willfulness had injured her chances of success." "If you have other girls, Miss Kemp, I would advise you to give them more opportunities for recreation," Helen admonished the vistor after reading the record. She was described as "furious" after reading Healy's summary and "insisted that no matter what anyone said she would go to school and not work in a factory or housework. She only wished she could get through without any help from CAS."

After a case conference on Helen, the visitor then attempted to have her return to the Judge Baker Foundation, where agents had expressed a willingness to "help her."[16] Helen, however, declined the offer and obtained a job in a medical office where men with venereal disease were treated. She liked the work, she said, because it gave her time to study. The visitor had observed both "a battered geometry book with scribbling and Canfield's book in evidence upon the table." Having lost her former admiration of Helen's studious commitments, however, the social worker now interpreted Helen to be merely putting on a "student pose." Helen then revealed that she was now "being coached and hoped to pass her college entrance exams. She had not been willing to speak of this for she wanted to surprise the visitor. Helen feels that if she could only be allowed to have some concessions as to meal payments she could accomplish her purpose of preparation for college." That concession, however, was not forthcoming. The matron of Franklin Square, a boarding home for working girls, felt Helen to be undeserving of favors.

During the ensuing months, the visitor saw Helen several times. She still told people that she was preparing for college and "exciting interest and admiration." In one of her last entries the visitor reported that she had met Helen on the street and that the girl looked "unkempt and rather in need of a bath. She still carries her notebook and Latin grammar to keep her student pose."

Despite receiving stifling interpretations by the Boston Children's Aid Society and the Judge Baker Foundation, and lacking class privileges and resources, Helen would not be moved. In 1931, after a five-year gap in the BCAS record, a "Miss Curt" of the North End Street Nursery inquired at the society about Helen. She had married and given birth to two children, yet she still wanted to go to college. Even though Miss Curt judged this ambition to be "a great handicap in her marital adjustment," she was swayed by Helen's devotion to her dream. She observed that Helen's conflict over her lack of education undoubtedly "dates back to when she was examined at Judge Baker and found to have an IQ of 100. At that time, she was anxious to go to school but did not seem to be the material for CAS to spend money on. Since then, she has been determined to show CAS and JBF that she could make the grade. Undoubtedly, she has a higher IQ then was given her at that time. But her attitude and lack of cooperation probably made her grade lower at that time."

Miss Curt suggested a housekeeper for Helen, but Helen said that she could not afford one because her husband was out of work and uncooperative about taking care of the children. She worried that Helen spoke about the children with a lack of affection and felt the outlook for them was "discouraging." She then told Helen that she ought to obtain a divorce but observed that Helen was "going to persist in her plans in getting an education and neglecting her children." Whether or not

Helen ever went to college was not noted in her case record. In 1962, however, an entry was made in Helen's case record of an inter-agency request for information. Helen was being seen for "emotional disturbances and fainting spells."

The case records of Rosa and Helen are moving because of the women's dreams and the strength of their resolve. Rosa's dream, however, was not as salient to her social worker as it is to a contemporary reader. Her dream, buried in a glut of accusations and reproaches, was not the story the caseworker chose to tell in constructing Rosa's life as a case; it is a subtext of that. The caseworker instead chose to build a tale in which the main storyline was formed around what she defined as Rosa's domestic failure. Similarly, Helen's lifelong ambition to obtain a college education became, in the eyes of her visitor, a sign of irresponsibility and impracticality rather than a testament to her fortitude.

Although fervently devoted to benevolence, caseworkers subscribed to the professional agendas and ideologies characteristic of their times, concepts that helped shape their notions of beneficence. Although deemphasizing detection, policing, and the bullying tactics of other agencies and approaches, caseworkers' unacknowledged class power and privilege hindered empathy and the more compassionate and generous descriptions of clients' dreams and dilemmas that might have accompanied it. Social workers' dreams of cross-class tutelage, trust, and friendships, of course, often went unrealized.

Charles Stillman, a social worker, aptly criticized typical social work methods of his era for rendering clients powerless by reducing them to types within demeaning categories. He lamented that

> reams of good paper were wasted in minute descriptions of clients' houses, the color schemes of their bathrooms, etc. The Visitor talks to the neighbors, listens to back-yard gossip, returns to the office and records every minute bit of scandal she has been able to gather. . . . Some of the families I visited personally and later read the records of their cases. In many homes, I learned touching lessons of patience, courage, and faith, and of old fashioned loyalty. But according to the record, most of the clients were of "low mentality." (1935, p. 546)

More recently, Kenneth Burke (cited in Monroe, Holleman, and Holleman 1992, p. 46) has contended that "terministic screens" such as "low mentality" preclude other, fuller ways of seeing, interacting, and rendering because they reveal "only such reality as is capable of being revealed by this particular kind of terminology." Maintaining in an often-quoted passage that "a way of seeing is also a way of not seeing," Burke argues that much of what we take as observations about "'reality'" may be "but the spinning out of possibilities implicit in our choice of terms." The attributions of Rosa's maternal neglect and the reduction of Helen's ambition to an affectation of a "student pose" are clearly the sort of "terministic screens" Burke had in mind. Sadly, they spun out certain possibilities and closed down others, with profound material consequences for both women.

As in the cases of Rosa and Helen, social workers frequently failed to persuade clients to adopt their ways of seeing or their advice. Consequently, many long-lasting relationships between social workers and clients terminated on peevish and brusque notes. Sometimes social workers found themselves compelled to close cases prematurely, as Miss Champine did when Hazel bolted from her supervision as soon as she was of legal age. In other cases they relinquished their struggles with clients in the light of what were perceived to be insurmountable hostility to "personal appeals" and were forced to revise their stories accordingly. They faced clients who threw lard pails, brandished axes, and threatened to sue them for slander, and many such encounters were concluded with words of finality: "Case Closed—as it was useless to persuade her."

Although they did not do so all the time, social workers, did provide needed support and action for many clients, even though the professional friendship they offered was always conditional. To leave a study of social work thinking that it only illustrates the turbulent, often dissatisfying, sometimes helpful relationships between individuals, where power and desires wrestle both to elevate the client and raise the discipline to professional status, is to mistakenly deny the larger context in which individual relationships could fail and yet social work, as a profession seeking legitimation, could succeed.

Attempts to attain client compliance and maintain genuine relationships, however, were only part of the professional mission demanded of social workers. Appeals to a skeptical public also had to be made, and case records, once they were finely edited and polished, promised to form a basis for campaigns to sway public sentiment in favor of social work and its preferred definitions of social ills and the professionalized solutions to them.

6

Tales of Accomplishment: Social Work and the Art of Public Persuasion

Paint us an angel . . . ; paint us a Madonna turning her mild face upward
. . . but do not impose on us any aesthetic rules which shall banish from
the reign of art those old women with work worn hands scraping
carrots. . . . It is needed we should remember their existence . . . let art
always remind us of them.

∾George Elliot, quoted in Hine (1909)

There is nothing like publicity
To further that lubricity
Which minted cartwheels need
To maximize their speed
In your direction.

∾Edmund Vance Cook, quoted in Stillman (1927)

Case records were not intended to collect dust in the filing cabinets of central offices. In addition to illustrating new professional techniques and organizational solutions for relieving distress, popularizing new classification categories, and training novice social workers, case stories also enjoyed wide circulation among the general public and played an indispensable role in the publicity and persuasive efforts of social workers. Mary Swain Routzahn, assistant director of the Department of Surveys and Exhibits at the Russell Sage Foundation and secretary of the Committee on Publicity Methods in Social Work, reminded social workers that people have a preference for "stories of individuals rather than of large numbers and for details rather than broad general statements" (1928, p. 28). Case narratives provided the details and human drama that could turn public sympathy toward social work's causes.

In 1893 Clarence Darrow noted the trend toward realism in newspaper reportage and literature: "The world has grown tired of preachers and sermons; today it asks for facts. It has grown tired of fairies and angels, and asks for flesh and blood" (quoted in Scudson 1978, p. 73). To meet this new demand for facts, early social workers—whether they thought of themselves as artists, scientists, detectives, protectors, surveyors, social engineers, or storytellers—experimented with a variety of ways of retelling case histories. In doing so they employed multiple forms of graphic, textual, and pictorial representations to present the basics of social work to the public. They employed a wide range of tropes to tell their stories and position themselves and clients favorably. Yet in reaching out to mobilize the public, social workers pursued contradictory and multiple agendas—whether to win sympathy for those they served, for example, or advance the credibility and prestige of the profession. In experimenting with a variety of forms of representation in persuasion, they struggled with a myriad of professional tensions and once again reentered the discursive arena for yet another round of debates about the science and art of the profession.

As a emergent genre of documentary discourse, social work case records were serviceable for conveying the drama involved in reform work and provided essential material for the plays, pageants, and human interest stories that social workers produced in order to open the hearts and pockets of the unconcerned. Elwood Street (1919, p. 680) contended that case records were human interest stories "telling in more or less detail the human dramas of people benefitted by the [social work] agency; stories telling of quaint characters." These stories, he believed, were the profession's greatest source of publicity. Alfred Whitman, general secretary of the Boston Children's Aid Society, concurred with Street and noted that "various organizations are learning that the wealth of material in case histories must not be neglected and that the public should be given the facts concerning the causes which make our work necessary as well as the stories of accomplishment" (Boston Children's Aid Society 1922, p. 33). Recalling the 1920s, Maggie Blake of the MSPCC reported that her agency, too, had learned that its "best publicity could be gathered in our own office from our case records" and that "our greatest need was then, and possibly still is, for publicity" (1947, p. 55). Accordingly, case stories came to be considered vital for infusing professionally constructed facts with texture, emotion, vitality, and immediacy.

Social workers employed a variety of metaphors; many publicity stories were built upon images of darkness and light. Pointing out that in Western literature light has been a long-standing metaphor representing truth and power, Mariana Valverde (1990, p. 68) argues that just as light appeared as the "torch for the Enlightenment or the Easter candle representing Christ," it typically took the form of a "searchlight held by someone in control in order to illuminate an external object" in representations of reform work. Social workers upheld those well-established metaphoric conventions in accounts replete with images that equated light with professional authority and social workers' knowledge of otherness and difference. Tousley (1927, p. 176), for example, referred to case records as the "lamp which illuminated" and as the "searchlight revealing much," and Lewis Hine (1909, p. 357) suggested that the dictum of the social worker should be "Let There Be Light."

Many social workers used darkness as a grounding metaphor to narrate glowing accounts of those rescued from dark circumstances that otherwise blocked out all sunshine and light.[1] Publicity stories used a variety of other metaphors as well, including images that portrayed social workers as "engineers" who salvaged clients from "garbage heaps" or, alternatively, "compassionate friends" who tenderly nourished clients portrayed as "delicate plants" struggling to blossom despite the lack of "sunshine and roses" in their lives. Regardless of the metaphoric conventions employed in publicity stories, however, clients were typically rendered as caricatures or types, appearing variously as predators, passive victims, reformable objects, or simply "raw material." Their complexity, struggles, dreams, and agency rarely provided the main storyline.

Early Models of Representation and Persuasion

Two exemplary but distinct poles of persuasive representation—sensationalized human interest stories and the cooler, more detached scientific exhibitions of the urban survey movement—provided the initial bearings for early social work publicity efforts. Although social workers eventually developed many genres of storytelling for persuasive purposes, Jacob A. Riis was one of the most important early pacesetters for later efforts to compose human interest stories, an artistic approach to persuasion that resonated with the impulse to write colorful case records. Riis began his journalistic career as a police reporter for the *New York Tribune* in 1877, where he learned the art of photography. Especially imaginative in combining photography and storytelling to further social reform campaigns, Riis pioneered in the use of photography and lantern slide exhibits and lectures in 1887 to dramatize and publicize the crime and misery he encountered among New York tenements.

Riis narrated popular slide exhibits with both humorous and adventuresome anecdotes of his excursions into city slums, which he portrayed as urban enclaves of otherness. Designed both to entertain and reassure middle-class audiences, *How the Other Half Lives* (1890) and *The Battle with the Slums* (1902) maintained this same tone of storytelling. Combining well-established interpretive conventions of popular literature with social explorations of deeply fragmented urban landscapes, Riis portrayed the American city of the 1880s as a bifurcated terrain; slums were represented as "another country" inhabited by "other races." Employing the concept of the "other half," Riis reinforced an imaginative distance between middle-class audiences and the inhabitants of slums. As Maren Stange (1992, p. 16) notes, "The 'other half' was not least among a battery of well-worn tropes evoking nether regions that presented an excursionist with scenes so alien, forbidden, or disgusting, that they required the mediation of artists or journalists."[2]

Throughout the late nineteenth century, many lurid accounts were written to describe excursions into the dark shadows of an urban underside that was pictured as teeming with menacing, primitive, exotic, and repulsive people. One example, *Darkness and Daylight; or, Lights and Shadows of New York Life* (1893) by Helen Campbell, was filled with "Hundreds of Thrilling Anecdotes, Personal Experiences, Humorous Stories, Touching Home Scenes, and Tales of Tender Pathos" from the dark side of New York (figs. 10–11). The book's numerous authors, who functioned as tour guides, included a variety of authorities, including a journalist, a police detective, and "a woman." (The latter was described as especially important because, as the editors asked, "Who but a woman could describe to women the scenes of sorrow, sin, and suffering among these people that have presented themselves to her womanly eye and heart?") *Darkness and Daylight* included 250 illustrations and told a wide range of exotic stories, including "How a Street Arab Went to Yale," "A Tour through Homes of Misery, Want, and Woe," "A Midnight Visit to Gambling Houses," and "The Foxes, Wolves and Owls of Humanity."

Because they represented their subjects from extreme and exotic angles, books such as *Darkness and Daylight* have been described as "defamiliarizing ethnography" (Reed 1988), a genre that makes otherwise familiar subjects seem strange and therefore requires authorial mediation. Thus the publishers of *Darkness and Daylight* pointed to the jeopardy that awaited those who ventured into the dark zones of New York on unmediated excursions without being safely escorted—buffered— by authoritative guides:

> The dark side of life is presented without any attempt to tone it down, and foul places are shown just as they exist. Any one who undertakes to see life in the haunts of vice and crime, especially by night, takes his life in his own hands, and courts danger in many forms. It is not pleasant, in underground dens, where hardened criminals and the vilest outcasts hide from the light of day . . . nor is it pleasant to spend day after day in vermin infested tenements and oozy cellars waiting for opportunities to portray some particularly desired scene. It is dangerous to breathe for hours an atmosphere poisoned with nauseating effluvia. (pp. 10–11)

Defamiliarizing ethnographies thus portrayed two subjects: life's dark "other" side and the benevolent, risk-taking mediators who guided readers through it. The dual focus suited social work's goal of educating the public and legitimating the profession.

Photographic shows by Riis and books such as *Darkness and Daylight* performed a buffering role for reform-minded, middle-class audiences who required a

Figure 10. "An Underground Stale-Beer Dive Late at Night in Mulberry Street Bend," 1893. Sensational accounts of degenerate and menacing urban populations were popular near the end of the nineteenth century. Campbell (1893, p. 230)

Figure 11. "Early Morning in a Shed Lodging-House in the Rear of Mulberry Street: Getting Ready for Another Day of Crime and Idleness," 1893. Campbell (1893, p. 429)

privileged, detached vantage point on slum life.[3] According to Stange (1992, p. 18), the approach Riis pioneered gave audiences elements of "the information need-ed to transform or control the slums, and the security and privilege of distance that obviates the 'vulgar, odious, and repulsive' experiences that the actual slums would inevitably present." Such a privileged gaze, signifying both possession and distance, structured "a range of disparate texts and heterogeneous practices which emerge in the nineteenth-century city—tourism, exploration/discovery, social in-vestigation, social policy" (Pollock 1988, p. 28). Presuming to inform as well as buffer, that style of representation would be reproduced by later social work pub-licists who retold case narratives to nonprofessional audiences.

Urban Surveys

The scientific urban survey movement also enlarged the genre of social work pub-licity because it was so well suited for showcasing professionally constructed "facts," scientific methodologies, and the centrality of expert interpreters. Urban surveys provided alternative conventions for social work publicity and also influenced the practice of social reform. In 1898 the New York Charity Organization Society es-tablished a tenement house committee, which held an exhibition in 1900 that in-cluded more than a thousand photographs, detailed maps of slum districts and disease zones, numerous statistical charts, and papier-mâché representations of tenement blocks. Stange (1992, pp. 44–45) notes that such an exhibit, in contrast to Riis's narrative style, was "grid-like rather than sequential, rational rather than narrative in structure. Fuller meanings emerge not in the course of narrative en-joyment, but rather when, like the exhibition organizers themselves, the viewer enters into an arduous process of cross reference, comparison, and analysis."

The Tenement House Exhibit was heralded as a pinnacle event, not only because of its success in conveying professional data to the public (the society claimed an attendance of ten thousand viewers in a two-week period) but also because of its practical results (it contributed to the passage of legislation establishing a state building and inspection commission). Other important early exemplars of the sur-vey genre were *The Hull House Maps and Papers* (Residents of Hull House 1895) and Robert Woods's *The City Wilderness* (1898), both of which emphasized the dis-tanced, rationalistic presentation of objective facts that had been collected, ordered, and professionally interpreted.

More imperturbable and remote than the human interest style pioneered by Riis, the survey genre emphasized bureaucratic and rational organization, scientific methodology, and the authoritative discourses of professionally trained experts. Intent upon showcasing scientific and expert procedures, the survey style provided social workers of the Progressive Era with a model for publicity efforts that was built on Riis's earlier publicity efforts, especially his use of photography, but it projected a more modernist tone of objectivity and expertise.

The Pittsburgh Survey, one of the largest, best-known of the urban surveys, was launched in 1906 with funds provided by the Russell Sage Foundation. After two years of fieldwork, an exhibition was set up to display the results of the survey, and six volumes were published on survey results and methodologies. Reflecting on the Pittsburgh Survey in 1929, Paul Kellog (1908), director of the Pittsburgh Survey and editor of the charity organization society magazine *Charities and the Commons,* stated that "the effort was to make a town real to itself; not in goody-goody preachment of what ought to be; not in sensational discoloration; not merely in a formidable array of rigid facts" (Stange 1992, p. 51). A believer in the didactic value of surveys, Kellog, who asserted that social revelation and reform required more than just "personal contact or picturesque and graphic form," described survey representation as an "adventure on the high seas between the census and yellow journalism" (p. 51).

Both the Pittsburgh Survey and the Tenement House Exhibit were important catalysts for the spread of the survey metaphor in social work publicity campaigns and in the practice of social reform. The Russell Sage Foundation published an influential series of how-to books on surveys and exhibits, including such works as *Traveling Publicity Campaigns* (1920) and *The ABC of Exhibit Planning* (1918), which encouraged reform agencies in smaller cities to adapt the survey form to local publicity efforts. Amos Warner (1922, p. 172) noted that after 1909, when the Pittsburgh Survey material was first distributed, there were numerous surveys of general scope and hundreds of smaller surveys throughout the country because "no intelligent movement is any longer undertaken without a survey."[4] Particularly noteworthy was a survey undertaken in Springfield, Illinois, in 1914 that stationed volunteer interpreters along a predetermined, ninety-minute course and used moving devices and special lighting effects to arouse interest in its maps and charts (fig. 12).

One of the survey movement's important practitioners, Amos Warner, noted (1922, pp. 169–70) that civic surveys were originally conceived by the Publications Committee of the New York Charity Organization Society as journalistic endeavors designed to "get the facts of social conditions and to put those facts before the public in ways that counted." And Stange describes (1992, p. 51) the survey approach as "radically expand[ing] the function and status of the investigator to include the role of explainer." Alan Trachtenberg (1989, p. 196) also maintains that the "survey was not only a method of investigation but an emphasis on communication, a belief in the 'efficacy of facts' and in the 'ultimate benevolence of an informed public.'"

The survey movement thus sought to enhance eyewitness authority with expert

Another interesting feature was the stopping points where exhibits of action might be seen, such as the school playground, motion-picture hall, and playhouse. These were well distributed around the hall, and on the "home stretch" were two places for rest, the "coffee house," and the "summary" or "last word" booth.

The floor plan on page 98b allowed freedom of movement in all directions, but provided an effective grouping of exhibits quickly understood by the visitor who on entering the hall faced arches, with illuminated title signs, leading into the five main divisions. This plan enabled the visitor to select the subject of immediate interest and to quickly locate the demonstrations on that subject.

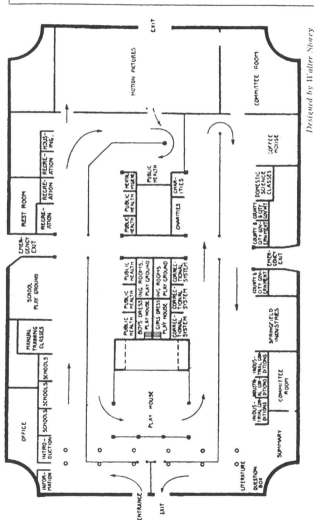

FLOOR PLAN OF THE SPRINGFIELD SURVEY EXHIBITION

Designed by Walter Storey

The floor plan on this page shows a one-way arrangement of booths and exhibits with guide rails dividing the aisles so that visitors could move in only one direction. The back walls of booths were brought out from the building wall, allowing for a variation in the depth of booths and for various uses of the space behind them.

Figure 12. "Floor Plan of the Springfield Survey Exhibition," 1918. Urban surveys and exhibitions were celebrated as a way of showcasing professional expertise. Routzahn and Routzahn (1918, p. 98c)

interpretation, but it parted ways with Riis's stylistic conventions by pursuing more solemn and less aesthetic means of communication predicated upon technocratic professional expertise and scientific objectivity. Surveys also employed representational tools such as maps, charts, diagrams, three-dimensional exhibits, and photographs (viewed as transparent vehicles for the objective corroboration of facts).[5] Despite its cool and detached tone, the survey movement borrowed the casework method of bringing "problems down to human terms" in order to illustrate the "flesh and blood" of social work (Edward Devine, quoted in Young 1939, p. 22; Watson 1922, p. 540).

Social Work and the Public

In the early docudramas of Riis and in urban surveys, social work publicists had at least two prominent stylistic precursors to imitate and refine. They sought not only to woo public financial support and enhance professional credibility but also to raise public awareness of social conditions. According to the early publicist Georgia Bowen (1924), social work was "not a private, distinct, and sacred little thing to be snuggled jealously to the trained breast of social workers" nor something "to be fondled in technical terms which confuse the public." Rather, it was "the concern of great masses of people . . . who must become thoughtfully intelligent on these matters if we are to move towards any betterment" (p. 505). W. Brooks Graves (1930) expanded those goals to include creating a feeling of personal responsibility and the willingness to contribute, developing public confidence in the honesty of purpose and general effectiveness of work done by a profession composed primarily of women, and selling expert treatment solutions. Maggie Blake put the matter more bluntly when she stated, "If we wanted funds, we must enter the field of publicity" (Blake 1947, p. 38). Mary Swain Routzahn (1931, p. 549) likewise encouraged social workers to "expose the inside of [their] professional mind[s] more often to public view."

Throughout the early decades of the twentieth century, social workers thus struggled with often-contradictory impulses to improve social conditions and increase professional prestige. At the same time, they experimented with—and debated—the relative merits of sensational "sob stuff" as opposed to reasoned and technocratic forms of persuasion. They employed a mélange of guises to depict clients, including contradictory portrayals of those clients as visual spectacles: odoriferous and polluting, exotic, romantic and heroic victims, worthy of pity, emblems of sufferings, or reformable and scientifically classified objects.

In 1907 the National Conference of Charities and Corrections helped advance publicity-seeking by forming a standing Committee on Press and Publicity.[6] Reporting on the committee's first year of activity, H. Wirt Steele (1908, p. 263) noted that only a few agencies were conducting publicity adequately according to a national survey of casework agencies. Although many organizations fed information on clients and professional activities to local newspapers, most had no idea of the "sequence or the psychology involved in effective publicity."[7] To remedy that, the committee sponsored short-story and play-writing contests and offered substantial prizes to caseworkers judged best able to dramatize situations they had encountered.

At the same NCCC session, Edward Shaw (1908), managing editor of the *Washington Times,* attempted to formulate such a psychology for social work. In a manner reminiscent of Riis, Shaw used the metaphor of tourism to evoke an analogy between social work publicity and sightseeing, stating that an effective tour guide points out all that is odd, dramatic, romantic, and pathetic. To arouse the public effectively, social workers should point out the humorous, dramatic, romantic, and pitiful happenings in their contacts with clients. For example, Shaw commended Upton Sinclair's *The Jungle* (1906), which he termed a prototype for case recording because it conveyed "pathos, suffering, self-denial, hopes raised up and shattered, hopes renewed, love and sacrifice that came trustfully up to the merciless Juggernaut of modern commercialism and were swept under and crushed. . . . What makes it stand out is the characters are so vividly, so lovingly, so intimately drawn that they became real flesh and blood" (p. 271). According to Shaw, social work had ample material for convincing publicity, but it needed to cast that material in such a way as to stir sympathies as effectively as Sinclair had done.

To illustrate persuasive writing, Shaw belittled a typical newspaper article— "$500.00 in One Lump Aids Charities Fund"—that had been submitted by a social reform agency. Instead, he suggested a more dramatic and effective story entitled "Family in Dire Need; Husband in Workhouse; Woman Tells Her Story," which would be built around popular themes of noble sacrifice and struggle on the part of the virtuous poor: "A woman and her two children are slowly dying while her husband lies in the workhouse for drunkenness and his relatives who are well to do refuse to relieve the mother and children's destitution by so much as a nickel. . . . The agent stood in silence, wondering at the courage of the poor. . . . Whatever beauty she had has been sacrificed long ago. Her hair is short and scant and is a stranger to hairpins or any sort of fastening. Her misery is lamentable" (1908, p. 275).

Shaw's version of a "family in dire need" was not universally applauded, however, because it clashed with the more rational forms of persuasion characteristic of the survey movement. For example, Charles Weller, general secretary of the Associated Charities of Washington, D.C., agreed that more concrete human stories were precisely what social work publicity required but acknowledged that he had "winced" when Shaw's story of the "Family in Dire Need" was presented because "it was overdrawn. . . . The woman was not dying or starving, but she had been for a long time *underfed*" (1908, p. 277, emphasis added).[8]

For a variety of reasons, social work made many people uncomfortable, although Shaw was effective in warning social workers of the obstacles they would face in seeking publicity. He pointed out (1908, pp. 268–69) that the average citizen tended to avoid charity involvement because "the sight of distress was unpleasant to him and he knows that if he is brought face to face with it he will inevitably sacrifice something of his time and money in an effort to alleviate it." Walter Lippmann likewise noted that social work's unpopularity stemmed from the fact "that people don't want to be reminded of their social sins as social work reminds them; they don't like the air of superiority of uplifters, and they don't understand the jargon" (quoted in Bowman 1923, p. 478). And a reporter observed that social workers "are nursing the unfit and subsidizing the poor players in the game, opposing the doctrine of the survival of the fittest" (Bing 1923, p. 486).

Social work publicists were also faced with a variety of negative public perceptions because of the gendered nature of the field. In a public opinion survey of newspaper reporters, two respondents said that "social workers (speaking of ladies) have no charm"; they were "well intentioned and enthusiastic but illy fitted novices of the class referred to in street parlance as 'bugs' . . . they slobber over and make a mess of the work" (Bowman 1923, p. 482). By the 1920s, contrary to the ambitions of social work publicists, social workers themselves were often depicted in popular characterizations as obsessive, heartless, and bureaucratic investigators rather than rational, scientific experts.[9] Routzahn (1931) conceded that since social workers were often unpopular figures in the public's imagination, they were also difficult to portray in fiction and drama. Although a defensive campaign could be waged to "bring to light unexpected characteristics now effectively concealed by our horn-rims, our low heels, and our latinized vocabulary," social workers would instead do better to "develop the art of telling what she sees, not what she does" (p. 541).

Indeed, social workers were energetic in their attempts to captivate the public by developing the "art of telling what she sees." Throughout the first three decades of the twentieth century, they engaged in a multitude of persuasion activities, including radio programs, pageants, stage and screen plays, street stunts, storefront exhibits, articles in newspapers and magazines, and novels.[10] Many reform organizations (the New York Charity Organization Society and the federations of both Cleveland and Cincinnati, for example) hired public relations staffs. Maggie Blake, a Massachusetts Society for the Prevention of Cruelty to Children stenographer, noted the effectiveness of the orations of that agency's janitor to "conservative male members of Beacon Hill families" as he swept and shoveled the sidewalks in front of the society's headquarters. All staff members, she urged, should think of themselves as publicity agents.

Influential books by Mary Swain Routzahn and Evart Routzahn (1928) and Charles Stillman (1927) provided agencies and social workers with overviews of publicity experiments, including a variety of exhibits that reform organizations had used effectively. For instance, a child welfare agency combined text and action in "Mrs. DoCare and Mrs. DontCare" (fig. 13), an exhibit that deployed the popular trope of contrasting opposites, in this case the homes of good and careless housekeepers. Exhibits were also structured by combining models of representation, such as "technical" charts picturing such stories as heredity and mental defects (fig. 14). "Come and see tours," street stunts, health improvement contests, exhibits on trains, and floats also proved to be effective ways to drama-

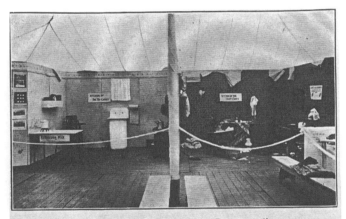

"MRS. DOCARE" AND "MRS. DONTCARE"

A number of child welfare exhibits have had displays in full size contrasting the kitchen or bedroom of the bad housekeeper with the good one who presumably has about the same means. A fault in the example shown above and in many other exhibits of the same kind is that the home of "Mrs. Dontcare," while not entirely overdrawn, since there are many such homes to be found, is too extreme to carry a lesson to most of the audience. Many a careless Mrs. Dontcare might be stimulated to greater effort by a reproduction of cleanliness and neatness that she would recognize as possible for her to carry out, contrasted with one of dirt and disorder that is true enough to be reminiscent of her own home. Mrs. Docare's kitchen here is inadequate, a fact she herself would know if she saw it. It lacks the proper equipment for the cooking, washing, and meal serving.

The idea is an excellent one, however, if it is carried out skilfully and tactfully.

Figure 13. "Mrs. DoCare and Mrs. DontCare," 1918. Social workers experimented with a variety of publicity techniques, including contrasting opposites to win public support. Routzahn and Routzahn (1918, p. 78b)

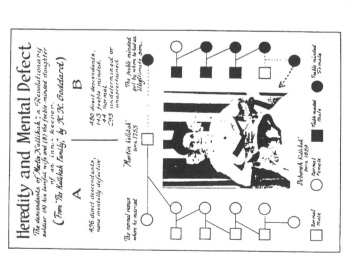

Figure 14. "Technical versus Popular Exhibit Forms," 1918. How-to books on publicity for social workers became increasingly popular during the 1920s. Routazahn and Routazahn (1918, p. 60, d-e)

tize social information (Routzahn 1920). In their examination of effective publicity, the Routzahns (1928, p. 270) gave special mention to "Mr. Cholera Germ," a street spectacle that consisted of a man on stilts and dressed in a long yellow robe. Mr. Cholera Germ had electrically lighted eyes and used a megaphone to point out unsanitary conditions and shout, "Cholera is at your door!" Most important, the Routzahns urged social workers to develop a nose for the news, look for the "good story," and not ignore the human interest that too often lay buried in case files or concealed under a mass of technical terms. Such stories, they argued, furnished golden opportunities to dramatize professional objectives.

Case Stories and Multiple Audiences

> I was just about to say, "My most interesting case last year was. . . ." But I realized that this is the point at which cases always begin to appear in this sort of article. I shall spare you the case therefore with only this much about it. She had no idea that she was a case at all. She came into the office to get some criticism on her poems. Her poetry was neither good or bad enough for any finality of judgement but it offered extra evidence of the emotional jam she was in.
>
> ∾Newsletter of the American Association of Psychiatric Social Work (1936)

When social workers turned attention toward influencing the public, they were already well rehearsed in the use of case records as persuasive means of exerting influence within the profession. Case records had for many years been used repeatedly to illustrate new professional techniques, promote professional solutions for distress, provide teaching material, and communicate new knowledge and classification categories. Case records had also forewarned the public of the dangers and perils posed by society's others. In the form of specimen, illustrative cases, and typical stories written both for public and professional audiences, case stories routinely appeared in a variety of places, including instruction manuals, professional presentations, and agency annual reports.

Sophonisba Breckinridge's *Family Welfare Work* (1924), a collection of forty-four edited case records compiled for teaching, introduced such "quaint" characters as "The Family of Peter Zuchola: A Skilled but Insane Cabinet Maker," "The Family of Lewis Morozoff: A Mental Defective and His Wife Ester, Who Is Diagnosed as Constitutionally Inferior," and "Julia Waldron: An Insane Woman Tramping with Three Small Children." *The Kingdom of Evils* (1922), a widely read book coauthored by social worker Mary Jarrett and E. E. Southard, a psychiatrist, consisted of the descriptions of a hundred exotic cases, including "Agnes Jackson, Pathetic Nuisance"; "Nora Campbell, Ladylike Adventuress"; "Bertha Greenwood, Hysterical Sex Delinquent"; "Theresa Beauvais, Girl of Bad Heredity, Victim of Hypersexualis"; "Maurice Eastman, Psychoneurotic Cigar Maker with Financial Worries"; and "Harriet Farmer, Psychopathic Typesetter, Attempted Suicide, Trained to Competence." Because the profession relied so heavily on the use of case stories for teaching and training, social workers were generally familiar with such stories (Bruno 1926).

Case stories were also commonly used to introduce and popularize new classification schemes and new groups of public menaces and idlers that required professional supervision and control, as, for example, in Margaret Powers's presentation at the 1920 National Conference of Social Work: "The Industrial Cost of the Psychopathic Employee" (pp. 343–46). In another address to the same conference, Homer Wichenden used a case illustration to demonstrate the importance of psychological study and direct attention toward a new classification category, the "constitutional psychopathic." Topical fare also included organizational success stories of courageous clients who, thanks largely to the proddings of social workers and, to a lessor degree, their strong wills and impeccable characters, managed to stay afloat amid the challenges of everyday life (Donahue 1917; Shuman 1915).

Local charitable agencies learned that case records could be used to win sympathy for professional missions. In its 1900 annual report to the general public, for example, the Boston Children's Aid Society reproduced seven complete specimen cases to illustrate the society's work. Each case representing a "specimen of the various types" brought to the society was headlined in order to direct readers to preferred meanings. For example, the heading of one case directed readers to appreciate a caseworker's efforts to keep a family together: "This case shows how by his own friendly counsel and by interested others, the agent kept a family together and was thus able to prevent them from becoming a burden on charity" (p. 13). Likewise, the Lexington [Kentucky] Child Guidance Service published six illustrative cases in its 1934 annual report, each with a summary intended "to aid the reader in grasping the essential nature of the problem, its causation, and the treatment methods employed" by the agency.

Organizational success stories drawn from case records thus became significant elements in the repertoire of social work discourse, and publicists drew upon them for annual reports. In time, few annual reports were fashioned without such success stories. The reports of the Massachusetts Society for the Prevention of Cruelty to Children, for example, presented a cross section of its successful cases in abbreviated form. One, involving a tyrannical father, ended well because "Anna and her mother are facing the future with new courage, confident that in [the MSPCC] they have a friend and protector." Another successful outcome involved a "little girl rescued from suffering and misery, perhaps from death, and started on the road to good health and happiness," and yet another showed that "industry, thrift, fidelity, and good home standards replaced the former disorders" (Massachusetts Society for the Prevention of Cruelty to Children 1926).

Even organizational failures found their way into publicity efforts. In the 1927 annual report of the MSPCC, for example, the case of a feebleminded women and another involving a fourteen-year-old sex delinquent, both of whom created sexual disorder in their respective communities despite the energetic ministrations of the society, were used to argue for the need to expand opportunities for the "protective" institutionalization of such community menaces.

Human Interest Stories

> The alternative title for this talk was: "Need Social Work Writing Be Dull?"
> That is a challenge and an insult. There is no predestination of dullness
> upon us. The work we do is not dull, this task of striving to make life
> happier and fuller for all of us.
> ∾Whipple (1927)

Not content merely to guide the public with excursions into worlds inhabited by the exotic others portrayed in such works as *How the Other Half Lives* and *Darkness and Daylight in New York,* later social worker publicists further embellished the plots of case stories to capture the human interest of social work situations. Some writers, to be sure, sought to present sympathetic rather than outlandish portraits of clients by emphasizing virtues shared with the middle class. Others, however, argued that although clients should be portrayed sympathetically, they nonetheless belonged to a different world than that of middle-class readers. Consequently, such cases still required the mediating role of social work experts for understanding, interpreting, and, ultimately, correcting urban problems.

Suspense, drama, and comedy were perceived as integral to successful human interest stories. For example, Routzahn and Routzahn (1928) warned social workers to be cautious in stories about narratively solving clients' difficulties too quickly with organizational solutions. Readers, they said, were often hooked by uncertainty and suspense; consequently, the lead paragraph of human interest stories was critical. The Routzahns criticized the following lead as being ineffective from a human interest angle: "Last week Miss — of the state board was called to investigate a case brought to the attention of her department." Instead, they suggested: "Long before the milkman made his rounds, Miss — hurried to a little frame house. . . . Death had come to the little house in the night leaving a grieving numbed woman and three frightened children" (1928, pp. 78–79).

Maggie Blake (1947, p. 56) suggested that humor also had an important place in human interest stories "to relieve the desperate tenseness" of social work situations, even though it was "dangerous to make fun at the expense of people in dire trouble." In her agency memoir (p. 56), she recorded several examples of how the MSPCC used humor: "His wife said that he was a heavy drinker; so the family moved every time the spirit moved him"; "A neighbor said the people are extremely cultured. Something should be done about their condition"; and, "Man hit by an automobile—speaks broken English." The Routzahns (1928) also urged social workers to appreciate that the public resents "having one's beliefs disturbed" and prefers the "familiar story." Even though many Appalachian children wore shoes, for example, showing them with those shoes reduced the children's public appeal.

In addition to the suspenseful, humorous, and familiar, other publicists such as Charles Stillman (1927, pp. 68–69) argued that human interest stories should be "dignified but heart-gripping." As a standard for social workers to follow in composing case stories for human interest reporting, Stillman canonized a story—"Red Tape to the Rescue"—that had appeared in the *New York Tribune* on April 30, 1922. The account, reproduced in many other stories, contrasted two defenseless boys, both "raw material" from the "scrap heap," a metaphor for their slum upbringings. Only one boy, however, was saved by professional ministrations. The other faced further degeneration because he did not receive the benefit of professional guardianship, or, in a nice reversal on the bureaucratic image of social work, the protection of "Red Tape."

> Joe and Harry were only eight when the die was cast for both of them. We asked for a chance at Joe and got it. He was a shy-acting chap. . . . His crimes? He loved to jump from roof to roof of the tenements; he lied to his parents and teachers who did not understand him. He was backward at school, as he had been specializing in bonfires in the back lots with some of his little truant friends. That was two years ago. Joe's father paid his way for one year with a foster mother of our choosing, far from the tenements and gangs and Joe was salvaged from the scrap heap.

In similar publicity stories, social workers became salvagers while clients were reduced to "wreckage," although potentially salvageable material. In a *Boston Herald* story in 1923, for example, the Boston Children's Aid Society boasted in a series of illustrations that it had "lifted the work of salvaging wrecked and sordid humanity into the realm of beauty." Social workers typically anchored such narrations with metaphors likening poor children to tender plants, buds, or flowers that would not flourish in the sordid, dark conditions of their impoverished homes and imposed by their incompetent parents. As in the case of Red Tape, children were often removed and families disrupted in order to lift such children to a "realm of beauty."

Yet compelling and long-standing stories were also written to describe how social work prevented the collapse of marriages and the gender order by keeping competent mothers—even the unhappy ones—with their children and spouses. Thus, the Boston Society for the Care of Girls provided a human interest story—"Society Reunited a Disrupted Family"—that appeared in both the *Herald* and the society's annual report in 1922. The story began when a mother left her three children one night because she was "tired of her responsibility." When her husband sought help, the errant mother was found working in a New York City restaurant. A visitor, dispatched with haste to New York for an interview, reported: "She said in nine years she had only one new suit and coat, and had, during that period, been out only twice, an afternoon and evening, and that her husband was inconsiderate in all things, making her work like a slave. She did admit that he provided proper food. Because the home was sold over their heads and she questioned his loyalty to her, she finally ran away" (p. 12). Because the visitor convinced the woman to try homemaking again, helped her find a suitable home, and invited both parents to the office for a reunion, the case ended on a positive note: "The woman has kept her promise that she would not leave her husband again, and the children are in possession of their heritage, the normal bringing up such as other children have."

One such human interest news story written about a Family Welfare Association of Minneapolis case provides an especially good look at how "heart gripping" stories were produced from sober case records. The case file is particularly informative because it contains both the standard case record diary of a social worker's involvement with the client as well as a copy of a human interest story that appeared in local newspapers and described the case. The case file also preserves a series of wretched letters written to the client's relatives by the social worker, which provide still another retelling of the case story—again for purposes of persuasion, only to a more specific audience. The case thus provides a rare opportunity to examine the presence of text on text within a single account as well as the multiple layers of persuasion involved in social work practice and publicity.

The case opened in 1908, when a landlord telephoned the Minneapolis Family Welfare Association to complain that 2, his tenant, had fallen behind on her rent.[11] Agent "Elizabeth Henry" visited and noted that 2 was:

> very hard of hearing and doesn't speak much English so I could learn nothing from her. Took "2" to "41" who interpreted for her; says "2" has managed to get along quite well for the last month or so but having to buy fuel she has gotten back on the rent and will be unable to pay it. Sells eight quarts of milk for 6 cents a quart and does an occasional washing and earns a dollar for that. Has plenty of fuel and groceries. Agent suggests to "2" that she do day work two or three days a week but she says she is not physically able to do it.

On the surface, this dry, bare-bones first-visit account seems to lack drama for human interest reportage, yet the client's gallant battles to raise chickens and vegetables, despite severe weather, could be portrayed as evidence of hardworking virtue that deserved agency support. In a news story dated December 8 and entitled "Real Santa Claus to Visit Children: Lady Bountiful Will Carry Cheer to Destitute Home," the case of 2 was embellished as follows:

> With hope that the many Santas that they have invited to their home will come, little Paul and Mary are waiting for the eventful night with childish squirms of anticipation. And they will not be disappointed for a certain Santa has made plans to be there. Peter and Mary are the eldest of five children and for almost a year the knowledge that their father was in prison had been hanging like a shadow over their little home. Their mother has met the problem of existence by raising chickens and a cow and by keeping a small vegetable patch. But when the last severe cold spell came, the chickens, one by one, succumbed to the cold and the little supply of garden stuff gave out.

In the news story, readers reencountered a popular plot for human interest stories that revolved around a family in poverty held together by an indefatigable and valorous mother who was no stranger to the toil and ingenuity required to make a home. The real-life 2 had done the right thing in the eyes of the Family Welfare Association, and rewards had been forthcoming. According to the newspaper story:

> The neighbors reported the case to FWA and mentioned that the children had been around town inviting various Santa Clauses they met to their home and were positive that one of the benign looking creatures would keep his promise. Their name was promptly given to a prominent society woman living on one of the fashionable boulevards who had asked for names of deserving poor children and she is planning to play Santa Claus and visit the home Christmas Eve. In her big limousine, this Lady Bountiful will take a tree with all the necessary decorations and help the children trim it. And of course, there will be all manner of suitable Christmas gifts of toys and clothing.

But while the virtuous resourcefulness of 2 gained the approving eye of the FWA, her intransigence in regard to her own ways of making ends meet eventually helped turn a tale of protection—that is, a story of passive virtue—into a tale of detection. A prosaic entry in the case file immediately following the colorful news-clipping contains a vapid recital of her misguided attempts to make ends meet, especially her steadfast refusal to sell her cow. Here, 2 was no longer presented as a worthy paragon of domestic virtue but rather as a source of irritation because of her refusal to follow professional advice.

The social worker, however, was not finished with 2 or the art of persuasion. She next wrote a series of letters to 2's relatives, pleading for their assistance. In one such effort to persuade the daughter of 2 to assist her mother, she wrote:

> I regret very much that it is necessary for me tell you of the sad case of your mother and three younger sisters. Your father and sister were arrested because of certain immoral relations between the two and have been sent to our state prison for several years. Meanwhile, your mother and sisters are left with practically no income. The rent, $8.00 a month, must be paid in some way so that your mother may keep a roof over her head. What would you advise her to do? Would it be possible for her to come down and live with you? What plan for her betterment would you suggest? Perhaps you can urge your mother to give the landlord her cow. She could then stay until April 1.

Refusing to give up her cow, 2 was no longer an acquiescent victim of poverty who lent herself to sentimental depictions. She had parted ways with her social worker, and her cleverness was now "irritating." Professional approval of her strategies for survival had evaporated. Not only did approval fade in this particular case story but also in many others in which recognition was never forthcoming for the efforts that working-class and poor clients made to make ends meet.

Apart from the realities of approval and condemnation that marked this case, the story of 2 furnished the same ingredients that made up what W. F. Axton termed a "glad story" in his preface to *Mrs. Wiggs of the Cabbage Patch.* The story of a widow and her children who lived in a poor neighborhood of Louisville, Kentucky, named "The Cabbage Patch" because of the many small plots where residents raised vegetables for sale, *Mrs. Wiggs* offered "nothing painful or depressing [that was] unmodified by pathos, humor, a sharp eye for bizarre comedy, or by the assurance of better times ahead if personal charity and homey virtues could prevail" (Rice 1901, p. xviii). In a similar vein, the human interest version of the story of 2 and her children was also tidied up as a glad story. The case record upon which the story was based, however, an ongoing saga of encounters between the social worker and 2, did not permit so easy and appealing a resolution. Rather, by resisting many of her social worker's suggestions and impositions, 2 disrupted an ongoing story of affable, cross-class relationships.

Together, the case recordings, news-clippings, and letters of appeal in the case of 2 illustrate how integral storytelling and persuasive efforts were to social work— and how easily selections of case stories could be detached and extended from casework to public work, from case management to public relations. Human interest stories, however, were not the only vehicles for staging social work cases and causes. Plays and pageants also were popular forms of publicity and information.

Social Welfare Theater

The production of plays and pageants occupied many social work publicists (fig. 15). As early as 1910, Mrs. W. I. Thomas urged social workers to regain control of the emotional and dramatic form of the five-cent theater that was taking the "en-

Figure 15. "Scene from a Play about Babies," 1918. Like surveys and exhibitions, plays and pageants gained prominence as vehicles for publicizing professional methods. Routzahn and Routzahn (1918, p. 86b)

tire machinery of appeal through dramatic appeal" and reducing it to mere amusement and unwholesome entertainment (p. 146). Thomas reminded social workers that both Greek drama and morality plays had functioned much like state constitutions to teach ethical lessons and social values, and she urged the restoration of these functions to popular entertainment. She chastised social workers for neglecting the need for wholesome emotional amusements and observed that "in the U.S., we have few holidays or bright gala day costumes." What predominated instead were primarily stories of Puritans and pioneers, reflecting "the whole dreary standard of American industrial and middle class life." Mrs. Thomas also lamented the dependence "upon our friends from overseas for all the highlights and picturesque touches and social games and dances" that enlivened urban life.

In a review of social work publicity efforts, the Routzahns (1928, p. 261) argued that the "everyday experiences of social work abounded in materials from which to fashion plays" and urged social workers to take control of this "machinery of appeal." Their preference was for allegorical plays and pageants that had straightforward, formulaic plots and revolved around the theme of the redemptive power of professional knowledge to conquer many forms of evil. "A child," for example, "lies down and takes a nap. While he is asleep a beautiful health fairy with silver wings waves a wand and conducts child to the land of good health. Here Imps, Goblins, Dragons, Demons, or Witches beset the child. His plight is dire, when in dash Knowledge, Doctor, Fresh Air. . . . The powers of evil are dispelled and good triumphs. The child emerges, pure and enriched by the experience" (p. 260).

The Narrow Door, an allegorical play staged in 1915 for Pittsburgh Baby Week, also received rave reviews from the Routzahns. The play unfolded as a plea for action against the growing menace posed by ignorance and the material conditions of slums, which stunted the growth of innocent victims:

> As the curtain raises two women, Vita and Hygeia are discovered spinning thread from a distaff while in the background the grim, shrouded figure of the Mors leans upon a great two-edged sword at the right of the Narrow Door. Groups of children are happily playing with colored balloons. Vita complains that the threads are brittle and snap too easily. Hygeia tells her this is so because of the plague bred in crowded alleys, ignorance, and neglect that have made the slender threads so weak and delicate that they are scarcely twilled before they break. . . . Soon the Mors calls the name of one child, who slowly moves towards the Narrow Door and passes through. In the course of the play, three of the children thus disappear and the others, puzzled because they can not follow ask the women to explain. The children are told that they must appeal to mankind to stop this criminal waste of young life. (1928, pp. 260–61)

In each play, social work is portrayed as a rescuer, triumphant in one and sorely missed in the other.

Pageants, like plays, tended to adhere to standard plots that celebrated the value of professional expertise. Two typical pageants were respectively entitled *King Health Slays the Dragon Disease* and *Queen Knowledge Rescues Children from the Den of Ignorance*. Despite the fact that such productions were often trite and would admittedly have benefited from the "imagination of a poet" (p. 266), the Routzahns argued that they were important sources of self-expression and involvement for large numbers of people.

The Routzahns noted, however, that the major difficulty that social work publicists faced was how to dramatize social work remedies and solutions effectively, because drama requires crises. In a health play, for example, they suggested that the dramatist should develop a situation fraught with emotion by having the destinies of several likable people converge when a husband and breadwinner dies. Depictions of the same man surrounded by social workers in a modern sanitarium, however, were certain not to produce a dramatic crisis of equal poignancy.

John Brown (1926, p. 76) urged social workers to keep themselves in the background of stories because "as Milton discovered, good angels must be made uninteresting and versatile devils must be put in the center of the stage." At the same time, however, Brown also acknowledged that the drab realities of many social situations were often too sordid and depressing for an average audience to endure. A typical reaction to productions that portrayed only unrelieved misery was that audiences refused to believe that such conditions were real.[12] Consequently, social work playwrights were advised to "introduce a ray of hope or some bright moment to offset the unbearable picture of suffering" (Routzahn and Routzahn 1928, p. 264).

Invariably, the "ray of hope" in social work dramaturgy was provided by social workers rather than by clients, who were perceived not to possess sufficient means or desire to embark upon a way up and out. No where in social work publicity or plays, for instance, does one find representations of the numerous self-help and mutual aid efforts that existed alongside professional charity work, nor does one find portrayals of the many ways in which neighbors and kin assisted in navigating the ups and downs of everyday life. Public portraits of clients, singularly pictured as unable to make do without professional interventions and wisdom, were thus highly essentialized and abridged. One commentator (Paradise 1932, p. 586) aptly lamented that clients too often became either "sugar-coated" or "grief-coated" dummies" in social work writings. But her recommendation that social workers "mull, meditate and imagine your characters . . . until you know and feel them from inside" before writing human interest stories was a far cry from the deep reflections upon the politics and responsibilities of professional narrative authority that such writing demands.

Because many professional social workers sought to render clients in dramatic and sensational ways, they rallied against the publicity efforts of charity programs that remained on the margins of the profession. Although publicity stories were seen as both the legitimate and necessary means for advancing professional ambitions and speaking for the poor was considered as a professional duty, the storytelling practices of the Salvation Army in particular were condemned by many social work professionals as exploitative, lurid, and unprofessional. Edwin Solenberger (1906), for example, denounced as especially repugnant a human interest story released by the Salvation Army and headlined "Women Cut off Toes with Knife—Was without Money to Pay Surgeon—Tragedy Revealed to Officers of Salvation Army—Maimed Wife and Mother Forced to Support Two Small Children."

The case of "Martha Dorsey," used by the Salvation Army to appeal for funds for a working girls' home in Cleveland and reported in the *Cleveland Press* on February 17, 1913, also aroused the ire of professional reform organizations and caused one of many battles between social workers and Salvation Army members for the control of benevolent solutions. In the controversy surrounding Martha Dorsey, the Salvation Army had received feature coverage for the case story of Martha, a country girl who had left a position as a domestic servant in order to seek her fortune in the city and found that no charitable organizations other than the Salvation Army would help in her endeavor. Soon after the story ran, however, a major investigation was launched by the Cleveland Committee on Benevolent Organizations to tell the "professionally" correct story, and several spokespersons for Cleveland's professional charity organizations wrote editorials and letters to correct public misunderstanding of their many worthy efforts on behalf of cases such as Martha's. Clearly, professional social workers sought to establish tight editorial control over publicity stories.

Let Us Now Praise and Admonish: The Poverty and Wealth of Social Work Representations

The naive empiricism that had initially characterized publicity efforts in social work began to fade during the 1920s when facts increasingly came to be viewed as both interested and constructed. Walter Lippmann noted, for example, that "the development of the publicity man is a clear sign that the facts of modern life do not spontaneously take a shape in which they could be known. They must be given shape by somebody" (quoted in Scudson 1978, p. 143).

Social workers were not immune to rising suspicions over the epistemological and ontological nature of "the facts," and some began to equate some of their profession's publicity efforts to "propaganda" and rebuke such efforts for being insufficiently educative. Even Charles Stillman, who had long advocated publicity, lamented that "it seems so easy to maximize 'human interest' and minimize the rational message" (1927, p. 64). Throughout the 1920s when social workers began to debate the politics of publicity they increasingly condemned the use of "sob stuff," emotional appeals, and blatant advertising methods as being unethical and unbefitting of professional decorum (Brown 1926; Stillman 1927; Whipple 1930).

During the 1930s, however, such prudence began to diminish as social workers' firsthand knowledge of poverty was sought out by a public that seemed to hunger for the massive documentation of specific human experience during the Great Depression. Under those circumstances, the publication of social workers' emotionally saturated case stories appeared to herald the existence of a comprehensive archive of local color. Eager to try their hands at writing, a significant number of social workers contributed magazine articles during the New Deal (Stott 1973); Frances Perkins, Grace and Edith Abbott, Paul Kellog, and Lillian Brandt were but a few.

By the 1930s those who wrote popularized case history had a myriad of stylistic precursors to emulate, because social work publicity was no longer a juvenile endeavor. The spectacular style of Riis and the solemn, technocratic style of the urban survey movement each could be used as departure points. Organizational success stories such as "Red Tape to the Rescue" or "Society Reunited a Disrupted Family" likewise could be imitated to build a case for the cool, efficient expertise of social work professionalism in saving clients from themselves and their circumstances. At the same time, stories in the vein of "Real Santa Claus to Visit Children" could be employed to emphasize social workers' compassion. Case histories of menacing clients could be used as well to promote the profession as a savior of public morality.

During the depression, as earlier, publicity efforts were divided between extolling the merits of the profession and winning public sympathy and support for clients and reform efforts. Among social workers who concentrated primarily on portrayals of clients, Clinch Calkins, who was also a poet, was especially noteworthy. She was the author of the first book on unemployment during the depression, *Some Folks Won't Work* (1930), a study based on the case histories of settlement workers. Calkins employed documentary techniques that allowed only occasional remarks from subjects, and she retold facts as she felt they needed to be represented. Her attempt to "isolate and visualize one statistic" so that human spirit does not "escape up a stairway of graphs" (p. 17) quickly deteriorated into sanitized, romantic stories of the unemployed, whom she portrayed as middle-class refugees clinging to the vestiges of their former lives. All of Calkins's subjects were idealized as virtuous types forced to forsake membership in the Mothers' Club and forgo the white lace curtains that had once adorned the windows of their immaculate houses. They thus provided a distinct counterpoint to the strange and menacing clients who had peopled earlier works such as *Darkness and Daylight; or, Lights and Shadows of New York* and *The Kingdom of Evils*. Calkins's accounts likewise yielded a meager, one-sided, and simplistic story in many of the same ways that mundane case records routinely stripped and abridged the lives of clients. In trying to evoke sympathy for the unemployed, she robbed subjects of individuality and complexity and subdued their individual voices because she instead spoke for her profession.

Despite the multitude of ways social workers recounted the lives of clients, their representations, both in case records and in documentary human interest writings, remained professionally bound and impoverished. One way to highlight the many inadequacies of social work documentary descriptions and representations is to compare them to James Agee's depression-era portrait of southern sharecroppers, *Let Us Now Praise Famous Men* (1939). Both Agee and Calkins (1930, p. 3) direct readers' attention at the beginning of their narratives to the appropriate relationship between privileged and "wretched" members of the community by using a quotation from act 3, scene 4 of *King Lear:*

> Poor naked wretches, whereso'er you are
> That bide the pelting of this pitiless storm
> How shall your houseless heads and unfed sides,
> Your loopt and window'd raggedness, defend you
> From seasons such as these? Oh! I have ta'en
> Too little care of this! Take physic, pomp;
> Expose thyself to feel what wretches feel. . . .

While both Agee and Calkins moved the relationship between text and reader away from the tourism model of Riis's representations, their commonality ends there. Only Agee provided an account that refused to present his subjects by way of standard plots, simple types, or taxonomy.

Agee's story of the Gudger family was not one of singularly valorous people such as those Calkins portrayed. They were neither objects of pity as in "Real Santa Claus to Visit Children" nor essentialized like so many subjects of other case records. Instead, Agee attempted to render the Gudgers in great depths of psychological complexity and human dignity. In order to shake readers from their preconceived codings of the poor, he described people when they were most in command of themselves, as when they imposed their wills upon their environments (Reed 1988). Although Agee made extensive use of the case study method, he did not solely dramatize subjects in their social roles or present them as symptomatic of essentialized types or hereditary stocks such as the "wayward" or the "chaste." Instead, he described them going to bed or to town and going about the many mundane and universal aspects of their lives. Although Agee's subjects were neither singularly heroic nor noble and free of degeneracy, readers were to respect their complexity rather than pity them or recoil from them (Reed 1988).

Unlike the writers of case records, Agee allowed himself to become a significant character of his book. He confessed his humanity and shortcomings throughout the text in order to encourage the same responses from readers. Virginia Robinson (1921, p. 256) had stated that although social workers have a "hangover of self-consciousness which restrains us from mentioning ourselves in the case record," personal factors should be standardized and objectified by impartial recording. Such objectified subjectivity was a far cry from Agee's confessional obsession and from his tendency to portray himself as unattractive and reckless. It is hard to imagine, for example, Agee's sexual confessions appearing in a case record as a worker's "personal factors."

Agee argued that the representation of a subject depended "as fully on who I am as on who he is" (p. 239), and he explicitly reflected on the inventive nature of documentary descriptions: "George Gudger is a human being, a man, not like any other human being so much as he is like himself. I could *invent* incidents, appearances, additions to his character, background, surroundings, future, which might well point up and indicate and clinch things relevant to him which in fact I am sure are true, and important, and which George Gudger unchanged and undecorated would not indicate and perhaps could not even suggest" (pp. 232–33).

Yet instead of abandoning the project of representation, Agee called for greater aesthetic and political reflexivity. He used a variety of devices to inject doubt about the ability of any text to provide authentic access to other worlds and "achieve immediacy, or full representation" (Reed 1988, p. 61). His text frequently offered contradictory versions of characters and scenes in order to convey the elusiveness of subjects. In contrast to the rigid chronological construction of case records, Agee describes his earliest encounters with the Gudgers at the end of the volume rather than at the beginning, a construction, according to Reed (p. 169), that conveyed the idea that readers had just begun, not concluded, a relationship with the Gudgers and provided a further reminder of the Gudgers' mysterious nature.

Unlike Agee, social workers did not acknowledge their subjects' mystery and elusiveness in either case records or human interest writings, nor did they dwell as deeply on the distinctive problems of professional narrative power. Yet questions of representation were important to social work. It was with professionally rare candor that Calkins concluded, "I can picture part of the story but parts of it are beyond my powers to picture" (1930, p. 129). A considerable literary distance thus existed between the essentialized renditions of the poor in social work publicity and Agee's self-conscious, complex portrayal of the Gudgers. Agee's story requires careful reading, because he refused to clarify the Gudgers' secrets or simplify their truths by writing compact case summaries.

Although social work is characterized by its focus on the lives of impoverished and marginalized populations, its lack of reflexivity on the politics of representation remains problematic because case recordings and publicity efforts are both highly political and ideological acts. The privilege of authorship and the professional practice of thinking, speaking, and writing about others have yet to be granted the centrality they deserve in social work education and practice. Reed (1988, p. 157) argues that *Let Us Now Praise Famous Men* "can be read as a detailed political allegory about the relations between those of us with the power to represent others and those we claim to represent." Furthermore, he maintains that it illuminates "the problem of representing 'disadvantaged' others, a problem played out between the danger of appropriation and reduction through representation on one hand and the equal danger on the other hand of leaving these 'others' unrepresented or represented less scrupulously and less justly" (p. 157).

Pauline Leader's autobiographical *And No Birds Sing* (1935) recounts her experiences as a resident of a home for unwed mothers. While there, she found a book that publicized the home. Her comments on the publicity material are incisive—and at odds with the publication's promotional nature. Leader first commented on the agency's reliance on marriage as a universal solution and as the evidence of professional accomplishment: "Many of the 'graduates' of the home were now respectable waitresses, stenographers, factory workers. Some were even married. The Home dwelled long and lingeringly on marriage. To get a girl, especially one who had a baby, married was the peak of the Home's achievement. What sort of hell went on after marriage, the Home did not concern itself with. Only to get the girl married. Surface. Surface. Let the surface be smooth" (p. 273). Attacking the pretensions of modern social work practice that the home boasted of implementing, she wrote: "I turned another page. The home was, above all things modern, I read. The Home stressed particularly the mental health of its girls. . . . Yet what did the psychiatrist do? Now and then she held hours when she poked fingers into the girls. Most of the time she was away. All that was done with the girls was to herd them together, girls who were prostitutes, girls who were syphilitic, girls who were merely delinquent" (p. 274). Chastised by a staff member for reading the booklet, Leader concluded, "These booklets, I should have known, were not for the girls themselves who would read and laugh cynically" (p. 274).

Agee's and Leader's lesson for social work is that social workers need both to interrogate the purposes and consequences of their writings and make ample room for clients' perspectives as well as for clients' reactions to such professional interventions as narrativity.

Afterword

When you see an object, you are not seeing the look.
∾Trinh T. Minh-ha (1992)

This volume has sought to recapture forms of narrativity in the case records of early social workers as well as the vigorous discourses and debates about record-keeping that flourished in social work during the first three decades of the twentieth century. Early social work leaders argued about professional maps, conceptual tools, narrative conventions, and recording practices for representing and translating clients' lives and the foundations for professional knowledge and writing. Lively debates were conducted over whether social work was a science or an art and how best it could be either. Such conversations were not only confined to social work. Rather, discussions of the problematics of documentary realism were conducted before a wider professional public, including sociologists and psychiatrists.

Although considered a primary professional obligation, case-recording during the early years of social work's professionalization remained a pliable genre and was examined frequently for underlying assumptions and protocols. Many influential social workers preoccupied themselves with questions of science, objectivity, comparability, and generalization, whereas others choose to infuse dramatic and literary qualities into their texts. Some social work authors sought a judicious blend of science and art by arguing that case records could be improved by tinkering with form and organization rather than content. Still others advocated sharing textual space with clients or personalizing professional authority by narrating the role social workers played in interactions with clients.

Consequently, early front-line social workers could write client descriptions in a variety of ways and use a plethora of terms and concepts to ground professional narrativity. They could choose questionnaires to structure their accounts, or they could seek to capture the flair of novels and dramatic works. Alternatively, they could choose to share textual space with clients' voices and perspectives, introduce themselves into the case record, and assess the impact of their presences. Or they could remain in the textual shadows by selecting a detached, scientific authorial pose, as when they wrote about themselves in the third person.

My examination of case records has shown that although social workers fashioned a broad array of techniques to represent clients, two genres of tales usually predominated. Tales of detection told of building cases against menacing clients, and a key element in those narrations involved describing how agents secured probative evidence. In tales of protection, social workers told somewhat different stories of convoluted relationships with promising and worthy clients. Considerable overlap existed between the two modes of narration, however, because changes in relationships between social workers and clients could easily transform a narration from one genre to another. Agency auspices also played significant roles in shaping front-line casework and therefore narrative practice, and the need to publicize agency and professional activities and perspectives led to a further round of narrativity: the professional tales of persuasion, which were efforts to legitimate social workers in the public arena.

Social work practitioners delved deeply into the everyday lives of clients and had protracted interactions with those individuals. They provided accounts of these relationships and approached the construction of knowledge in ways that sharply contrasted with typical practices in male-dominated professions such as psychiatry. Regardless of their means of inquiry and representation, social workers saw more of life—and saw it differently. In a field in which women predominated, social workers were able to grasp certain realities of clients' lives in a deeply contextualized fashion. As routine visitors to the living rooms and kitchens of impoverished clients they witnessed the ups and downs of family fortunes and the ways in which clients tried to stay afloat. Social workers knew what clients ate and how they spent their days and hence were no strangers to the domestic arrangements and intimate spheres of the poor.

In comparison to their counterparts in psychiatry, social workers were less encapsulated in tightly ordered conceptual frameworks and thus confined by theoretical models. Even though they made a host of normatively determined judgments about the clients they labeled "wayward," "feeble," or "immoral," they were less likely to frame clients with the terminology of professionally significant syndromes and less likely to reduce them to categorical types than medical and psychological practitioners. Consequently, social case records were more typically encyclopedic renderings of selected details, impressions, and events snatched from the daily lives of clients.

Yet social workers' representations were nonetheless professionally driven constructions and as such were far from innocent of the privileges emanating from race, class standing, and professional authority. Although the dynamics of race, class, and professional power were for the most part unacknowledged in case records and professional debates, many early social workers were reflexive about other important aspects of the politics of representation, including the problems of reduction and abstraction and the hazards of pigeonholing clients in clinical diagnostic categories.

Early social workers, sociologists, and psychologists were thus far from unified on questions of the places of science, realism, facticity, and objectivity, and their debates anticipated many contemporary interdisciplinary debates about science, textuality, representation, and neutrality. Modern scholars are exploring the connection between ideology and cultural translation and are taking up questions of whether and when it is possible or justifiable to speak for others (Alcoff 1991–92; Minh-ha 1989; Roof and Wiegman 1995; Said 1979; Spivak 1988). Linda Alcoff, for example, argues that if there are many dangers in speaking for others, including the "possibility of misrepresentation, expanding one's own authority and privilege, and a generally imperialist speaking ritual," then "speaking with and to can lessen these dangers" (p. 23). Acknowledging nonetheless that marginalized groups often need "'messengers'" to advocate for their needs, Alcoff concludes that it is important to interrogate the "bearings of our location and context" as well as examine the effects of our representations by asking, "Will [they] enable the empowerment of oppressed people?" (p. 29).

Contemporary writers are also exploring more empowering and less constrictive ways of knowing and writing, including collaborative models for textual productions such as shared and self-representations (Byerly 1986; Collins 1990; Davidson, with the women of Mutira 1989; Fields and Fields 1985; Menchu 1984; Personal Narratives Group 1989; Shostak 1983). With a few notable exceptions, relatively little attention has been paid to case-recording in the field of social work, however, because for the most part recording is taken for granted. That poverty of attention is a far cry from the seriousness and suspicion with which early social workers regarded record-keeping practices. As a consequence, social work has been forced to the sidelines of current interdisciplinary debates about epistemology, representation, the construction of knowledge, and professional practices for thinking, writing, and knowing about others.

The characteristic position of social workers with regard to clients' demands has sustained interrogation of their roles as messengers. In a discussion of professions involved in health care, for example, Poirier et al. (1992, p. 15) point out that today's social worker "is perhaps the professional who stands readiest to listen to the multiple, often conflicting and ambiguous accounts of the patient's life in the community, the most likely repository of 'extraneous' details, and the most constrained by the necessity to document the social 'facts' detached from their rich context." Such contradictory demands and opportunities, however, have not inspired sufficient reflection. Instead, much recent conversation about recording and representation has been confined to questions of liability, risk, reasonable client access to records, and technical improvements in record-keeping for the purposes of cost-efficiency and accountability. Bureaucratic concerns have outweighed theoretical ones.

Avoiding liability on the part of agencies rather than the many risks to clients that can be attributed to unreflexive recording-keeping is often a central concern. Based on his study of recording practices in England's largest voluntary childcare agency, Sheldon Gelman (1992), for example, asserts that case records are a critical element in risk management because of the potential consequences of record-keeping for agency liability. In order to improve recording practices so they can contribute to risk reduction rather than risk exposure, Gelman urges social workers to pursue "purposeful" recording and "differentiate between entries that are factual and objective and entries that are subjective and possibility biased" (p. 75). He also advocates informing clients about what records an agency maintains on them and providing them with opportunities to inspect, correct, and amend such records. Having evaluated client assessment policies at childcare centers, Gelman concludes that clients who were "actively involved in sharing records identified strongly with the project and became advocates for the project and organization." These same clients were "less likely to challenge decisions and therefore posed less of a risk than did those clients alienated from the agency" (p. 77).

The increasing pressures on contemporary social workers to abstract, standardize, objectify, and quantify are resulting in an ever-increasing disembodiment of professional knowledge. From state-mandated "structured recording systems" that require social workers to record case information under particular categories (Edwards and Reid 1989) to insurance companies' pressure on clinical social workers to employ the psychiatric diagnostic classification system elaborated in Kutchins and Kirk (1988), record-keeping is fast becoming controlled by business, management, and state interests. The pressure to conform is significant and threatens diversity in social work practice. Nancy Matthews (1995), for example, notes that an organization called Santa Cruz Women against Rape lost funding as result of resisting California's record-keeping and data-collection requirements.

Marie Campbell (1992, 1993) has documented a trend toward increased management-introduced technologies that make quality assurance a matter of documentary procedures relating to cost reduction and operational efficiency. Because social workers are spending more time reporting their work in forms designed to accentuate cost reduction and operational efficiency, social work is rapidly being transformed from an "experience-based practice into a document-based practice." As Edwards and Reid found in their survey of child welfare workers, social workers are spending "more time with paper than people" (1989, p. 49).

Concurrent with the trend toward a document-based practice is the parallel trend toward computerized case management. Here, social work assessments of clients' progress and prognoses are organized and reported in ways that maximize cost-effectiveness and yield intervention decisions based on computer-generated probabilities of predictable outcomes for improvement. According to a consultant to the Metro Toronto Children's Aid Society's computerized case management system, such systems yield "probabilities of what to expect for each client type when sufficient historical data are accumulated. The computer could be programmed to generate costs per client and to project what combination of treatments is most likely to bring cost-effective results" (Campbell 1992, p. 513). The uncritical embrace of objective and quantified description for efficiency purpose has become conspicuous, and it is assumed that predicting outcomes for specific "client types" will not only save time but also help standardize decision-making:

> Availability of data would speed up interaction between worker and client by cutting down time spent on the initial assessment and subsequent interviews. The system makes it possible for social workers to choose client interventions on the basis of statistically significant indicators. The technological capacity to program decision-making about client services is derived from the ability to conceptualize and document the features of clients' history, problem treatment choices, and interaction objectively; then, any particular client's profile can be scanned, in relation to standard decision criteria. (Campbell 1992, p. 513)

In a study of the record-keeping practices of 114 social service agencies, Jill Doner Kagle (1993) has observed that a majority of the agencies studied have begun to use computer technologies for client tracking and case management. She reports that eighty-eight human service managers were "enthusiastic" about computers' ability to standardize information-gathering, provide ready access to information, and analyze data rapidly. Solely from the standpoint of efficiency—ignoring important questions about the role of documentation in disqualifying various knowledge and practices—Kagle concludes that the use of computers to support case management has had "mixed results" because savings that might have been realized by greater efficiency in information-processing are often absorbed by increased demands for recording. In the cause of efficiency enhancement Kagle thus argues for "outlines, checklists, or brief forms" that "place space limitations on documentation and signal the worker as to what and where information is to be documented" (p. 194). She makes this recommendation without examining the silent control exercised by such forms themselves or the universalizing tendencies of computerization and also overlooks a potential loss of client individuality and social workers' creativity and insight.

State and business mandates increasingly dictate the nature of social work writing, as do long-standing allegiances to science. Jane Gorman, for example, observes (1993, p. 248) that the predominance of a scientific ethos in social work has deval-

ued the local and the personal and thus negates a social worker's pivotal responsibility "as a messenger—a bearer of interpretive, fragmentary, personal, emotional, heart-wrenching tales of oppression, of silenced voices." Along with scientism,
Charles Cowger (1994, p. 262) notes that because "deficit, disease, and dysfunction"
are deeply rooted in all facets of social work practice, the political act of making
social work assessments of clients is geared toward finding client inadequacies
rather than strengths, which silences large portions of clients' stories and erases
their personal strengths. Ellie Pozatek (1994) points out that when assessments that
dwell on inadequacies are awarded the status of truth they influence other practitioners and determine what helpers think is possible in a case. Clients are often
uninformed of such professional practices.

In light of objectivism, scientism, and other "dysfunctional" trends, it is refresh-
ing to find that at least a few social workers still advocate a more critical approach
to case-recording. Infrequent as it is, however, that discussion has focused largely
on how to involve clients in constituting their own case records and telling their
own stories. Advocates of the approach, however, do so with trepidation over the
possibility of losing scientific objectivity. Nancy Badding (1989, p. 539), for example, proposes that caseworkers allow clients to participate in the making of case
records, and, "using professional judgement, the practitioner then writes the client input into the case recording, adding his or her own assessment. The procedure is best suited for writing progress notes at the end of casework or therapy
sessions, rather than for extensive summaries or reports." Kagle argues (1984, p.
104) that client-prepared records such as diaries or logs—"client memoranda"—
are important resources, but she warns that they are "inherently subjective in content." Thus, she advises, "To enhance reliability and objectivity of decisions, client memoranda should be used in conjunction with other sources of information."

Stating correctly that human experience and professional practice do not conform to the "ontological assumptions and methodical requirements of the scientific method," Thomas Holland (1991, p. 33) maintains that social workers can develop greater sensitivity to the themes and issues underlying practice problems by
reflecting on the narratives that people tell about themselves and also employing
a hermeneutical approach to the interpretation of clients' behavior. By "listening
carefully to the client's story, identifying underlying themes and suggesting possible alternative explanations, the practitioner becomes a collaborator with the client in a living story that is in process of being rewritten. The resulting product is
itself an interwoven text, a jointly authored story of lives coming into temporary
intersection and then diverging" (p. 39).

As in much of the wider social work literature, missing in Holland's idealized
discussion are critical reflections about interests and inequalities at work in the
social worker–client relationship, the ideological presuppositions of the profes-

sion that a social worker carries, class differences, the dynamics of expert power in professional narration, and the narrative presence of social workers in case records.

Especially problematic are the many obstacles that, although unacknowledged, prevent social workers from hearing client stories.[1] Dennis Saleebey, for example, points out that "the static of our own theories and presumptions, agency canon, and the informal stories about clients and client groups make it difficult to hear with clarity" (1994, p. 355). Catherine Kohler Riessman (1987) argues along similar lines. Many gender, class, and cultural incongruities affect both the form and content of life stories, which can function as obstacles to hearing what is important to the narrator. Most important, as Howard Goldstein observes (1992, p. 50), client stories, like those of social workers, reveal "with purpose or intention a particular world view." A practitioner who acknowledges the treatment value of client narratives and perspectives cannot begin to collaborate with or represent a client without raising penetrating questions about professional power and ways of hearing and not hearing.

Some of these issues of power and representation have received critical attention within medicine. Rita Charon (1992), for example, points out how physicians interpret patients' stories according to professionally generated rules of causality and signification. Kathryn Hunter argues (1992, p. 173) that a case history is a physician's story because "there is always an observing eye and a well-observed, if unspoken, I behind the case, a professional self that grounds case narrative with a readily perceptible display of skill and knowledge." As T. Hugh Crawford observes (1992, p. 148), "Who gets to tell whose story when and where—is bound up with social privilege." Scrutiny of professional concepts of signification and the privileged location of professional narrators are key elements in learning to speak and write in ways that empower clients.

In a similar vein, insightful articles by Terry Holbrook (1995, 1983) provide some of the few discussions in social work literature that raise questions about power in social case-recording. Holbrook observes (1983, p. 651) that case records are admissible in courts of law, where they determine who "to a great extent, gets welfare and who does not, who gets probation and who does not, who gets charged with neglect and who does not, and who receives training, day care, public housing, and food stamps." He argues that social workers have neglected to think about and anticipate future uses for the kinds of information contained in records, and he criticizes the tendency to attribute moral and political neutrality to official agencies and professional thinking. Furthermore, Holbrook believes that case records objectify subjective impressions through language while glossing "over many of the subjective human qualities of their authors" (p. 650). Drawing upon the work of Judith Lee (1980), Holbrook urges social workers to begin to reflect on the descriptive terms and generalizations they use to describe clients. He points, for example, to a variety of deleterious professional descriptions used to characterize "multiproblem" families: "Rarely are both parents in the home. Generally, the mothers have lived in a common-law relationship with a number of men. . . . The families multiply rapidly. . . . The mothers . . . are, for the most part psychologically too self-centered and impulsive to have sufficient interest in and responsibility for their children. Incest, narcotic addiction, prostitution, homosexuality, and criminal acts have been part of their family background" (pp. 654–55). He warns that "language, words, classifications, and diagnoses define, limit, and in part, actually determine what we are capable of seeing" (p. 655).

Work by Saleebey (1994), Holbrook (1995), Pozatek (1994), and Gorman (1993) indicates an emerging trend toward a politically grounded questioning of professional power and privileges. These scholars point out the variety of ways that client narratives, knowledge, and experience are banished in social work and how social workers might help to empower clients, arguing that social workers can avoid being narrative adversaries with clients. Dennis Saleebey, for example, contends that "the initiatory act of helping would seem to be the suspension of canon or theory . . . or 'the old saw about beginning where the client is'" (1994, p. 355). Jane Gorman suggests (1993, p. 253) that social work needs methods of writing that involve clients as much as practitioners in order to further the "articulation of local knowledge from multiple perspectives—with all its uncertainty, complexity, conflict, nongeneralizability, and paradox." Similarly, Ellie Pozatek states (1994, p. 399) that a social worker must "hold open a space in his or her mind for uncertainty, to question how his or her subjective experience may be causing the worker to privilege some aspects of the client's story and marginalize or disqualify others." Articulating what is known in social work as a "strengths perspective," Saleebey (1994, p. 358) argues that social workers must "help individuals and collectivities restore and restory themselves." He points out, for example, that tales of public housing, which so often focus on danger, disorganization, and drugs, have encouraged social workers to find and spread "counter stories," that is, tales of survival, strength, and possibility (Weick and et al. 1989).

Two excellent examples of counter-stories and client self-representation are *Rose's Story,* written by a self-termed "Survivor of Our Social Services" (Rose 1991) and detailing a woman's experiences with foster care and children's protective services, and Theresa Funiciello's *The Tyranny of Kindness: Dismantling the Welfare System to End Poverty in America* (1993), a critique of the welfare system from the perspective of a former welfare recipient. Such writing illustrates the significance of clients reframing social work discourse in light of experience and knowledge.

Representation and narrativity cannot be avoided, but practices of representation that fail to challenge uncritical professional ways of thinking, observing, writing, and speaking that colonize clients' experiences are forms of domination and, ultimately, violence. Renewed attention to the politics of narrativity gives social workers an opportunity to move beyond narrow, defensive questions of efficiency and risk management toward the critical scrutiny of their conceptual foundations for knowing, interpreting, and writing about clients' lives.

Giving centrality to the consequences of such documentation necessitates once again the sustained critical interrogation of case-recording practices as they were practiced during the 1920s. But social workers must now look deeper—at the power and privilege of writing and the partiality of their professional truth claims. The promotion of self-representation and storytelling promises to benefit not only clients but also social workers. Finally, it is necessary to challenge the trends toward a document-based practice of social work and the move toward administrative models for standardized record-keeping because both disempower clients and front-line social workers.

Social workers must ask themselves how and why they employ textual authority. The questions a client posed in 1930 remain a good starting point: "The charity workers come around and they write, write, write, write. And they ask questions, questions. They ask 'what your father work at?' What's the use of that when he has been in the grave twenty years? Why don't they ask how much my children's shoes cost? How much wages lost this week when the baby was sick? They write history, history, history, pages of it—and what good that do me?" (Young 1930, p. 153).

Asking what good case-writing does for clients begins a process of critical reflection. The process does not automatically lead to needed resources for clients, but it does provide a departure point for examining the politics of professionalism and the hegemony of social welfare discourses that pathologize clients and mask social injustices. The examination of narrativity brings into focus not only the object of professional attention but also the politics of looking. Such attention brings awareness of what otherwise is taken for granted in a socially constructed world: how clients are constituted and their knowledge excluded. From such a starting point, clients are more likely to be seen as bearers of significant truths rather than as objects of professional knowledge. Thus they become allies in an ongoing struggle for equality that social workers are more likely to recognize as their true calling.

Appendix

Case Inventory

Boston Children's Aid Society
    Type of agency: child-placing.
    Total number of cases examined: twenty-nine.
    Average duration: 8.1 years (no closing date noted in four cases).
    Percentage of cases opened before 1920: 32 percent.
    Percentage of cases opened 1920 and after: 68 percent.
Massachusetts Society for the Prevention of Cruelty to Children
    Type of agency: child protection.
    Total number of cases examined: forty-six cases were from ledger books. (All were
        opened between 1901 and 1903, and almost all consisted of only one or two entries
        of only a page or two in length; none lasted more than a few months.) Forty case
        narratives were also examined. (All were opened after 1905; six were opened in 1906,
        six in 1911, six in 1915, six in 1919, six in 1923, six in 1925, and four in 1929.)
    Average duration of the forty case narratives: 4.5 years.
Minneapolis Citizen's Aid Society—Girls' Department
    Type of agency: child-placing (in existence from 1920 to 1930).
    Total number of cases examined: five.
    Average duration: six months.
    Percentage of cases opened before 1920: 0.
    Percentage of cases opened 1920 and after: 100 percent.
Minneapolis Child's Protective Society
    Type of agency: child protection.
    Total number of cases examined: fifteen.
    Average duration: 11.8 years.
    Percentage of cases opened before 1920: 38 percent.
    Percentage of cases opened 1920 and after: 62 percent.

Minneapolis Family Welfare Association

Type of agency: family casework, relief.

Total number of cases examined: twelve.

Average duration: 9.6 years.

Percentage of cases opened before 1920: 66 percent.

Percentage of cases opened 1920 and after: 34 percent.

Notes

Introduction

1. Caroline Bedford (1924), assistant general manager of the St. Louis Provident Association, employed a daily chronological log of workers' activities and a cost analysis to decrease "useless motions" and increase the amount of time available for the reading and study of case records.

2. Wenocur and Reisch argue that not only was the charity organization society movement aided by developments in the larger political economy and culture but also that a confluence of forces allowed the casework segment of social work to become dominant over social reform work, which emphasized living among the poor and immigrant populations, community participation, and broad themes of social justice. Examples of such forces include superior organization and resources of casework and the fact that most training programs in social work had the mark of the charity organization movement in terms of sponsorship and curriculum, with the notable exception of the University of Chicago's program. Books by casework leaders such as Mary Richmond and Amos Warner dominated the curriculum, and graduates were more likely to find jobs at agencies influenced by the movement than elsewhere. Social reform work faced a variety of obstacles to establishing professional dominance, all of which contributed to the prominence of casework over settlement house work: difficulties in interpreting the broad spectrum of settlement activities, more egalitarian notions of client relationships, more emphasis on neighborliness rather than professional expertise, and the use of sponsorship to advance reform legislation rather than their own professional status. The continuing impact of settlements on the rhetoric and practice of social work cannot be ignored, however.

3. Peggy Pascoe (1990, p. 86) observes that the records of welfare institutions often have "such thick rhetorical veils" that historians have found them more useful for understanding reformers rather than clients. The work of Duggan (1993), Kunzel (1993), and Terry (1990, 1991), however, opens new possibilities for reading against the grain of dominant accounts by looking for narrative traces of clients' subjectivities in the openings provided by the conflictual interplay of professionals and clients.

4. Beginning in 1923, for example, the Milford Conference, a committee of casework executives and agency board members, met annually to determine whether common skills and methods existed across disparate social work settings, including family welfare agencies, hospitals, and child welfare agencies. In 1928 the committee concluded that a generic casework methodology did exist, providing a common base for social casework across specialty areas. Leighninger (1987) also notes other attempts at unifying the diverse field of social work, including the founding of professional associations such as the National Conference of Charities and Correction (established in 1873) and the American Association of Social Workers (established in 1921). She concludes, however, that the story of social work was the "story of strains between different segments and of tensions between forces for cohesion and pulls for separateness" (p. 20).

5. The intimate involvements of social workers in the daily life and struggles of poor clients—a more feminized and less prestigious site of knowledge than that which psychiatrists and psychologists typically habituate—impeded the professional legitimization of social work. Sociologists, for example, challenged the reliability and objectivity of social caseworkers as witnesses and recorders. Psychiatrists expressed similar reservations, even though they found social workers to be useful as semiprofessional handmaidens and time-savers. Thus, in one of the more charitable renditions of the usefulness of social work, Richard Cabot, M.D., noted that doctors were "content with the fragments of a story," and that it was the task of social work to "neutralize the necessary evils of medical specialism; to pick up the dropped stitches" (Cabot 1970, p. 35).

According to this view, social workers were important mediators between physicians and patients, allowing psychiatrists to maintain professional detachment and distance from the domestic details of their clients' lives. Social workers' case recordings, however, were judged to be less scientific than those physicians made, because they primarily focused on localized, concrete descriptions of the experiences of women and highlighted the commonplace issues of child-rearing, hygiene, and household economy.

6. Many agencies, such as the Boston Children's Aid Society, had a department of study that analyzed case records of former clients to evaluate the effectiveness of professional interventions as well as the adequacy of case narratives. Also included in many case records I examined were casework supervisors' critiques of caseworkers' investigations and records.

7. In her time-motion study of a family welfare agency, Caroline Bedford (1924) noted that district secretaries spent four hours a week studying case records of workers, one hour a week at dictation, ten hours a week on clerical tasks, and two hours a week in the field. Based on a comparative study of those offices with and without dictaphones, their value as time-savers was thought to be immense. As a result, they were installed in all the district offices.

8. Maggie Blake (1947) boasted that the meticulous keeping and preservation of case records not only afforded the Selective Service access to important information during World War II but also enabled individual clients to benefit from the MSPCC's archives. She recounted the story of a woman, adopted at an early age and soon to be married, who was reassured after reading her record that not all of her biological ancestors were morally blemished.

9. This study is indebted to the work of Michel Foucault (1978, 1979) and Dorothy Smith (1990, 1992), who provide new angles for exploring the history of professionalization of social reform by focusing on professional texts and discourses. Foucault's writing on the connections between knowledge claims (especially knowledge presumed to be neutral and universal) and power, the disciplinary origins of power, and the matrix of micro-practices that support power and knowledge regimes such as social work led me to the study of case records. His approach calls for a closer inspection of techniques of expert power such as the microscopic webs of observational, assessment, and documentary techniques used to classify, arrange, interpret, and order people as "cases." Such expert techniques impose a heightened visibility upon those in need of correction and place them in a "field of surveillance" and a "network of writing" that "engages them in a whole mass of documents that capture and fix them" (Foucault 1978, p. 189).

Foucault's work also provides a framework for thinking about professional or disciplinary power as "constitutive" rather than merely "repressive" by calling attention to how new social pathologies are defined within expert discourses. Professional knowledge, according to Foucault, constitutes the problems to which it is applicable. Smith (1990, p. 70), however, argues correctly that Foucault's conception of power and knowledge, although important for an understanding of society, is "mystified." Foucault's power "has no ontology, no form of existence." Instead, power and knowledge are always "the mobilization of people's concerted activities." Smith's insight has shown me the importance of what social workers did on a daily basis and the importance of reading of their records.

10. Barbara Herrnstein-Smith notes that narrative "versions" have two meanings: "as retellings of other narratives and as accounts told from a particular or partial perspective" (1981, p. 211). The form and features of any version stems in part from the motives that invoked it, as well as the interests it was designed to further. Social case records were clearly reflective of a partial perspective, because client versions were routinely submerged, silenced, and made sporadic in order to render a professionally preferred account that advanced the authority and knowledge of the social work community.

11. Steven Stowe notes the historical shift that occurred within physicians' clinical stories to tightly framed narratives that reduce the biographic particulars of patients' lives to general demographic factors. Stowe also points out that unlike contemporary, tightly framed diagnostic medical writing, medical narratives in the mid-nineteenth century constituted a different genre of writing and can be characterized as "common-sense work stories" (1996, p. 43). They were autobiographical, vernacular, and contextual, suggesting a less developed professional authority over the practice of medicine.

12. Nancy Fraser suggests that there are many competing ways of talking and interpreting people's needs, which reflect relations of dominance and subordination. Professions such as social work, part of a myriad of authoritative "expert-need" vocabularies, frequently reposition people as recipients of "predefined services rather than as agents involved in interpreting their needs and shaping their life conditions" (1989, p. 174). Although people often internalize these expert interpretations of their needs, Fraser identifies examples of resisting and reshaping expert needs talk on the part of subordinated groups. She points to Linda Gordon's work on the clients of child protection agencies, who were able to use an ex-

pert-recognized need of child abuse to gain recognition for domestic battering, an unacknowledged need.

13. In a contemporary training book for social workers, *Social Work Records,* Jill Doner Kagle acknowledges that "the role of the record keeper carries power with it" (1984, p. 103). Her discussion of power, however, goes no further than this. She merely advises social workers that they have two choices for dealing with power: "The worker may use this factor either to alter or maintain the existing balance." Content with merely acknowledging narrative power, Kagle sidesteps the significant political questions that any exercise of professional power ideally would entail.

14. Regina Kunzel's studies of unmarried mothers (1988, 1993) highlight the gendered nature of transformations in benevolent work by tracing the conflict between notions of "redemptive femininity" and female difference in religiously based charity and the neutered, secular language and practice of later professional social workers. As Kunzel's studies show, evangelicals differed profoundly from professional caseworkers in their approach to benevolence. Social workers sought to redefine maternity homes as places of treatment and replace evangelical sisterly ties with a professional-care relationship. Instead of our "fallen sisters," residents were constituted as "cases."

Such attempts to make benevolence more efficient and scientific—and thus less feminine—characterized many battles over professionalization, for example the rivalry between the Christian Commission and the Sanitary Commission in the late nineteenth century (Ginzberg 1990). Early-twentieth-century struggles waged by the proponents of scientific charity against the methods of the Salvation Army provide another example and also illustrate the importance of gender and of record-keeping in such battles for benevolence (Tice 1992).

15. Elizabeth Lunbeck (1994) provides another view on the contrast between psychiatry and social work in her illuminating study of the changing contours of psychiatric practice, including psychiatric social work, as it unfolded at the Boston Psychopathic Hospital during the early decades of the twentieth century. She reveals the gendering of professional knowledge and methods by showing that social work practice yielded a close view of clients' lives, which in turn resulted in knowledge that differed from that of psychiatrists, who typically focused on patients confined to wards and divorced from family and networks of relationships. Social workers' contacts with clients, by contrast, were not detached from the context of everyday life because their methods took them outside the confines of institutional walls to witness life as it unfolded in homes and kitchens, on doorsteps, and on neighborhood streets.

16. Andrew Abbott argues that high status in the professions "went with being able talk purely professional talk, being able to rule out the confusions and difficulties that clients often present to professional knowledge schemes" (1995, p. 550).

17. Linda Gordon, however, observes that "male-and female-dominated welfare campaigns arose from and then confirmed highly gendered modes of welfare work." In a comparison of rhetorics of reform, she maintains that "if the welfare writings of the early twentieth century were read with authors' names hidden, we might be able to pick the sex of the writer with a high degree of precision. Women's writings sounded the social work approach to poverty—a concern with personal maladjustment" (1994, p. 157).

18. Throughout this study, actual clients' names have been changed to protect their anonymity.

19. In chapter 1, I maintain that benevolent femininity as a predominant model for reform was superseded by a scientific and professionalized one. As with many facets of reform practice and thinking, however, benevolent femininity did not simply disappear. It coexisted in a variety of transmuted forms embedded in ascendant scientific and professional discourses.

Chapter 1: "I'll Be Watching You"

1. A recurring motif in the writings of movement advocates concerned the craftiness and laziness of clients. George Holt (1891), for example, narrated the story of a family who had long enjoyed the fruits of religious giving. Things came to a head when a request for wood was made to the charity organization society. Unsplit wood was given. Subsequently, the society worker discovered that two able-bodied boys were in residence at the home and that the wood had not been split. When the mother refused to let the workers in, a social worker "pushed her way into the house and found the woman's two sons smoking cigarettes, contented as lords" (p. 120).

In his study of typical relief problems, Edward Devine (1914, p. 262) recounts another case of chicanery. The antagonist was a Madame Katherine D'Arago, whose "patience with organized charity was exhausted and henceforward she studied to evade it." Madame D'Arago was so skilled at composing "begging letters" that she eventually was able to make a living for herself by applying for aid for her friends and receiving a fee when she was successful in her quest. Mary Richmond, then secretary of the Philadelphia Society for Organizing Charity, noted, "I know that there are a great many people born lazy who will never do one stroke more of the world's work than direct necessity forces them to" (quoted in Wenocur and Reisch 1989, p. 31).

2. Ginzberg (1990) argues that although the ideology of benevolent femininity included a strong critique of male dominance, this ideology obscured class relations. Defining class solely as a moral condition, the ideology camouflaged the considerable authority exercised by charitable women, their class identities, and the extensive interconnections among women and men of the same class.

3. The New York Association for Improving the Conditions of the Poor, established in 1843 with an emphasis on coordination of relief and supervision, not only served as a model for many relief societies in the 1840s but also developed principles that would be the bedrock of charity organization societies in the 1870s (Lubove 1965). Men not only made up the executive board and staff but were also charity visitors.

4. As a legacy of this approach, see, for example, Oscar Lewis (1966) on the culture of poverty and Tice and Billings (1991) for a critique of the application of the approach to Appalachia.

5. Mrs. John Glenn defined casework in a similarly condescending manner: It "deals with life lived unsuccessfully." She also likened clients to "objects" and "pawns" (1913, p. 353). The fortitude of many clients in navigating the ups and downs of family fortunes, howev-

er, can be sensed from case records, but rarely did their achievements get much explicit attention in social work accounts.

6. Many early charity organization society movement leaders defended the practice of friendly visiting against those who argued that friendships and affection were not possible in such an artificial relationship. Watson (1922, p. 152) quoted an anonymous superintendent of friendly visiting who celebrated the many cheerful friendships that had been established in her district. Although such acquaintances began with "hesitancy and misgiving," they would "ripen into ones of confidence, trustfulness, and hopefulness." She eventually saw "tired mothers turn with gratitude and words of praise to young women who cheer their homes and tenderly minister to their feeble offspring. I see the eyes of invalid mothers brighten when cheerful friends make frequent calls. I see young women becoming companions to those who need an older sister's counsel and support. I see the heroic efforts of visitors who are trying to lift to the purer atmosphere of self-dependence those whose low standard of life accepts pauperism and beggary. I see earnest visitors carrying a real heart sorrow that as yet there is no evidence of better impulses in stubborn, intemperate, or wayward lives."

7. Madeline Breckinridge, one of the founders of the Lexington, Kentucky, Associated Charities in 1900, routinely used the women's pages of the local newspaper to celebrate the efficiency of documentary accumulation. On one occasion she boasted that "about seventy-five people were taken care of at the office yesterday. Nearly all the persons applying for assistance were well-known to the agents, and a very small investigation was necessary, as compared to what had to be done five or six years ago when the office was first opened" (*Lexington Herald,* Jan. 31, 1909).

8. Despite their critique of the record-keeping and investigative practices of the movement, settlement workers were also, according to Boyer (1978, p. 157), equally enthralled by statistics but chose to collect information on neighborhoods, political environments, and industry as their units of investigation.

9. Robert Park, a sociologist, was among the many professionals who carried on the tradition of evoking the Jukes and the tribes of Ishamael when he observed: "In this great city [Chicago] the poor, the vicious, and the delinquent, crushed together in an unhealthful and contagious intimacy, breed in and in, soul and body, so that it has often occurred to me that those long genealogies of the Jukes and the tribes of Ishmael would not show such a persistent and distressing uniformity of vice, crime, and poverty unless they were particularly fit for the environment in which they were condemned to live" (Cappetti 1993, p. 44).

10. The work of Odem (1991, 1995), Broder (1988), Crocker (1992), and Gordon (1988) are especially important for refuting arguments that conclude that middle-class reform work can be understood solely as the one-way intervention of the middle class upon a passive working class.

11. Confidential exchanges were reminiscent of the New York City Police Department's Rogue's Gallery, a major tourist attraction, which had the portraits and records of several thousand professional criminals on display. Police superintendent Thomas Byre boasted that it was "probably the most complete criminal directory in the country" (quoted in

Stange 1992, p. 19). In like fashion, the Gerry Society of New York, the first society for the prevention of cruelty to children, boasted of its sensational display of abused and neglected children. Upon intake, each case was registered in the "great books" of the society and then photographed. After one day of care by the society, cases were re-photographed. Based on the use of contrasting vignettes, a rhetorical display used frequently in persuasion campaigns throughout the Progressive Era, these before-and-after photographs, in addition to case information, were put on exhibit in the Gerry Society gallery, along with "whips, knives, canes, broomsticks, and all weapons of torture . . . many of them still bloodstained or bent from the force of blows given" (Campbell 1893, p. 183).

Blake (1947, p. 37) observed that the MSPCC carried on such traditions but limited pictures to "only certain portions of a child's body, such as angry welts on the back or an emaciated child with a blank thrown across the eyes to prevent identification," until the *Boston Post* informed the society that it could no longer accept such pictures for readers "to absorb with their coffee. Evidently, good coffee and horror conflicted and indigestion resulted." The BCAS also publicized before-and-after pictures of the children in its care. Such shifting conventions for ordering and exhibiting dangerous others and showcasing professional authority later came to be woven into the case stories and professional exhibits of social workers as they sought to persuade the public of their good works and professionalism throughout the Progressive Era (chapter 6).

12. A notable exception to this trend was the Chicago School of Civics and Philanthropy, which fostered a broader sense of practice beyond casework. Even those social workers, however, were not immune to pressures to adopt movement and casework techniques, especially during the late 1920s when the Commonwealth Fund made training stipends contingent upon the teaching of particular courses, including psychiatric casework.

13. Quarrels between the charity organization society movement and the settlement movement can be likened to a "family spat" (Boyer 1978). At professional meetings there was indeed a great deal of quarreling back and forth. Mary Richmond, for example, argued that settlement workers were naive because they accepted uncritically the positions of those they lived among. She disdainfully observed that "they are bowled over by the first labor leader, or anarchist, or socialist they meet" (Boyer 1978, p. 156). Mary McDowell, in response to a charity organization society paper on the moral deficiencies of the poor, responded by commenting that she could not condemn a dirty tenement as indicative of the moral failings of the poor when she knew that nearby factories were producing the problem.

Nonetheless, workers from both charity organization societies and settlement houses shared many practices, especially fact-gathering and documentation. Although the societies emphasized the investigation and documentation of families and individuals, settlements investigated, surveyed, and documented neighborhoods, communities, and industry. Boyer concludes that although the settlement house movement shared many of the moralistic tendencies of the charity organization society movement, it was less preoccupied with individual weaknesses and more focused on environmental factors. In a study of seven settlements in Indianapolis and Gary, Crocker (1992) shows that agendas for reform and activities for residents varied widely, preventing easy conclusions about social control and class politics in settlement work.

14. The association's report noted that "entirely inadequate records were kept. The matron has a little book in which they simply put the child's name and age. The importance of a record was shown recently when an uncle took two nieces of his from the institution promising them a good home. He ruined them. . . . This is of course also an indication of the wrong of returning girls to relatives without sufficient evidence of their character. . . . An inquiry in regards to the person's character is made beforehand but not a sufficiently thorough one" (American Association for Organizing Charity 1918).

15. Pascoe (1990, p. 189) notes an 1889 survey of charitable work that lamented the unwillingness of Protestant churches to participate in the consolidation efforts of scientific charity. The surveyors accounted for this reluctance by noting that churches were "probably less disposed to value organization because the charities of a church are rarely in the hands of business men, but of the clergy and women, who, while energetic and competent enough, have not the bent towards organized combination acquired in the constant handling of large affairs."

16. Although some charity organization societies maintained a general relief fund, many did not because relief was seen by some as an abomination on the individual and society. By the 1920s, however, many family welfare or associated charities had modified that stance and saw relief as a vital treatment tool. See, for example, Moore (1927) and Lubove (1973).

17. World War I ushered in a new market for "casework above the poverty line" through the work of the Red Cross's Home Service public health hospitals and services to soldiers and their families. Many charity organization society leaders such as Mary Richmond were involved in the national training program of the Red Cross, and those wartime activities helped consolidate a larger focus on family treatment for all families in the community rather than only those who were poor.

18. One of the factors in the waning of reform was a growing emphasis on administration and bureaucratic routines in social work practice. During the 1926 presidential address to the National Conference of Social Work, Gertrude Vaile attributed the decline of "crusading leadership to the emergence of a new kind of institutional leader, more an administer and an organizer than a person likely to be distinguished by penetrating insight or broad social vision" (Chambers 1963, p. 94). In his presidential address in 1929, Porter Lee endorsed the trend toward administration and organization in social work.

19. Chapin and Queen (1937, p. 22) observed changes in family welfare agency recordings because of shifting practice priorities as well as socioeconomic factors. They argued that case recordings began as "literally relief rolls" which expanded to "brief comments on clients and aid granted." Such records were "self-justifying reports on cases handled" and used as "aids to the memory of workers and for transmission to new workers." Later records became "elaborate and intimate accounts of the clients, their situations, relations to workers, services rendered and results attained." These detailed records, however, were "reduced by necessity during the depression to brief topical summaries."

20. Timothy Gilfoyle (1986) notes that preventive societies such as the SPCC differed from other nineteenth-century anti-vice and moral reform movements not only in terms of gender composition but also in methods. Given limited law enforcement powers and the prac-

tice of employing undercover and vigilante tactics, SPCC agencies typically defined the social work problem as one of lax law enforcement.

21. Lines of responsibility, however, were often blurred because stenographers often were asked to function as caseworkers (Blake 1947). Many reform tasks were clearly gendered; men typically controlled finances and held administrative positions, whereas women did personal visiting, moving eventually into professional casework (Cumber 1988; Kellogg 1893). Men moved more frequently to lecturing, social investigation, and local politics. Early social workers shared little agreement around questions of gender. Virginia Smith (1891, p. 231) maintained that women did not have "similar inheritances" or the practical education to fit them for public life, yet with the dawning of more educational opportunities and women's superior knowledge of domestic affairs they should be appointed to charitable boards.

In a roundtable discussion of the report of the Committee on Cooperation of Women in Management of Charitable, Penal, and Correctional Institutions (1891, pp. 337–45), a "Mrs. Jacobs" noted that women were often more successful in cleaning streets because they had the time to devote to the task, whereas businessmen had no such time to spare. Mary Richmond said that men can do "personal" work as well as women and sometimes better and that the question was not one of "sex but capacity." Mrs. Charles M. Walker, however, argued that "women can come closer to sinful women than any man and the mother's heart can come nearer to the heart of a girl than any man."

Social workers continued to wrestle with questions of gender and the profession. In 1901 Edward Devine, director of New York Charity Organization Society, proclaimed that women, the "daughters of Eve," were better suited for personal visiting than were men, because their "presence lends its warmth and health to all who come before it. If women lost us Eden, such as she alone can restore it" (quoted in Chambers 1986, p. 8). In 1923 James Tufts also pointed out that women were better fitted to visit homes because they were less likely to "disturb the public order." Less devoted to existing institutions, women were therefore less likely "calmly [to] assume that cities must be smokey, that streets must be filthy, that industry must kill and maim" (p. 73).

Many other social workers maintained, however, that professional credibility required the recruitment of men to the profession, although some, such as Neva Deardorff (1925) and Esther Brown (1938), opposed discrimination in favor of men. Deardorff recommended a "modification of that attitude of mind which assumes when a job which pays more than $3,000 is to be filled, that an ordinary man will be worth that much, but it will take a whale of a women to earn it" (p. 642).

22. Lightner Witmer (1915), a psychologist, noted that the all-women social service department of the Psychological Clinic of the University of Pennsylvania consisted of a head social worker, an assistant social worker, and a recorder who was present at all examinations to take dictation from the examiner.

23. Popular songs reworded into Salvation Army songs, along with marching bands and uniforms befiting a fighting unit, were used to formulate a distinctive image and guide the hunt for those in need of reclamation. The Salvation Army also often established deeper

involvements in the everyday lives of the poor and the outcast than did professional social workers. It launched a program of slum work in which teams of "slum sisters" lived in depressed areas all year. In setting up such a slum post in Cincinnati, they "brought no pictures to hang on their walls, no carpets for their floors, no flowers to grow in their window. Other people in slumdom did not have these things and the newcomers meant to live there as their neighbors across the hall did" (Slum sisters file, undated, Salvation Army National Archives and Research Center). Unlike their charity organization counterparts, slum sisters would assist in domestic chores. As one put it, "Our ammunition of war consisted of a broom, a scrubbing brush, a pail, and a Bible" (*Social News,* July 1911).

24. As Kunzel points out (1988, p. 93), the dilemma of professional detachment and objectivity proved difficult to navigate in many of the relationships that social workers established with clients (chapter 5). Professional discourses did not totally eclipse evangelical understandings and methods; like many other more traditional understandings, they were interwoven, often in a contradictory and convoluted fashion and with emergent ways of theory and practice (Kunzel 1988, 1993).

Chapter 2: The Construction of Case Records and Professional Legitimation

1. Single-factor works on professionalism such as Roy Lubove's *The Professional Altruist: The Emergence of Social Work as a Career, 1880–1930* (1973) under-read diversity within social work and wrongly assume a cohesive professional culture unified in its ambition to imprint the profession with bureaucratic principles and routines (Leighninger 1987). Instead, Leighninger maintains that social workers themselves debated a variety of key issues, including the relative emphasis to be placed on public service versus profession building, the role of the professional in social and political change, the nature of the relationship to the federal welfare system, and the breadth of the profession's intellectual and membership base, all of which played key roles in the development of social work from the 1930s onward.

2. Women social workers took the politics of professional fashion seriously, another manifestation of insecurities around professional acceptance and the construction of women's professional identity. In her memoirs of forty years at the Massachusetts Society for the Prevention of Cruelty to Children, Maggie Blake recounted the importance of dress for women who wanted to fit in at an agency that had no women until 1908. The first women agents all wore "high buttoned or laced boots with black cotton stockings, there was none of the so-called giddy footwear to disturb the client on whom the agent must make a very stern and overpowering impression. To give austerity to the costume, a professional appearing and large leather bag similar to a nurse's bag was carried all day by women. High necked shirtwaists, a black bow in the hair at the nape of the neck. . . . To make the women more like policemen, a bolt of navy blue broadcloth was purchased from the Police Department" (1947, p. 19). Regarding stenographers, whom men on the staff initially viewed suspiciously, Blake pointed out that "women's place in life from the cradle to the grave is improved by her individual fashion of choosing and donning wearing apparel . . . and a short-sleeved dress, jewelry worn in business hours, or too gay a bird on the hat were not considered good form for the business women who wanted to get ahead, so to speak" (pp. 47–48).

3. See also Esther Brown (1938), who argued that less educated men were given preference in social work hiring over better qualified women.

4. Leighninger (1987) also notes that sociologists of the 1920s and 1930s were also preoccupied with the scientific advancement of their field. By the 1940s, however, sociology had moved closer to applied work in policy and social problems. With the establishment of the Society for the Study of Social Problems in 1951, many sociologists established closer ties with practitioners from all disciplines, including social workers.

5. Social workers were quick to retort to such challenges and thus responded with a variety of maneuvers and volleys of their own. Taft (1918, 1922), for example, described numerous defects in the practice of psychiatry, including analyzing people out of context, obtaining one-sided pictures of clients, and lacking firsthand knowledge. Border wars also found their way into social work fiction. For example, Stern and Stern (1923, p. 226) echoed a recurring theme in social work's characterization of psychologists as unapproachable and disconnected from real life. Their fictional psychologist had "filled his office with pictures of travel or achievement, attributes to his professional and social standing . . . no wonder he felt people of every day were of another world! They were; they were not of his world at all. . . . No wonder he looked upon these people as—experiments, problems, foreigners, whose speech he did not share, although he was interested and intrigued with them." The Sterns praised two real-life psychiatrists, Richard Cabot and William Healy, however, for their rare combination of "love and science" (p. 228).

6. Social work had not achieved the status of a true profession that had educationally communicable skills and techniques of its own (Flexner 1915). Instead, it was a "keyboard" and in touch with many professions rather than a profession itself. Because professions were limited and definite in scope, Flexner concluded, and social work engaged in a broad array of activities, it could not be considered a profession.

That conclusion provoked much debate within social work. Mary Richmond declared (1917, p. 114), "But as we listened to Mr. Flexner [thereby shearing the doctor of his professional status] we were more or less aware that quietly and behind his back, apparently, there was developing a skill quite different in method and aim from the work he described. We are not behaving like the telephone girl at the switchboard who pulls out one plug and pushes in another; many of our social agencies were something better than animated clearinghouses."

Flexner's conclusion was evoked frequently. It was discussed at the 1917 National Conference on Charities and Correction and also was highlighted at the 1925 National Conference of Social Work (see, for example, Hodson 1925), as well as in numerous writings of social work leaders who advocated a variety of pathways to the achievement of professional status (Hagerty 1931; Karpf 1931; Walker 1928).

7. The Boston Children's Aid Society, for example, boasted as early as 1914 that it was no longer content to collect and report the facts but was now engaged in "skilled weighing of facts" (1914, p. 37).

8. In contrast to the naive empiricism that informed these understandings of science, Thomas Kuhn (1970) has pointed out that there are no neutral facts, nor are there neutral, non-rhetorical, and disinterested languages in which to report such facts. Scientific facts are not independently waiting "out there" to be discovered but are produced through the ap-

plication of theories, assumptions, conventions, methods, procedures, beliefs, and narratives held by the scientific community. Linda Hutcheon (1989, p. 57) notes that "facts are events to which we have given meaning," and Hayden White (1987, p. 14) observes that in "any account of reality"—whether its genre is science, history or fiction—"narrativity is present," because the world does not present itself to perception in the form of stories that have main subjects, beginnings, middles, and ends. White adds that "every narrative, however seemingly full, is constructed on the basis of a set of events which might have been included but were left out." Fictional elements encompass not just feigned elements but the "forming, shaping and molding elements: the crafting of a narrative" (Davis 1987, p. 3).

9. Psychiatric social work, a new casework specialization, had a major impact on social practice throughout the 1920s. The high status of psychiatry and the opportunities for expansion of social work services to persons above the poverty line helped ensure its growth. The establishment of a school for psychiatric social workers at Smith College in 1918, courses in mental hygiene and social psychiatry at the New York School of Social Work and Pennsylvania School of Social and Health Work, and the establishment of the Commonwealth Fund facilitated the spread of such knowledge. Field (1980), however, has argued that social work theory and practice were not as "deluged" by psychoanalytic theory, as Lubove (1973), for example, had maintained.

Throughout the 1920s there was growing collaboration among a variety of child welfare and child guidance clinics in the form of referrals for mental testing. In 1929, for example, the Massachusetts Society for the Prevention of Cruelty to Children required a mental examination for all children seen by the society, and throughout the 1920s the Boston Children's Aid Society regularly referred children under their care to the Judge Baker Foundation for psychological analysis. Face sheets for these agencies were revised to include psychological evidence of mental defect.

10. Many social workers believed that improved case-filing systems and indexing would increase practice efficiency and improve record-keeping. See, for example, Watson (1922), Bristol (1936), and Ralph (1915). Ralph devotes an entire chapter of *Record Keeping for Child Placing Organizations* to filing and referencing case records. Both Hamilton (1936) and Bruno (1916, p. 458) devote time to the logistics of style. Bruno observes that in many records social workers' practice of using "numbers in the record to indicate individuals, that is, '1' to indicate the man, '2' the woman, '3–10' the children is unnecessarily impersonal." Likewise, Hamilton devotes a chapter in *Social Case Recording* to the problems of tense, elliptical sentences, and phrasing. Problems of bulk, verbosity, and coherence were also recurring concerns (Brown 1933; Wead 1932). Wallerstein (1920b, p. 18) observed that much social investigation and documentation is akin to "an overladen ship on an uncharted sea"; it needed to be streamlined and better directed. See also Hazelton (1927), who argued that the incoherence and verbosity of case records can be reduced by emphasizing a central figure to which everything else is subordinated, and Bedford (1921, p. 248), who advocated the use of "prognoctic" summaries at frequent intervals.

11. Kline (1922) and Myrick (1924) each recommended the use of William White's outlines of psychiatry for social case records, and Hardy (1926) devised a schedule for social workers to use in recording the methods mothers use to train children.

12. As ways of ordering case narratives, Sheffield (1931, p. 469) suggested identifying "sentiments that contribute to right living" and "situation patterns" such as the "home as a cushioned retreat for men."

13. Leighninger (1987) and Leighninger, Leighninger, and Pankin (1974) argue that the relationship between sociology and social work vacillated. Among the factors contributing to their separation was a conceptual distinction introduced by Robert McIver in 1931, which defined the relationship of sociology to social work as that of a "science to an art," although one benefiting from cooperative endeavors (Leighninger, Leighninger, and Pankin 1974, p. 81). Leighninger, Leighninger, and Pankin maintain that this way of conceptualizing the difference between sociology and social work camouflages not only commonalities but also developments in theory and methods, which, by raising new suspicions around science and objective knowledge, undercut the assumption of a neat divide between science and art.

14. I have drawn heavily on the work of many scholars for my analysis of nineteenth- and twentieth-century urban explorers and guardians. I am particularly indebted to the work of Meyerowitz (1988), Nord (1987), Stansell (1987), and Walkowitz (1992).

15. Paradise (1923, p. 319) was an ardent proponent of local color writing and implored social workers to go beyond merely reporting statistics and look into the lives of clients. Her condemnation of the widespread reliance on statistical reports of facts as "wiping the tears away" was borrowed from a poem by Helen Wilson, a government worker:

Little black figures in rows
Little crooked black figures
Numberless columns
To add,
To distribute into little spaces.
Strutting black insects,
Impostors,
Who juggle our tragedies.
"Vital Statistics"
Marriages,
Babies dead,
Broken lives,
Men gone mad,
Labor and crime,
All treated in bulk, with the tears wiped off.
Numbered.

16. Robert Park, in a play on the domestic visits that distinguished social work practice and social case narratives, noted that life histories were essential in sociology. Otherwise, a sociologist was "like a man in the dark looking at the outside of a house trying to guess what is going on inside." According to Park, the life history approach was akin to "a man who opens the door and walks in, and has visible before him what previously he had merely guessed at" (Young 1935, p. 96).

17. John Van Maanen (1988, p. 64) observed that closure in what he termed "realist tales" is essential to conveying the authority of a text and that the focus of a realist tale is frequently restricted to a specific problem posed early on and more or less resolved by the end. Closure is "an argument for certain knowledge. Leaving matters indeterminant, up in the air, ambiguous or otherwise uncertain might be disturbing to the readers and might undermine the authority of the text." Closure can be achieved in many ways, including "pigeonholing" materials into professional concepts and constructing archetypes such as Burgess and Shaw's "Stanley." In contrast, social workers in the case records I examined frequently were ambiguous about the outcomes of cases or even suggested that their professional activities may have been in vain. As Wheeler (1925, p. 256) pointed out, one could find a "veritable cemetery" of files marked "case closed. Family uncooperative" among the records of social workers.

18. Thomas observed (1923, p. 125) that in life histories, "girls will often point to an unfortunate love affair or a betrayal in their representations," and these should be discounted because "girlhood and womanhood have been idealized to the degree that this explanation is to be expected and the girl wishes to give it; for betrayal is the romantic way of falling, the one used in storybooks and movies."

19. In her study of maternity homes, Kunzel (1993, pp. 103–4) likewise argues that resistance as well as accommodation characterized how unmarried mothers told their stories to social workers. Even when asked within those coercive contexts where social workers had the power to withhold resources, direct questions about how they became pregnant presented clients with the "possibility for appropriation, subversion, and sometimes outright resistance to expected narratives of seduction and abandonment."

Chapter 3: The Rescue of "Juvenile Fragments"

1. C. C. Carstens, director of the Child Welfare League of America, boasted of the many advances in the burgeoning field of child welfare by 1927. He noted the development of the Federal Children's Bureau; new consciousness on the part of institutions for children not only within their confines but also in "extra-mural relationships"; the development of "intake, adjustment," and mother's aid in connection with both child-placing societies and institutions; more systematic methods of discharge; the growth of medical, psychological, and psychiatric services as an adjunct to casework for children; new children's casework in the area of delinquency; and the establishment of state-run child welfare commissions.

2. Although case records of the Minneapolis Citizen's Aid Society are available at the University of Minnesota Social Welfare Archives, administrative records are not part of this collection. Therefore, my efforts to trace biographical information on Miss Champine were not successful. Given trends in social work staffing, however, it is safe to assume that like the other front-line workers whose case records I examined, she was white, unmarried, and middle class.

Some social workers were graduates of professional schools of social work. The board minutes for December 1922 of the Boston Children's Aid Society, for example, note that at least three of the ten woman on the staff were graduates of Simmons College of Social Work, and the general secretary, Alfred Whitman, was a Harvard graduate. By contrast, the Massachusetts Society for the Prevention of Cruelty to Children fell behind in this aspect of professionalization, boasting no graduates of professional social work schools in its employ at the time. Maggie Blake (1947) noted that during his tenure as general secretary, C. C. Carstens briefly required new staff to have college training. Katherine O'Rourke and Helen Marsters, the first women hired as agents rather than stenographers at the MSPCC, were college graduates. Blake recalled, however, that few men applied, and "only a limited number of women were desired" (p. 8).

3. This argument grows out of recent work that explores the conflict and contradictions among discursive systems. Jennifer Terry, for example, explores the production of "counterdiscursive deviant subjectivity" forged in opposition to medico-scientific discourses that pathologized homosexuality, a resistive discourse that allowed possibilities for expression and self-representation. Queer subjects of a study of homosexuality during the 1930s in New York City, sponsored by the Committee for the Study of Sex Variants, were not reduced to a "medicalized identity, on the contrary, while they participated in a scientific study which assumed from the onset that they were not normal, they were never docile victims" merely written upon. Instead, "they deployed interventionist strategies within and against a medical discourse in relation to which the subjects—often with humor, anger, excess, and irony—asked questions of self and at the same time eluded the determined and finally frustrated gaze of the doctors" (Terry 1991, p. 68). See also Lisa Duggan's (1993) study of the narratives surrounding the 1892 murder of Freda Ward by Alice Mitchell, which similarly concludes that although the case histories and newspaper accounts of that trial were "strategic constructions," they were not free of "the shaping influence of women like Alice Mitchell and of the story she told her family, lawyers, trial experts, and court. They were, that is, not simple impositions but appropriations" (p. 880). Kunzel (1993) and Gordon (1988) both argue that the perspectives of clients were apparent in many case records, as were the strategies clients employed to pursue their own needs, countering a widespread tendency in other historical accounts to position them as being merely passive in the hands of social workers.

4. Holloran (1994) rightfully observes that psychiatric social workers who worked in hospitals and clinics played an ancillary role within these settings, primarily collecting and recording data for psychiatrists and making home visits. Holloran further maintains that workers from Boston's child welfare agencies such as Boston Children's Aid Society showed "deference" to the more skilled psychological insights of child guidance clinics. As in the case of Hazel, my analysis of case records from the BCAS shows that it referred many cases to the Judge Baker Foundation for evaluation and participated in many case conferences conducted by the clinic to hammer out diagnosis and treatment recommendations. On many occasions, however, caseworkers merely inserted case conference reports from the JBCG into the larger case record while ignoring the suggested treatment plan.

5. Eric Schneider (1980) notes that typical practice during the 1920s at the Judge Baker Foundation consisted of a single, hour-long client interview. The meetings, designed to obtain own stories and make diagnoses, were a far cry from the out-of-office, long-term casework relationships typical of social work. Among the twenty-seven cases written by the staff of the Boston Children's Aid Society during the 1920s, eleven spanned ten to twenty-two

years, seven ran from three to nine years, and only seven were two years or less. Most that did not span at least two years were open only a few months, suggesting in most instances that once BCAS cases were well established they tended to involve long-term relationships.

6. Slingerland (1919a) reported that children were placed in boarding homes in one of three ways: in free homes without payment of board, with expenses being supplied by the foster parents; in "working homes" at wages that did not necessarily produce a surplus beyond the child's board and clothes; and on a "board" basis, where parents, guardians, or agencies paid a fee. C. C. Carstens recalled (1927, p. 123) problems with free home placement because older dependent children were often expected to contribute too much to the household, and, as a result, such placements were most vulnerable "to the danger of child exploitation." Regardless of the form of placement, boarding out typically meant long hours, hard work, and little free time. Uniforms were often required, signifying to many girls their servitude and problematic status within the "homes" of others. For a classic study of the theory and practice of boarding out, see Theis and Goodrich (1921).

7. Miss Champine's struggles with Hazel over appropriate clothing bring to mind parental power and after-school shopping sprees with my mother. On one outing, I insisted on a pink taffeta dress resplendent with rhinestones for the first day of school. Instead, I received a woefully plain sailor's suit. Not only did I weep openly in the store but a later picture of me in the hated dress documents my "disagreeableness," a favorite depiction of Miss Champine's for Hazel's moods after similar shopping trips.

Chapter 4: To Make a Case

1. In the tradition of acknowledging narrativity in all forms of writing, Eric Rabkin (1986) applies a classification of story genres to the psychological case history.

2. The long-term nature of social workers' relationships with clients was facilitated in protective cases, in part by the heavy reliance on continuances by the courts, a judicial disposition that allowed agents to oversee clients' homes and gather evidence over long periods. In one case the court agreed not to remove the children if their mother complied with the following agreement: "The children's hair must be cleaned up. She must do her duty and keep them in school. She must conduct herself so that she is a good influence on her children." The disposition allowed social workers to supervise the home for almost a decade.

Because staff turnover was high, long-term clients usually had more than one caseworker over the course of time, a problem that many social work leaders hoped to alleviate by increasing the training and education of social workers and hence the salaries paid to those who were skilled.

3. In 1927 the MSPCC reported the following breakdown on cases requiring court action. Of 5,396 families investigated, with 13,823 children involved, 1,169 families required court action, 2,512 children were protected by court action, and 9,405 children were protected without court action. In 227 cases there was a failure to "accomplish purpose because the evident was insufficient or because the law did not reach the conditions disclosed" (Annual Report 1927, p. 41).

4. The general secretary of the MSPCC, Frank Fay, was a founder of the Lancaster School,

a reform institution for delinquents, and a member of the Massachusetts Prisoner's Aid Association. Theodore Lothrop, general secretary after Carstens, was an attorney. The MSPCC had more male agents throughout its history than the BCAS, probably reflecting its commitments to law enforcement functions. Of seven male agents in 1908, one was a former police officer, and one was Alfred Whitman, who soon went on to head the BCAS. In 1910 the secretary and assistant secretary were both men, all eight of the special agents were men, and the two newly hired supervising agents were women. They both had college degrees, the first among MSPCC agents. The examining physician was a woman, as were the matron and assistant matron of the MSPCC's temporary home. In 1921 the secretary and assistant secretary were male, as were the two supervising agents, whereas ten out of eighteen general agents were women.

There were greater numbers of women at the agent and visitor levels throughout the history of the BCAS. In 1909 the staffing was as follows: the general secretary was male, as were one out of four investigation agents, one out of eight placing-out agents, and one out of four agents-in-training. In 1921 the general secretary was a man, the two assistant secretaries were women, and only one of sixteen visitors was male.

5. For example, at the MSPCC, which typically had the most adversarial relationships and approaches to clients of all agencies I examined, one agent urged a client to join the union at the shoe factory where she was employed in order to secure better wages and more humane working conditions. Both Stadum (1992) in her study of the Minneapolis Family Welfare Association and Gordon (1988) in her study of the MSPCC and the Judge Baker Foundation observed the flexibility of individual agency workers in their interpretations, decisions, and relationships.

6. The statistical reporting by the agencies I examined was inconsistent across time and agencies, making direct comparisons difficult. Even by 1921, when other agencies such as the Minneapolis Family Welfare Association provided a great deal of specific detail about clients, including race, living conditions, and wages earned, the MSPCC merely reported overall numbers of clients served, sources of requests for its services, and a ranking of factors in the neglect of children. Neither the MSPCC nor the BCAS provided information on the financial background of clients.

7. *Social Diagnosis* was the bible for social education and training throughout the 1920s and 1930s (Wenocur and Reisch 1989). Mary Richmond's connection to Russell Sage and her national presence in the Red Cross, as well as the successful marketing of *Social Diagnosis*, helped ensure the book's influence. The BCAS, MSPCC, and Minneapolis Family Welfare Association all used it in their agency training. Pearl Salsberry, director of Relief and Service at Minneapolis Family Welfare Association, noted (1927, p. 154) that the "broken backs and the dog-eared, thumbed copies of Social Diagnosis on our office shelves—and most of all, our important improvements in the techniques of casework—point to the contribution which Social Diagnosis makes." Despite the volume's canonical status, however, Mary Richmond was defeated as a candidate for president of the National Conference of Social Work, perhaps because she was viewed as being out of step with the growing passion many felt for the importance of psychological interpretation throughout the 1920s (Chambers 1963; Wenocur and Reisch 1989).

8. Despite differences in their missions and methods, agencies shared case records, and workers regularly read those of different agencies. In this case, staff from the Judge Baker Foundation read the MSPCC record in 1933.

9. In all of the case records I examined, only two caseworkers were male, both employed by the MSPCC.

10. Merely interviewing a wide range of witnesses was not, however, enough to win professional accolades. Some social work leaders advised mastering the more advanced prosecutorial skills of cross-examination and sifting testimony for fallacies. Refining the arts of interviewing and interpreting evidence was considered indispensable by social workers such as Helen Myrick (1926, p. 121), who argued that much could be learned from lawyers, including the "tricks and traps used in cross examination."

11. For this insight I am indebted to an extensive body of scholarship on women, gender, and reform and to the fine work of many feminist historians. Among them are Barbara Brenzel, Sherri Broder, Linda Gordon, Joanne Meyerowitz, Peggy Pascoe, Kathy Peiss, Elizabeth Pleck, and Christine Stansell.

12. In 1929, 1,220 among the MSPCC's 5,056 cases were referred by other agencies, 1,062 by the general public, 677 by the police, 568 by schools, 492 by families, 327 by relatives, 382 by courts, 285 anonymously, and 43 by churches. The BCAS received a higher percentage of applications for service made by clients, families, or friends. In 1914 the BCAS reported that of 548 child-placing cases, 516 cases were referred by family or friends, 6 by settlement workers, 6 by mothers' societies, 7 by churches, 9 by civic agencies, and 4 by lawyers. In 1912 at the MFWA it was noted that applicants' initiatives accounted for 2,705 applications for service, organizations for 1,157, and business firms accounted for 61 applications.

In my sampling of twenty-nine BCAS cases, fourteen were referred by parents themselves and two by relatives. The most frequent form of parent referral came from fathers who wanted to board out their children. The 1920 annual report of the BCAS noted that out of 207 children supervised in foster homes, 83 were received due to the death or disability of the mother and 24 had been left to "distracted fathers who, after trying indifferent housekeepers or unwilling relatives, had in desperation sought a child-placing agency" (Annual Report 1920, p. 11). Of ten cases from the Minneapolis Family Welfare Association, five were self-referrals, one was from a church, and four were from other agencies.

Pleck (1987) also notes the high numbers of referrals of children to juvenile court by family members, and Brenzel (1983) points out many family-initiated commitments to the State Industrial School for Girls in Lancaster, Massachusetts—many on complaints of stubbornness.

13. Social workers, however, were not the only ones who observed and recorded impressions of clients' faces and physical features. The Judge Baker Foundation also regularly reported impressions of client appearances. In 1932, for example, the case summary of "Laura" reported that she was "very well-developed, good strength, Octoroon, regular negroid features, pleasant expression, rather attractive."

14. Sexual management was a predominant theme in the stories of social workers, who commonly confronted "sex-saturated" girls thought to be "prostitutes in the making." They expended great amounts of energy to supervising what they perceived to be ominous ten-

dencies toward sexually unruly behavior in girls under their charge. What Frank Mort (1987, p. 190) noted in regard to England was equally apt for the United States in the early decades of the twentieth century: "It was no longer the 'professional prostitute' who was isolated as the source of danger but a new form of threat—the promiscuous girl who gave sex for free. As Lucy Bland has shown, the 'amateur prostitute,' as she was christened, was the source of a series of moral panics during the First War, condensing fears about the rising tide of immortality, illegitimate births, and the spread of VD."

15. In 1917, according to the MFWA, 229 families included persons who had mental defects, compared to only two of eighteen MSPCC cases from the 1920s were referred to the Judge Baker Foundation for consultation, and none mentioned IQ testing.

17. For evidence that many social workers were acutely aware of potential sex dangers to boarded-out girls, see Theis and Goodrich (1921, p. 82). For another example, see Martha Falconer's Social Hygiene Committee report to the National Conference of Charities and Corrections in 1915, which also pointed to the danger of cross-class boarding where men were known to consider wayward girls "lawful prey." She noted further that "conscientious people who have tried to place girls in family homes will testify that the girl is often in great danger from the husband in that household. Though the home has been carefully investigated, the girl will need constant and careful supervision" (p. 252).

Chapter 5: Tales of Protection

1. The social worker of a client named "Helen," however, neglected to read in advance the reviews of a play she had chosen to attend with her impressionable ward. Consequently, she "spent the evening with [Helen] at the public library studying pictures of the Holy Grail and taking out Tennyson's *Idylls of a King* for the girl to read to offset the cheapness of the afternoon's performance."

2. Those who write psychoanalytic case histories often turn to archetypes in organizing them. In his studies of hysteria, for example, Charcot analyzed clinical phenomena by dividing them into archetypes of psychological disease. Years later, in a commentary on Charcot's methodology, Freud observed (de Marneffe 1991, p. 74) that archetypes "could be brought into prominence with the help of a certain sort of schematic planning, and with these archetypes as a point of departure, the eye could travel over a long series of ill-defined cases—the *'formes frustes'* which branching off from one or another characteristic feature of the type, melt away into indistinctness." Freud also noted, "Even at the stage of description it is not possible to avoid applying certain abstract ideas to material in hand, ideas derived from somewhere or other but certainly not from observation alone" (quoted in Malcolm 1990, p. 315). By contrast, social workers employed deeply theorized archetypes far less frequently in their case histories than psychiatry did to organize plots for the multitude of disparate behaviors and appearances they encountered and narrated.

3. Ellen Raynard, a missionary reformer in nineteenth-century England, claimed that women charity workers were often more effective in establishing a presence in working-class neighborhoods than male clerics and medics because they were capable of "getting down, down, deeper down into the hearts of the poor. . . . Why are they so wretched in their circumstanc-

es and in their habits in our great metropolis of civilization? Because the middle-class which ought to civilize them has known so little of them. This knowledge is now being attained in a womanly way" (quoted in Mort 1987, p. 57). Raynard was wrong, of course, to have related these "womanly ways" of reform to essential differences between women and men, but she did grasp that women, because of the gendered structure of everyday life, went about their work and charitable relationships in ways that were distinctly their own.

4. In her studies of the Minneapolis Family Welfare Association, Stadum (1987, 1992) found that agency standards for motherhood and wage work were nebulous and inconsistent. At the same time that many MFWA workers believed that maternal wage work caused spousal shiftlessness and delinquency among children by disrupting natural gender obligations, they were nonetheless inclined to promote self-sufficiency through wage work. They had no unified line on questions of paid employment, divorce, and the marriage of pregnant women. For example, in marked contrast to many social workers who sought to stop mothers from wage work, one MFWA agent focused her efforts on encouraging a married woman with a six-month-old child to go to work rather than the woman's husband. The work of Nancy Hewitt (1984) also challenges assumptions of the presumed uniformity of women's activism by pointing out important class and philosophical differences among reformers.

5. Stadum (1992, p. 219) points out that the charity organization leader Amos Warner (1930, 290–92) observed that between the 1890s and the 1920s there was a tendency for fewer cases to receive material assistance, but those who did received larger amounts. Warner also pointed out that Joanna Colcord, once the director of the Minneapolis Family Welfare Association, noted that giving small amounts of relief on demand was less effective than establishing adequate budgets for clients. Other caseworkers, such as Madeline Moore of the New York Charity Organization Society, pointed out (1927, p. 186) the ongoing dilemma between social casework principles that sought to "apply treatment to the individual in accordance with all his lacks-emotional, intellectual, social, and economic" while facing the "specter of the saturation-point in relief budgets." In a study of casework for the New York Charity Organization, Grace Marcus argued (1929) that relief and casework could be integrated successfully because relief provided an opening for establishing the good will of clients. According to this new thinking, relief did not automatically produce character decline as the charity organization society had earlier asserted. Relief, however, was viewed as being useless without casework, because casework was vital for ferreting out and treating nonmaterial maladjustments and moving clients to a higher level of functioning than merely providing relief could do.

6. The caseworker was following the conventions of social work practice of the period by engaging in an extensive documentation of history and testimony throughout the duration of the case. A series of letters and reports was written to family welfare agencies in other cities in which the family was "known," and the agent talked to their minister, employers, and friends. When the family took in a boarder, the MFWA investigated that individual. At the same time, the visitor provided other forms of help throughout the case, ranging from rides to the hospital to books on menstruation for Hilda's daughter when Hilda was reluctant to discuss that topic with her.

7. Virtuous sisterhood was reserved for white women only; common cause with middle-class black women was not possible because of their perceived immorality and inferi-

ority. One southern writer asserted, "I sometimes read of a virtuous Negro women, hear of them, but the idea is absolutely inconceivable to me . . . I can not imagine such a creature as a virtuous black woman. . . . They are the greatest menace possible to the moral life of any community where they live" (quoted in Guy-Sheftall 1990, p. 46). Slingerland (1919b, p. 30) warned that "diseased colored cooks and housemaids who are more numerous than the writer dares indicate impartially spread the germs of their maladies" among the white people for whom they work. African American women thus had to contend with a plethora of bigotry that concerned their bodies, sexuality, and womanhood (Carby 1992; Higginbotham 1992).

They also had the burden of rewriting the powerful text of their presumed immorality and otherness. As Josephine St. Pierre Ruffin noted in a speech in 1895 to delegates of African American women's clubs, "Too often we have been silent under unjust and unholy charge. . . . Year after year southern women have protested against the admission of colored women into any national organization on the ground of the immorality of these women, and because all refutation has only been tried by individual work, the charge had never been crushed, as it could and should have been at first" (quoted in hooks 1981, p. 131). In 1901 Mary Taylor Blauvelt, a self-described "woman of no negro blood" (1901, p. 662), attended a meeting of the Michigan State Federation of Colored Women's Clubs. Although she was impressed by many things, including the fact that delegates were "dressed like ladies with very little of the tendency towards gaudy or inharmonious colors which has been supposed to characterize the race" and that they gave "addresses so eloquent that they would have electrified an assembly of white college women," she nonetheless concluded that the delegates represented the "aristocracy of the race and not the rank and file."

8. Questions regarding the suitability of white workers to this project of racial redemption, however, were voiced in light of notions that cast blacks as the quintessential other. Mary Russell (1921, pp. 60–61), secretary of the Memphis Associated Charities, maintained, for example, that because most social workers were white and numerous "complications" blocked white workers from "real" understanding of black clients, it was essential that "well-rounded," "adequately trained," and white-supervised black workers who understood the "handicaps" of their race be enlisted in reform efforts.

Many casework organizations had no black staff, and at the BCAS as well as the MSPCC there was no mention of black staff throughout the 1920s. At the Minneapolis Family Welfare Association, however, the number of African American clients increased from 28 in 1917 to 107 in 1926 (Family Welfare Association 1917–26). A black visitor had been approved at the September 1918 board meeting to work exclusively with black families, and in 1926 another black worker was hired, Audre McCullough. By 1928 there were not enough black families for two workers, so Audre McCullough, in an unprecedented move for the time, was sent to visit white clients and in 1931 was made a district supervisor in charge of white clients and workers (Salsberry 1933).

Holloran (1994) noted that when Charles Birdwell became general secretary of the BCAS in 1886 he helped the society become more racially sympathetic. In a 1902 address before the National Conference of Charities and Correction, Birdwell presented the case of a fifteen-year-old black prostitute to demonstrate the soundness of the society's policy of crossing the racial line in child-placing. In 1914 the society's annual report noted that 41 of 583 children seen were black. Nativity had replaced the reporting of race by 1921. And the next year, the society reported that it had provided homes for children "irrespective of age, color, or sect" (Annual Report 1922). In 1921 the Massachusetts Society for the Prevention of Cruelty to Children asserted that it, too, served "without discrimination as to race," however the society's annual reports do not document race. A BCAS social worker Holloran interviewed observed that the agency by the 1920s "accepted colored cases on an equal basis and tended to stick with them no matter how difficult they become" (1994, p. 152).

9. Although much attention was directed toward assimilating immigrants and to preserving some elements of their cultures, many social work organizations either neglected African Americans or excluded them from caseloads. Many white caseworkers perceived blacks to be less worthy of uplift efforts than ethnic immigrants, and notions of blacks as possessing inferior morals, psyches, and customs littered professional social work writings and shaped inter-racial practice (Sherman 1923). Mary Russell (1921) observed that casework among blacks was merely a fledgling effort and black mothers received mothers' pensions less frequently than white women, and Priscilla Clement (1992) noted that black women typically had a harder time obtaining material relief. Lasch-Quinn (1993) found that even within the more environmentally oriented settlement house movement, explanations of black dysfunction still lead to attributions of inferiority and segregated reform efforts.

10. For example, Slingerland (1919b) concluded that child-placing organizations were not very successful in the black community, an opinion that ignored such successes as the Lexington [Kentucky] Colored Orphans Industrial Home. Run by a board of managers, all African American women, the home was deeply woven into the life of the community and functioned not only as a school and orphanage but also as a bank, a church, an old-age home, and a day care center. The women were also adept at fundraising and collected necessary funds to rebuild after a fire destroyed the home in 1912. It still continues as a community center (Byars and Tice 1992). Also see the fine scholarship on African American reformers by Brown (1989), Giddings (1984), Gordon (1991), Lasch-Quinn (1993), and Neverton-Morton (1989).

11. By contrast, Joanna Colcord felt (1930, p. 214) that identifying family strengths and "wise parenthood among the humble folk" was important. She highlighted the case of a presumably white family of eight on relief due to the illness and blindness of the breadwinner, a situation resembling Rosa's. Here, however, the record was "bright" because the family was bonded by sterling characteristics such as "fortitude" and "utilization of opportunities." Boasting that the mother worked in order to prevent the daughter from having to leave Normal School, Colcord clearly found the woman to be a paragon. There were no traces of "self-pity, self-seeking, or complaint" in the family when "pain, cold, and hunger had to be endured," because "one makes the best of these things, fortified by religion and hope." Such a compassionate and generous description of dreams, dilemmas, strengths, and sacrifices, however, was not extended to Rosa by her Minneapolis Family Welfare Association caseworker.

12. In an address at the National Conference of Social Work, William Healy, director of the Judge Baker Foundation in Boston, maintained (1921b, p. 271) that mental testing of

women and girls was especially important, because "men are being tried out in the world continually, and one knows pretty well what they are; they are losing jobs or holding them, or they are good or poor earners, etc.; but women lead such comparatively protected lives that when it is necessary for them to go out and earn a living, or when one considers their qualifications for bringing up children, it seems all the more necessary to know something of their general and special mental abilities."

13. Martha Falconer (1915, p. 248) noted that it was especially urgent that girls of low mentality be given more "protection" in the form of segregation, because they have a "commodity to sell" and therefore are "asset[s]." A feebleminded girl is not always "an idiot or an imbecile, but . . . the girl who is most dangerous to society is the attractive, high-grade feebleminded girl."

14. Augusta Fox Bronner, one of the first women psychologists in the United States, received a Ph.D. in the mid-1910s from Columbia University, where she had studied female delinquency with Edward Thorndike. She codirected the Judge Baker Foundation from 1917 to 1949 with William Healy.

15. Sometimes clients enjoyed a reversal of fortune as their IQ scores miraculously increased. That was true for Ruth, who was given an examination in 1926, found to have an IQ of 47, declared feebleminded, and boarded at Rose Cottage in Minneapolis, pending placement. In 1928, however, she was retested, and her IQ score rose to 86, but the outcome was not recorded in Ruth's case record.

16. At this case conference on Helen, a worker from the North Bennett Industrial School observed that "there is something abnormal about the girl mentally. She is still encouraging the girl to think about high school next year but there does not seem to be in the present anyway of realizing this ambition." Helen's visitor stated that she doubted the wisdom of allowing "two years of dilatory studies with the opportunity for occupying the stage in a variety of ways." Mrs. W., also of the Children's Aid Society, stated that she felt "compelled to say something she rarely said of any girl and that was that she was 'hopeless.'" She felt that there was "nothing to do but watch her go to pieces and then step in and take whatever actions seem necessary."

Chapter 6: Tales of Accomplishment

1. Many examples of accounts draw from the well-established metaphoric conventions of light and darkness and overflowing filth to paint pictures of menacing, sinister, and foreign landscapes. For example, Elsa Herzfeld's *Close-Range Studies of Darkest New York* (1905), a year-long investigation of the lives of tenement-dwellers in one of the "submerged" districts of the city, is deeply indebted to notions of light and dark. Herzfeld reported (pp. 26–28) that thousands of people were still in "mental darkness and narrowness that was scarcely exceeded in the Middle Ages." She wrote that "all this darkness and unenlightment is not only true of the older generation," and that the "garbage can and ash barrel standing before the doors are always running over." Such metaphoric traditions also appeared in the case records of social workers, who narrated tales of clients who were in shadowy conditions that necessitated the enlightening influence of a social worker. It was also assumed

that the public needed experts to illuminate these dark conditions and lead the way toward their resolution.

2. Deborah Nord (1987) notes the widespread use of the England-Africa analogy that appeared frequently in middle-class explorations of slums. She argues that the most explicit use of this tactic of comparing the urban poor of England with Africans or other non-Western people was Gen. William Booth's *In Darkest England and the Way Out*. Booth, the founder of the Salvation Army, made the connection clear when he queried, "As there is a darkest Africa is there not also a darkest England?" (quoted in Nord 1987, p. 125). Reformers such as Booth had to convince the public that urban slum-dwellers were of "English society though separate from it, related to the middle class but a race apart" (p. 132), and could be civilized and reformed.

3. Alongside urban slum narratives, Richard Brodhead (1993, pp. 115–16) observed that the second half of the nineteenth century witnessed a profusion of "regional fiction" that ushered in a "new set of social knowledges." The genre required "a setting outside the world of modern development, a zone of backwardness where locally variant ways still prevail" and demanded "characters" perceived to be "ethnologically colorful, personifications of the different humanity produced in such non-modern cultural settings." The southern Appalachian mountain region, for example, was one such site of experiential imperialism (Billings and Blee 1996).

4. Bulmer, Bales, and Sklar (1991) note that 2,775 social surveys were carried out between 1912 and 1927, but by 1930 their frequency diminished. A weakening of the connections occurred between reform impulses and the survey movement during the heyday of surveys and social mapping (Cohen 1991). Unlike the nineteenth century and the early years of the twentieth century, disdain for reform and a turn to "real" science grew during the 1920s. Robert Park of the University of Chicago Department of Sociology observed that the sociological approach, because the world is filled with reform crusaders, should "be that of a calm, detached scientist who investigates race relations with the same objectivity and detachment with which the zoologist dissects the potato bug" (quoted in Cohen 1991, p. 264). Sklar (1991) and Deegan (1988), however, maintain that women played a major role in early social science. Women were active in the American Social Science Association, and its surveys, especially the noteworthy and reform-inspired *Hull House Maps and Papers* (Residents of Hull House 1895), were unacknowledged precursors to the university-based sociological studies of the 1920s.

5. Stange has noted that the camera played a key role in reform publicity of the Progressive Era by offering "scientific exactitude . . . linked metaphorically with the supposed neutrality of technical expertise" (quoted in Trachtenberg 1989, p. 205). Maggie Blake recalled that in telling their protective stories agents "found pictures to be almost one hundred percent effective, but to secure them in our case work is difficult and to publish them often times dangerous. In spite of this we did publish them in picture leaflets, trusting to chance that no harm would come. Pictures of 'before and after' were most acceptable and the results almost unbelievably good" (1947, p. 40).

6. Later, an annual section of the National Conference of Charities and Correction was devoted to the Mobilization of Social Forces in order to carry on the work of the earlier

Press and Publicity Committee. At the 1920 meeting of the National Conference of Social Work, a Committee on Publicity Methods in Social Work was established and in 1929 became the Social Work Publicity Council. With the assistance of the Harmon Foundation, the council held publicity contests and conducted publicity clinics annually at the National Conference of Social Work.

7. In a "clinical examination" of the annual reports of social work agencies, Karl de Schweinitz of the New York Charity Organization Society concluded (1915–16, pp. 509–10) after examining five hundred "specimens of the genus annual report" that most of these "creatures are suffering from unsightliness, malformations, obesity, and multiple personality. These defects are hereditary." One malformation was the "habit of reporting in terms of organization rather than in terms of accomplishment. . . . That means one straightway story" (see also Street 1919).

8. Other social work leaders also voiced Weller's anxieties over emotionalism and sentimental appeals. Questions regarding the purpose and content of social work publicity and its difference from propaganda would occupy social work publicists and their critics for years (see, for example, Brown 1926).

9. The film *It* (1927) portrayed two social workers as "'hard-boiled,' ignorant looking—women who seize a woman's baby and tell the mother they must put the child in a home until she is well enough to take care of it" (quoted in Walkowitz 1990, p. 1069). The American Association of Social Workers launched a protest campaign against the film and succeeded in winning the demand that placards for it replace the term *social workers* with *meddling neighbors*.

10. In 1939, for example, the Massachusetts Society for the Prevention of Cruelty to Children produced a film based on the case of Dora Hutton.

11. In many case records clients were referred to by a number only. Although some social work leaders viewed such a system as unnecessarily impersonal, many front-line social workers used it.

12. Because many social work situations were outside the experience of the middle class, they were often misunderstood. Evart and Mary Swain Routzahn (1928) pointed out that the term *child labor* was often mistakenly perceived to mean household chores rather than the harsh life of children who worked, for example, in beet fields. Therefore, to enhance middle-class understanding of the field of social work she stressed the importance of clear mental pictures and skillful visualization so readers would have a keener sense of the harsh reality of the lives of the poor.

Afterword

1. See Mayer and Timms (1970) for a discussion of the differing expectations and interpretations of casework encounters between clients and social workers.

Bibliography

Manuscript and Archival Collections

American Association for Organizing Charity. 1918. Report on the charities of Lexington, Kentucky, by Margaret Byington. Special Collections, Margaret I. King Library, University of Kentucky, Lexington.

Boston Children's Aid Society, case records, Collection 21; Boston Society for Care of Girls, case records, Collection 21; Children's Aid Association, case records, Collection 21; and Massachusetts Society for the Prevention of Cruelty to Children, case records, Collection 2. All in Archives and Special Collections, Healey Library, University of Massachusetts, Boston.

Child Guidance Service. Report and description of the child guidance service of Lexington, Kentucky, 1934–1940. Special Collections, Margaret I. King Library, University of Kentucky, Lexington.

Citizen's Aid Society, case records; Associated Charities/Family Welfare Agency, case records; Child Protective Society, case records; and Child Protective Society-Institutional Bureau, case records. All in Social Welfare History Archives, Microfilm Collection, Walters Library, University of Minnesota, Minneapolis.

Edith and Grace Abbott Papers. 1927. Memo to teachers of casework. Box 18, folder 6, Department of Special Collections, Joseph Regenstein Library, University of Chicago.

Madeline Breckinridge Papers. Boxes 693, 698, Manuscript Division, Library of Congress, Washington, D.C.

Salvation Army. *An introductory course in social welfare work*. 1933. New York: Salvation Army National Headquarters. Salvation Army National Archives and Research Center, Alexandria, Va.

———. Replies to your questions, Lecture notes, and Lecture 11: Record writing. Anita Robb Papers, Salvation Army National Archives and Research Center, Alexandria, Va.

———. Secrets of success in slumland, and Slums and the slum sisters. Slum Sisters file, Salvation Army National Archives and Research Center, Alexandria, Va.

————. Social Welfare Work: Family relief [lecture notes]. Ca. 1930s. Salvation Army National Archives and Research Center, Alexandria, Va.

Sophonisba Breckinridge Papers. Department of Special Collections, Joseph Regenstein Library, University of Chicago.

Annual Reports and Miscellaneous Documents

Associated Charities of Lexington and Fayette County. 1915. *The Vanguard* [annual report]. Special Collections, Margaret I. King Library, University of Kentucky, Lexington.

Associated Charities of Lexington, Kentucky. 1911. Annual report. Case reports, box 693. Sophonisba Breckinridge Papers, Manuscript Division, Library of Congress, Washington, D.C.

Blake, Maggie. 1947. Down the memory lane. Archives and Special Collections, Healey Library, University of Massachusetts, Boston.

Boston Children's Aid Society. 1900. Specimen cases, illustrative cases and forms. [Annual report.] Archives and Special Collections, Healey Library, University of Massachusetts, Boston.

————. 1905, 1909, 1912, 1913, 1914, 1916, 1918, 1920, 1921, 1922. Annual reports. Collection 4, box 1, Archives and Special Collections, Healey Library, University of Massachusetts, Boston.

Boston Society for the Care of Girls. 1922. Annual report. Collection 4, box 1, Archives and Special Collections, Healey Library, University of Massachusetts, Boston.

Breckinridge, Madeline. 1917. Fayette County Court Transcript, Hearing on Funding for the Salvation Army. Box 698, Library of Congress, Washington, D.C.

Division of Family Adjustment. 1919. Study of Americanization. Box 1, folder 16, Sophonisba Breckinridge Papers, University of Chicago.

Massachusetts Society for the Prevention of Cruelty to Children. 1909, 1910, 1914, 1921, 1926, 1927. Annual reports. Collection 2, box 257, Archives and Special Collections, Healey Library, University of Massachusetts, Boston.

Memorandum to teachers of casework in the Association of Schools of Social Work. Box 18, folder 6, Edith and Grace Abbott Papers, Department of Special Collections, Joseph Regenstein Library, University of Chicago.

Minneapolis Family Welfare Association. 1909, 1912. Annual reports. Social Welfare History Archives, Walters Library, University of Minnesota.

————. 1917–26. Family Welfare Association in action. Social Welfare History Archives, Walters Library, University of Minnesota.

Osborne, Thos. 1904–5. Organized charity. *Proceedings of the Kentucky State Conference on Charities and Corrections.* Special Collections, Margaret I. King Library, University of Kentucky, Lexington.

Pine Mountain Settlement School Archives. Berea College Microfilm Collection, Berea, Ky.

Other Sources

Abbott, Andrew. 1995. Boundaries of social work or social work of boundaries? *Social Service Review* 69(3): 545–62.

Abramovitz, Mimi. 1989. *Regulating the lives of women: Social welfare policy from colonial times to the present.* Boston: South End Press.

Agee, James. 1939 [reprint 1988]. *Let us now praise famous men.* Boston: Houghton Mifflin.

Alcoff, Linda. 1991–92. The problem of speaking for others. *Cultural Critique* 20 (Winter): 5–32.

Anderson, Nels. 1923. *The hobo: The sociology of the homeless man.* Chicago: University of Chicago Press.

Aronovici, Carol. 1916. Wider use of case records. In *Proceedings of the National Conference of Charities and Correction,* 468–73. Chicago: Hildmann Publishers.

Badding, Nancy. 1989. Client involvement in case recording. *Social Casework: The Journal of Contemporary Social Work* 70 (Nov.): 539–48.

Bain, Read. 1925. The impersonal confession and social research. *Journal Of Applied Sociology* 9(4): 356–61.

Bazerman, Charles, and James Paradis, eds. 1991. *Textual dynamics of the professions: Historical and contemporary studies of writing in professional communities.* Madison: University of Wisconsin Press.

Beattie, Anna. 1925. A fiction reading list. *The Family* 6(1): 24–25.

Bedford, Caroline. 1921. Methods of assembling material. In *Proceedings of the National Conference of Social Work,* 247–49. Chicago: University of Chicago Press.

———. 1924. The daily log. *The Family* 4(10): 239–44.

Berg, Barbara. 1978. *The remembered gate: Orgins of American feminism.* New York: Oxford University Press.

Bernheimer, Charles, and Claire Kahane, eds. 1990. In *Dora's case: Freud-hysteria-feminism.* New York: Columbia University Press.

Billings, Dwight, and Kathleen Blee. 1996. "'Where the sun set crimson and the moon rose red': Writing Appalachian and Kentucky mountain feuds." *Southern Cultures* 2(3–4): 329–52.

Bing, Lucia Johnson. 1923. What the public thinks of social work. In *Proceedings of the National Conference of Social Work,* 483–87. Chicago: University of Chicago Press.

Blauvelt, Mary Taylor. 1901. The race problem as discussed by Negro women. *American Journal of Sociology* 6 (March): 662–72.

Bliss, George. 1916. The danger of classifying as merely backward children who are feebleminded. In *Proceedings of the National Conference of Charities and Correction,* 263–66. Chicago: Hildmann Publishers.

Booth, William. 1890. *In darkest England and the way out.* London: International Headquarters of the Salvation Army.

Bordin, Ruth. 1981. *Women and temperance: The search for power and liberty, 1873–1900*. Philadelphia: Temple University Press.

Bowen, Georgia. 1924. Interpretative publicity as a function of social work: What part can the federation take in its development? In *Proceedings of the National Conference of Social Work*, 504–9. Chicago: University of Chicago Press.

Bowman, LeRoy. 1923. How far has social work influenced public opinion: What the press thinks of social work. In *Proceedings of the National Conference of Social Work*, 477–83. Chicago: University of Chicago Press.

Boyer, Paul. 1978. *Urban masses and moral order in America, 1820–1920*. Cambridge: Harvard University Press.

Braungard, Marion. 1929. Clinical field work in social service as presented in the psychological clinic at the University of Pennsylvania. *The Psychological Clinic* 18(5): 133–46.

Brecknridge, Sophonisba. 1921. *Madeline McDowell Breckinridge: A leader in the new south*. Chicago: University of Chicago Press.

———. 1924. *Family welfare work: Selected case records*. Chicago: University of Chicago Press.

Bremner, Robert. 1956a [reprint 1972]. *From the depths: The discovery of poverty in the United States*. 1956. New York: New York University Press.

———. 1956b. Scientific philanthropy, 1873–1893. *Social Service Review* 30 (June): 168–73.

Brenzel, Barbara. 1980. Domestication as reform: A study of the socialization of wayward girls, 1856–1905. *Harvard Educational Review* 50(2): 196–213.

———. 1983. *Daughters of the state: A social portrait of the first reform school for girls in North America, 1856–1905*. Cambridge: MIT Press.

Brisley, Mary. 1924. An attempt to articulate processes. *The Family* 5(6): 157–61.

Bristol, Margaret Cochran. 1936. *Handbook on social case recording*. Chicago: University of Chicago Press.

Broder, Sherri. 1988. Informing the "cruelty." *Radical America* 21 (4):34–47.

Brodhead, Richard. 1993. *Cultures of letters: Scenes of writings and reading in nineteenth-century America*. Chicago: University of Chicago Press.

Brown, Elsa Barkley. 1989. Womanist consciousness: Maggie Lena Walker and the independent order of Saint Luke. *Signs* 14(3): 610–33.

Brown, Esther L. 1938. *Social work as a profession*. New York: Russell Sage Foundation.

Brown, JoAnne. 1986. Professional language: Words that succeed. *Radical History Review* 34: 33–51.

———. 1991. Mental measurements and the rhetorical force of numbers. In *The estate of social knowledge*, 134–51. Edited by JoAnne Brown and David VanKeuren. Baltimore: John Hopkins University Press.

Brown, John. 1926. Publicity versus propaganda in family work. *The Family* 7(3): 75–79.

Brown, Josephine. 1933. *The rural community and social casework*. New York: Family Welfare Association of America.

Bruno, Frank. 1916. What a case record is for. In *Proceedings of the National Conference of Charities and Correction,* 452–60. Chicago: Hildmann Publishers.

———. 1926. Objective tests in case work. *The Family* 7(6): 183–86.

———. 1928. Some case work recording limitations of verbatim reporting. *Social Forces* 6(4): 532–34.

———. 1936. *The theory of social work.* Boston: Heath.

———. 1948 [reprint 1957]. *Trends in social work, 1874–1956.* New York: Columbia University Press.

Bulmer, Martin. 1991. The decline of the social survey movement and the rise of American empirical sociology. In *The social survey in historical perspective, 1880–1940,* 291–315. Edited by Martin Bulmer, Kevin Bales, and Kathryn Kish Sklar. Cambridge: Cambridge University Press.

Bulmer, Martin, Kevin Bales, and Kathryn Kish Sklar. 1991. The social survey in historical perspective. In *The social survey in historical perspective, 1880–1940,* 1–48. Edited by Martin Bulmer, Kevin Bales, and Kathryn Kish Sklar. Cambridge: Cambridge University Press.

A bundle or a boost. 1915. *Charity Organization Bulletin* 6(2): 17–21.

Burgess, Ernest. 1928. What case records should contain to be useful for sociological interpretation. *Social Forces* 6(4): 524–32.

Burke, Kenneth. 1969. *A grammar of motives.* Berkeley: University of California Press.

Burleigh, Edith, and Frances Harris. 1923. *The delinquent girl.* New York: New York School of Social Work.

Byars, Lauretta, and Karen Tice. 1992. The politics of difference: Race and class differences among women reformers in a southern community. Presented at the Council on Social Work Education, Kansas City.

Byerly, Victoria. 1986. *Hard times cotton mill girls: Personal histories of womanhood and poverty in the south.* Ithaca: ILR Press.

Cabot, Richard. 1911 [reprint 1970]. Social work and nursing. In *The child in the city,* 25–40. Edited by Sophinisba Breckinridge. New York: Arno Press.

———. 1919. *Social work: Essays on the meeting-ground of doctor and social worker.* Boston: Houghton Mifflin.

Calkins, Clinch. 1930. *Some folks won't work.* New York: Harcourt, Brace.

Campbell, Helen, Thomas Knox, and Thomas Byrnes. 1893. *Darkness and daylight; or, Lights and shadows of New York life.* Hartford: A. D. Worthington.

Campbell, Marie. 1992. Administering child protection: A feminist analysis of the conceptual practices of organizational power. *Canadian Public Administration* 35(4): 501–18.

———. Embodied knowledge. 1993. *The Women's Review of Books* 10(5): 24–25.

Cannon, Mary Antionette, and Philip Klein. 1933. *Social casework: An outline for teaching.* New York: Columbia University Press.

Cappetti, Carla. 1993. *Writing Chicago: Modernism, ethnography, and the novel.* New York: Columbia University Press.

Carby, Hazel V. 1992. Policing the black women's body in an urban context. *Critical Inquiry* 18(Summer): 738–55.

Carstens, C. C. 1927. Child welfare work since the White House conference. In *Proceedings of the National Conference of Social Work,* 122–31. Chicago: University of Chicago Press.

Case monographs of South Italians. 1917. *Charity Organization Bulletin* 8 (Sept.): 98–131.

Chambers, Clarke. 1963. *Seedtime of reform: American social service and social action, 1918–1933.* Minneapolis: University of Minnesota Press.

————. 1986. Women in the creation of the profession of social work. *Social Service Review* 60(1): 1–34.

Chapin, Stuart, and Stuart Queen, eds. 1937 [reprint 1972]. *Research memorandum on social work in the depression.* Bulletin 39, Social Science Research Council. New York: Arno Press.

Charities and Commons. 1909. To change the name of charities and the commons. *Charities and the Commons,* March 27, 1251–53.

Charon, Rita. 1992. To build a case: Medical histories as traditions in conflict. *Literature and Medicine* 11(1): 115–32.

Childrey, Rachel. 1933. Case recording: A committee report. *The Family* 13(9): 299–301.

Clark, Jane. 1926. The adolescent terminology of social work. *Journal of Applied Sociology* 11(1): 32–37.

Clement, Priscilla Ferguson. 1992. Nineteenth-century welfare policy, programs, and poor women: Philadelphia as a case study. *Feminist Studies* 18(1): 35–37.

Cohen, Sol. 1983. The mental hygiene movement, the development of personality, and the school: The medicalization of American education. *History of Education Quarterly* 23(2): 123–49.

Cohen, Steven R. 1991. The Pittsburgh survey and the social survey movement: A sociological road not taken. In *The social survey in historical perspective, 1880–1940,* 245–68. Edited by Martin Bulmer, Kevin Bales, and Kathryn Kish Sklar. Cambridge: Cambridge University Press.

Colcord, Joanna. 1927. Case work in 1926. *The Family* 8(1): 12–15.

————. 1928–29. A study of the techniques of the social work interview. *Social Forces* 7 (Sept.-June): 519–27.

————. 1930. Strengths of family life. *The Family* 11(7): 211–16.

Colcord, Joanna, and Ruth Mann, eds. 1930. *The long view: Papers and addresses of Mary Richmond.* New York: Russell Sage Foundation.

Collins, Pat Hill. 1990. *Black feminist thought: Knowledge, consciousness, and the politics of empowerment.* Boston: Unwin Hyman.

Committee on Cooperation of Women in the Management of Charitable, Penal, and Correctional Institutions. 1891. Discussion on cooperation of women. In *Proceedings of the National Conference of Charities and Correction,* 337–45. Boston: Geo. H. Ellis Press.

Conyngton, Mary Katherine. 1913. *How to help: A manual of practical charity.* New York: Macmillan.

Cowger, Charles. 1994. Assessing clients' strengths: Clinical assessment for client empowerment. *Social Work* 39(3): 262–68.

Crawford, T. Hugh. 1992. The politics of narrative form. *Literature and Medicine* 11(1): 147–62.

Crocker, Ruth Hutchinson. 1992. *Social work and social order: The settlement movement in two industrial cities, 1889–1930.* Urbana: University of Illinois Press.

Cumber, John. 1988. The politics of charity: Gender and class in late-nineteenth-century charity policy. *Journal of Social History* 14(1): 99–111.

Davidson, Jean, with the women of Mutira. 1989. *Voices from Mutira: Lives of rural Gikuyu women.* Boulder: Lynne Rienner Publishers.

Davis, Natalie Zemon. 1987. *Fiction in the archives: Pardon tales and their tellers in sixteenth-century France.* Stanford: Stanford University Press.

Deardorff, Neva R. 1925. The objectives of professional organization. In *Proceedings of the National Conference of Social Work,* 636–43. Chicago: University of Chicago Press.

Deegan, Mary Jo. 1988. *Jane Addams and the men of the Chicago school, 1892–1918.* New Brunswick: Transaction Books.

de Marneffe, Daphne. 1991. Looking and listening: The construction of clinical knowledge in Charcot and Freud. *Signs* 17(1): 71–111.

D'Emilio, John, and Estelle B. Freedman. 1988. *Intimate matters: A history of sexuality in America.* New York: Harper and Row.

de Schweinitz, Karl. 1915–16. Some reflections upon a clinical examination of the "annual report" as a social document. *The Survey* 35 (Oct.-March): 509–10.

Devine, Edward. 1901. Principles and method in charity. In *Proceedings of the National Conference of Charities and Correction,* 321–34. Boston: Geo. H. Ellis Press.

———. 1914. *The principles of relief.* New York: Macmillan.

———. 1939. *When social work was young.* New York: Macmillan.

Dewson, Mary. 1911 [reprint 1970]. Probation and institutional care of girls. In *The child in the city,* 355–70. Edited by Sophonisba Breckinridge. New York: Arno Press.

Dixon, Elizabeth, and Grace Browning. 1938. *Social case records: Family welfare.* Chicago: University of Chicago Press.

Donahue, A. Madorah. 1917. The case of an unmarried mother who has cared for her child and succeeded. In *Proceedings of the National Conference of Social Work,* 282–87. Chicago: Rogers and Hall.

Dugdale, L. Robert. 1875 [reprint 1910]. *The Jukes: A study in crime, pauperism, disease, and heredity.* 4th ed. New York: G. P. Putnam.

Duggan, Lisa. 1993. The trials of Alice Mitchell: Sensationalism, sexology, and the lesbian subject in turn-of-the-century America. *Signs* 18 (Summer): 791–814.

Dunham, Esther. 1930. Scattered-brained Sally. *The Survey* 64 (July 15): 362–63.

Edwards, Richard, and William Reid. 1989. Structured case recording in child welfare: An assessment of social workers' reactions. *Social Work* 34(1): 49–52.

Eliot, Thomas. 1928. Objectivity and subjectivity in the case record. *Social Forces* 6(4): 539–44.

Ehrenreich, John. 1985. *The altruistic imagination: A history of social work and social policy in the United States.* Ithaca: Cornell University Press.

Epstein, Barbara Leslie. 1981. *The politics of domesticity: Women, evangelism, and temperance in nineteenth-century America.* Middletown: Wesleyan University Press, 1981.

Estabrook, Arthur H. 1923. The Jukes in 1915. In *Social problems and social policy,* 376–92. Edited by James Ford. Boston: Ginn.

Estabrook, Arthur, and C. Davenport. 1912. *The Nam family.* New York: Eugenics Records Office.

Falconer, Martha. 1915. Social hygiene: Report of the committee. In *Proceedings of the National Conference of Charities and Corrections,* 241–52. Chicago: Hildmann Publishers.

Farmer, Gertrude L. 1921. *A form of record for hospital social work.* Philadelphia: J. B. Lippincott.

Field, Martha Heineman. 1980. Social casework practice during the psychiatric deluge. *Social Service Review* 54(4): 482–507.

Fields, Mamie Garvin, and Karen Fields. 1983 [reprint 1985]. *Lemon Swamp and other places: A Carolina memoir.* New York: Free Press.

Flexner, Abraham. 1915. Is social work a profession? In *Proceedings of the National Conference of Charities and Correction,* 576–90. Chicago: Hildmann Publishers.

Foucault, Michel. 1978. *The history of sexuality: An introduction.* New York: Pantheon.

———. 1979. *Discipline and punish: The birth of the prison.* New York: Vintage Books.

Fowler, Rosalie. 1922. Motion picture shows and school girls. *Journal of Applied Sociology* 7(2): 76–83.

Francis, Vida Hunt. 1906. The delinquent girl. In *Proceedings of the National Conference of Charities and Correction,* 138–45. N.p.: Fred Herr Press.

Frankel, Noralee, and Nancy Dye, eds. 1991. *Gender, class, race, and reform in the progressive era.* Lexington: University of Kentucky Press.

Fraser, Nancy. 1989. *Unruly practices: Power, discourse and gender in contemporary social theory.* Minneapolis: University of Minnesota Press.

Freud, Sigmund. 1905. Dora: Fragment of an analysis of a case of hysteria. In *The Complete Psychological Works of Sigmund Freud,* vol. 3. Edited by James Strachey. London: Hogarth Press.

Funiciello, Theresa. 1993. *The tyranny of kindness: Dismantling the welfare system to end poverty in America.* New York: Atlantic Monthly Press.

Geertz, Clifford. 1988. *Works and lives: The anthropologist as author.* Stanford: Stanford University Press, 1988.

Gelman, Sheldon. 1992. Risk management through client access to case records. *Social Work* 37(1): 73–79.

Giddings, Paula. 1984. *When and where I enter: The impact of black women on race and sex in America.* New York: William Morrow.

Gieryn, Thomas. 1983. Boundary-work and the demarcation of science from non-science: Strains and interests in professional ideologies of scientists. *American Sociological Review* 48 (Dec.): 781–95.

Gilfoyle, Timothy J. 1986. The moral origins of political surveillance: The preventive society in New York City, 1867–1918. *American Quarterly* 38(4): 637–52.

Ginzberg, Lori. 1990. *Women and the work of benevolence: Morality, politics, and class in the nineteenth-century United States.* New Haven: Yale University Press.

Glenn, Mrs. John. 1913. Case work disciplines and ideals. In *Proceedings of the National Conference of Charities and Correction,* 353–62. Chicago: Hildmann Publishers.

Glueck, Bernard. 1919. Special preparation of the psychiatric social worker. In *Proceedings of the National Conference of Social Work,* 599–606. Chicago: Rogers and Hall.

Goddard, Henry. 1916. *The Kallikak family.* New York: Macmillan.

Goldstein, Howard. 1992. If social work hasn't made progress as a science, might it be an art? *Families in Society: The Journal of Contemporary Human Services* 73(1): 48–55.

Goodman, Nelson. 1981. Twisted tales; or, Story, study, and symphony. In *On narrative.* Chicago: University of Chicago Press.

Gordon, Linda. 1988. *Heroes of their own lives: The politics and history of family violence.* New York: Penguin Books.

———. 1991. Black and white visions of welfare: Women's welfare activism. *Journal of American History* 78(2): 559–90.

———. 1994. *Pitied but not entitled: Single mothers and the history of welfare, 1890–1935.* New York: Free Press.

Gorman, Jane. 1993. Postmodernism and the conduct of inquiry in social work. *Affilia* 8(3): 247–64.

Graves, W. Brooks. 1930. The factual basis of social work publicity. In *Proceedings of the National Conference of Social Work,* 583–96. Chicago: University of Chicago Press.

Green, Byron. 1983. *Knowing the poor: A case-study in textual reality construction.* London: Routledge and Kegan Paul.

"Growing pains": Diary of a family welfare secretary. 1934. *The Family* 15(8): 263–67.

Gusfield, Joseph. 1976. The literary rhetoric of science: Comedy and pathos in drinking driver research. *American Sociological Review* 41 (Feb.): 16–34.

Guy-Sheftall, Beverly. 1990. *Daughters of sorrow: Attitudes towards black women.* Brooklyn: Carlson Publishing.

Hacking, Ian. 1986. Making up people. In *Reconstructing individualism: Autonomy, individuality, and self in western thought,* 222–36. Edited by Thomas Heller, Sosna Morton, and David Wellbery. Stanford: Stanford University Press.

Hagerty, James Edwards. 1931. *The training of social workers.* New York: McGraw-Hill.

Hamilton, Etta. 1925. Beauty and case work. *The Family* 6(7): 196–99.

Hamilton, Gordon. 1923. Progress in social casework. In *Proceedings of the National Conference of Social Work,* 334–37. Chicago: University of Chicago Press.

————. 1936. *Social case recording.* New York: Columbia University Press.

Hardwick, Katherine. 1922. Minimum educational requirements which should be demanded of those beginning family case work. In *Proceedings of the National Conference of Social Work,* 245–53. Chicago: University of Chicago Press.

Hardy, Sophie. 1926. What measures have we for growth in personality? *The Family* 7(8): 254–58.

Hartman, Ann. 1992. In search of subjugated knowledges. *Social Work* 37(6): 483–84.

Haskell, Thomas. 1984. *The authority of experts: Study in history and theory.* Bloomington: Indiana University Press.

Haskins, Anna. 1923. Progress in social case work in child welfare. In *Proceedings of the National Conference of Social Work,* 339–41. Chicago: University of Chicago Press.

Hazelton, Mabel. 1927. The picture behind the record. *The Family* 7(9): 283–85.

Healy, William. 1917. The bearings of psychology on social case work. In *Proceedings of the National Conference of Social Work,* 104–12. Chicago: Rogers and Hall.

————. 1921. Problems of mental subnormality in family social work. In *Proceedings of the National Conference of Social Work,* 268–72. Chicago: University of Chicago Press.

————. 1929. *Reconstructing behavior in youth: A study of problem children in foster families.* New York: Alfred A. Knopf.

Herrnstein-Smith, Barbara. 1981. Narrative versions, narrative theories. *On Narrative,* 209–32. Edited by W. J. T. Mitchell. Chicago: University of Chicago Press.

Herzfeld, Elsa. 1905 [reprint 1978]. Close-range studies of darkest New York. In *Women: Their changing roles.* The Great Contemporary Issues Series. New York: Arno Press.

Hewins, Katherine. 1916. Shaping the record to facilitate research. In *Proceedings of the National Conference of Charities and Correction,* 460–68. Chicago: Hildmann Publishers.

Hewitt, Nancy. 1984. *Women's activism and social change: Rochester, New York, 1822–1872.* Ithaca: Cornell University Press.

————. 1990. Charity or mutual aid? Two perspectives on Latin women's philanthropy in Tampa, Florida. In *Lady bountiful revisited: Women, philanthropy, and power,* 55–69. Edited by Kathleen McCarthy. New Brunswick: Rutgers University Press.

Higginbotham, Evelyn Brooks. 1992. African-American women's history and the metalanguage of race. *Signs* 17(2): 251–74.

Hine, Lewis. 1909. Social photography: How the camera may help in social uplift. In *Proceedings of the National Conference of Charities and Correction,* 355–59. Fort Wayne: Fort Wayne Printing.

Hobson, Barbara Meil. 1987. *Uneasy virtue: The politics of prostitution and the American reform tradition.* New York: Basic Books.

Hodder, Jessie. 1920. Disciplinary measures in the management of the psychopathic delinquent woman. In *Proceedings of the National Conference of Social Work,* 389–96. Chicago: University of Chicago Press.

Hodson, William. 1925. Is social work professional? A re-examination of the question. In *Proceedings of the National Conference of Social Work*, 629–36. Chicago: University of Chicago Press.

Hoffman, L. 1990. Constructing realities: An art of lens. *Family Process* 29: 1–12.

Holbrook, Terry. 1983. Case records: Fact or fiction? *Social Service Review* 57(4): 645–58.

———. 1995. Finding subjugated knowledge: Personal document research. *Social Work* 40(6): 746–51.

Holland, Thomas. 1991. Narrative, knowledge, and professional practice. *Social Thought* 17(1): 32–40.

Holloran, Peter. 1994. *Boston's wayward children: Social services for homeless children, 1830–1930*. Boston: Northeastern University Press.

Holt, George. 1891. The relation of charity organization to social problems. In *Proceedings of the National Conference of Charities and Correction*, 118–23. Boston: Geo. H. Ellis Press.

hooks, bell. 1981. *Ain't I a woman? Black women and feminism*. Boston: South End Press.

Horn, Margo. 1989. *Before it's too late: The child guidance movement in the United States, 1922–1945*. Philadelphia: Temple University Press.

Hull, Ida. 1914. South Italians. *Charity Organization Bulletin* 6(1): 2–17.

Hunter, Kathryn Montgomery. 1992. Remaking the case. *Literature and Medicine* 11(1): 163–79.

Hutcheon, Linda. 1989. *The politics of postmodernism*. New York: Routledge.

Jarrett, Mary. 1919. The psychiatric thread running through all social case work. In *Proceedings of the National Conference of Social Work*, 587–93. Chicago: Rogers and Hall.

Johnson, Alexander. 1923. *Adventures in social welfare*. Fort Wayne: Fort Wayne Printing.

Johnson, Fred. 1916. Case records: Discussion. In *Proceedings of the National Conference of Charities and Correction*, 471–72. Chicago: Hildmann Publishers.

Joint Committee on Methods of Preventing Delinquency. 1926. *Three problem children: Narratives from the case records of a child guidance clinic*. New York: Joint Committee on Methods of Preventing Delinquency.

Kagle, Jill Doner. 1984. *Social work records*. Chicago: Dorsey Press.

———. 1993. Record-keeping: Directions for the 1990s. *Social Work* 38(2): 190–96.

Kahn, Dorothy. 1929. The limitations of domestic discord case records for research. *Social Forces* 7(4): 512–15.

Karpf, Maurice. 1931. *The scientific basis of social work: A study in family case work*. New York: Columbia University Press.

Katz, Michael. 1986. *In the shadow of the poorhouse: A social history of welfare in America*. New York: Basic Books.

Keiser, Laura Jean. 1927. Analysis of an interview. *The Family* 8(1): 17–20.

Kellogg, Charles. 1893. Charity organization in the United States: Report on the history of charity organization. In *Proceedings of the National Conference of Charities and Correction*, 52–93. Boston: Geo. H. Ellis Press.

Kempton, Helen. 1932. First contact and social history. *The Family* 13(4): 111–15.

Kline, Lila. 1922. The personal psychiatric history. *Mental Hygiene* 6(1): 70–124.

Konrad, George. 1969 [reprint 1978]. *The case worker.* Translated by Paul Aston. New York: Harvest/HBJ.

Koren, John. 1908. Statistics: Report of the committee. In *Proceedings of the National Conference of Charities and Correction,* 214–19. Fort Wayne: Fort Wayne Printing.

Kuhn, Thomas. 1970. *The structure of scientific revolutions.* Chicago: University of Chicago Press.

Kunzel, Regina. 1988. Professionalization of benevolence: Evangelicals and social workers in the Florence Crittenton homes, 1915–1945. *Journal of Social History* 22(1): 21–43.

———. 1993. *Fallen women, problem girls: Unmarried mothers and the professionalization of social work, 1890–1945.* New Haven: Yale University Press.

———. 1995. Pulp fictions and problem girls: Reading and rewriting single pregnancy in the postwar United States. *American Historical Review* 100(5): 1465–87.

Kutchins, Herb, and Stuart Kirk. 1988. The business of diagnosis: DSM-III and clinical social work. *Social Work* 33(3): 215–20.

Ladd-Taylor, Molly. 1994. *Mother-work: Women, child welfare, and the state, 1890–1930.* Urbana: University of Illinois Press.

Larson, Magali Sarfatti. 1984. The production of expertise and the constitution of expert power. In *The authority of experts: Studies in history and theory,* 28–80. Edited by Thomas Haskell. Bloomington: Indiana University Press.

Lasch-Quinn, Elizabeth. 1993. *Black neighbors: Race and the limits of reform in the settlement house movement, 1890–1945.* Chapel Hill: University of North Carolina Press.

Lawton, Ruth W., and J. Prentice Murphy. 1915. A study of results of a child-placing agency. In *Proceedings of the National Conference of Charities and Correction,* 164–74. Chicago: Hildmann Publishers.

Leader, Pauline. 1932. *And no birds sing.* London: Routledge.

Lee, Judith. 1980. The helping professional's use of language in describing the poor. *American Journal of Orthopsychiatry* 50(Oct.): 580–84.

Lee, Porter. 1920. Providing teaching materials. In *Proceedings of the National Conference of Social Work,* 465–73. Chicago: University of Chicago Press.

Leiby, James. 1978. *A history of social welfare and social work in the United States.* New York: Columbia University Press.

Leighninger, Leslie. 1987. *Social work: Search for identity.* New York: Greenwood Press.

Leighninger, Robert, Leslie Leighninger, and Robert Pankin. 1974. Sociology and social work: Science and art? *Journal of Sociology and Social Welfare* 1 (Winter): 81–89.

Lewis, Oscar. 1966. The culture of poverty. *Scientific American* 215(4): 19–25.

Lewis, Ruth. 1931. A medical case record form. *The Family* 12(3): 72–73.

Lewis, Sinclair. 1933. *Ann Vickers.* Garden City: Doubleday, Doran.

Lies, Eugene. 1914. The family and the community: Report of the committee: Charity organization ideals. In *Proceedings of the National Conference of Charities and Correction,* 62–68. Fort Wayne: Fort Wayne Printing.

Lowrey, Lawson. 1928. The contribution of mental hygiene to the differentiated fields. In *Proceedings of the National Conference of Social Work,* 360–66. Chicago: University of Chicago Press.

Lowry, Fern. 1939. *Readings in social casework, 1920–38: Selected reprints for casework practitioners.* New York: Columbia University Press.

Lubove, Roy. 1973. *The professional altruist: The emergence of social work as a career, 1880–1930.* 4th ed. New York: Atheneum.

Lunbeck, Elizabeth. 1994. *The psychiatric persuasion: Knowledge, gender and power in modern America.* Princeton: Princeton University Press.

Lyons, Suzie. 1920. The training of social service workers in psychiatric field work. In *Proceedings of the National Conference of Social Work,* 396–98. Chicago: University of Chicago Press.

MacIver, R. M. 1931. *The contribution of sociology to social work.* New York: Columbia University Press.

Magnuson, Norris. 1977. *Salvation in the slums: Evangelical social work, 1865–1920.* New York: Scarecrow Press and American Theological Library Association.

Malcolm, Janet. 1990. Reflecting: J'appelle un chat un chat. In *Dora's case: Freud-hysteria-feminism.* Edited by Charles Bernheimer and Claire Kahane. New York: Columbia University Press.

Marcus, George, and Michael Fischer. 1986. *Anthropology as cultural critique.* Chicago: University of Chicago Press.

Marcus, Grace. 1923. The psychiatric point of view in social work. *Mental Hygiene* 7(4): 755–61.

———. 1929. *Some aspects of relief in family casework: An evaluation of practice based on a study made for the New York Charity Organization Society.* New York: Charity Organization Society of New York.

Mastin, J. T. 1912. The prevention of juvenile dependency. In *Proceedings of the Southern Sociological Congress,* 44–51. Nashville: Brandau-Craig Dickerson.

Matthews, Nancy. 1995. Feminist clashes with the state: Tactical choices by state funded rape crisis centers. In *Feminist organizations: Harvest of the new women's movement,* 295–305. Edited by Myra Marx Ferree and Patricia Yancey Martin. Philadelphia: Temple University Press.

Mayer, John E., and Noel Timms. 1970. *The client speaks: Working-class impressions of casework.* New York: Atherton Press.

McCulloch, Oscar. 1888. The tribe of Ishmael: A study in social degradation. In *Proceedings of the National Conference of Charities and Correction,* 154–59. Boston: Geo. H. Ellis Press.

McLean, Francis. 1908. How may we increase our standard of efficiency in dealing with needy families? In *Proceedings of the National Conference of Charities and Correction*, 99–110. Fort Wayne: Fort Wayne Printing.

Menchu, Rigoberta. 1984. *I, Rigoberta Menchu: An Indian woman in Guatemala*. Edited by Elizabeth Burgos-Debray. Translated by Ann Wright. New York: Verso.

Meyerowitz, Joanne. 1991. *Women adrift: Independent wage earners in Chicago, 1880–1930*. Chicago: University of Chicago Press.

Miner, Maude E. 1915. The Girls' Protective League. In *Proceedings of the National Conference of Charities and Correction*, 260–67. Chicago: Hildmann Publishers.

Minh-ha, Trinh T. 1989. *Woman, native, other: Writing postcoloniality and feminism*. Bloomington: Indiana University Press.

———. 1992. *Framer framed*. New York: Routledge.

Moi, Toril. 1990. Representation of patriarchy: Sexuality and epistemology in Freud's Dora. In *Dora's case: Freud-hysteria-feminism*, ed. Charles Bernheimer and Claire Kahane, 181–99. New York: Columbia University Press.

Monroe, William Frank, Warren Lee Holleman, and Cline Marsha Holleman. 1992. Is there a person in this case? *Literature and Medicine* 11(1): 45–63.

Moore, Elon. 1934. How accurate are case records? *Social Forces* 12(4): 498–507.

Moore, Madeline. 1927. Though not by bread alone. *The Family* 8(6): 186–89.

Mort, Frank. 1987. *Dangerous sexualities: Medico-moral politics in England since 1830*. New York: Routledge and Kegan Paul.

Muncy, Robyn. 1991. *Creating a female dominion in American reform, 1890–1935*. New York: Oxford University Press.

Munro, Marguerite. 1951. Modern casework recording: Integrating casework and supervision through case records. *Social Work Journal* 32(4): 184–97.

Murray, Virginia. 1920. The runaway girl and the stranded girl. In *Proceedings of the National Conference of Social Work*, 175–80. Chicago: University of Chicago Press.

Myrick, Helen. 1924. Methods employed in an experiment in advising a general social casework agency on psychiatric social problems. *Mental Hygiene* 8(2): 522–29.

———. 1926. Cross examination and case work interviewing: An art. *The Family* 7(4): 121–24.

Neverdon-Morton, Cynthia. 1989. *Afro-American women of the south and the advancement of the race*. Knoxville: University of Tennessee Press.

Newton, Hazel. 1930. Miss case-worker goes scientific. *The Survey* 63(8): 464–65.

Nord, Deborah Epstein. 1987. The social explorer as anthropologist: Victorian travellers among the urban poor. In *Visions of the modern city: Essays in history, art, and literature*, 122–34. Edited by William Sharpe and Leonard Wallock. Baltimore: Johns Hopkins University Press.

Odem, Mary. 1991. Single mothers, delinquent daughters, and the juvenile court in early twentieth-century Los Angeles. *Journal of Social History* 25(1): 27–43.

————. 1995. *Delinquent daughters: Protecting and policing adolescent female sexuality in the United States.* Chapel Hill: University of North Carolina Press.

O'Donnell, Sandra. 1994. The care of dependent African-American children in Chicago: The struggle between black self-help and professionalism. *Journal of Social History* 27(4):763–76.

Odum, Howard. 1923. The scientific journal of interpretation. In *Proceedings of the National Conference of Social Work,* 487–92. Chicago: University of Chicago Press.

Oppenheimer, John. 1925. *The visiting teacher movement.* 2d ed. New York: Joint Committee on Methods and Delinquency.

Paradise, Viola. 1923. Behind the statistic. In *Proceedings of the National Conference of Social Work,* 314–21. Chicago: University of Chicago Press.

————. 1932. Creative writing for social work. In *Proceedings of the National Conference of Social Work,* 575–88. Chicago: University of Chicago Press.

Pascoe, Peggy. 1990. *Relations of rescue: The search for female moral authority in the American west, 1874–1939.* New York: Oxford University Press.

Peiss, Kathy. 1986. *Cheap amusements: Working women and leisure in turn-of-the-century New York.* Philadelphia: Temple University Press.

Personal Narratives Group. 1989. *Interpreting women's lives: Feminist theory and personal narratives.* Bloomington: Indiana University Press.

Phelps, Harold. 1927. The case record and scientific method. *The Family* 8(4): 103–9.

Pleck, Elizabeth. 1987. *Domestic tyranny: The making of social policy against family violence from colonial times to the present.* New York: Oxford University Press.

Poirier, Suzanne, Lorie Rosenblum, Lioness Ayres, Daniel J. Brauner, Barbara F. Sharf, and Ann Folwell Stanford. 1992. Charting the chart: An exercise in interpretations(s). *Literature and Medicine* 11(1): 1–22.

Pollock, Griselda. 1988. Vicarious excitements. *New Formations* 2 (Spring): 25–50.

Powers, Margaret. 1920. The industrial cost of a psychopathic employee. In *Proceedings of the National Conference of Social Work,* 342–46. Chicago: University of Chicago Press.

Pozatek, Ellie. 1994. The problem of certainty: Clinical social work in the postmodern era. *Social Work* 39(4): 396–404.

Preston, George. 1927. The view from the fence. *The Family* 8(7): 233–34.

Price, Frances. 1929. The need for standardization of family case records for research purposes. *Social Forces* 7 (4): 516–18.

Pruette, Lorine. 1928. The family and the modern novel. *The Family* 9(2): 46–50.

Queen, Stuart. 1927. Nonstatisical studies of social work. In *Proceedings of the National Conference of Social Work,* 459–66. Chicago: University of Chicago Press.

Rabkin, Eric. 1986. A case of self-defense. *Literature and Medicine* 5(2): 43–53.

Ralph, Georgia. 1915. *Elements of record-keeping for child-helping organizations.* New York: Russell Sage Foundation.

Reed, T. V. 1988. Unimagined existence and the fiction of the real: Postmoderist realism in *Let us now praise famous men. Representations* 24 (Fall): 156–76.

Residents of Hull House. 1895. *Hull House maps and papers: A presentation of nationalities and wages in a congested district of Chicago, together with comments and essays on problems growing out of the social conditions.* Boston: Thomas Crowell.

Reynolds, Bertha Capen. 1963. *An uncharted journey: Fifty years of growth in social work.* Silver Springs: National Association of Social Workers Press.

Rice, Alice Caldwell Hegan. 1901. *Mrs. Wiggs of the cabbage patch.* New York: Century.

Richardson, Teresa. 1989. *The century of the child: The mental hygiene movement and social policy in the United States and Canada.* Albany: SUNY Press.

Richmond, Mary. 1901. The message of associated charities. In *Proceedings of the National Conference of Charities and Correction,* 327–29. Boston: Geo. H. Ellis Press.

Richmond, Mary. 1907. Friendly visiting. In *Proceedings of the National Conference of Charities and Correction,* 307–15. Fort Wayne: Fort Wayne Printing.

———. 1917. *Social diagnosis.* New York: Russell Sage Foundation.

———. 1922. *What is social case work?* New York: Russell Sage Foundation, 1922.

———. 1925. Why case records? *The Family* 6(7): 214–16.

———. 1930a. Case worker and client. In *The long view: The addresses and papers of Mary Richmond,* 385–96. Edited by Joanna Colcord and Ruth Mann. New York: Russell Sage.

———. 1930b. What is charity organization? In *The long view: The addresses and papers of Mary Richmond,* 131–43. Edited by Joanna Colcord and Ruth Mann. New York: Russell Sage.

Riessman, Catherine Kohler. 1987. When gender is not enough: Women interviewing women. *Gender and Society* 1(2): 172–207.

Riis, Jacob. 1890 [reprint 1957]. *How the other half lives: Studies among the tenements of New York.* New York: Hill and Wang.

———. 1902. *The battle with the slums.* New York: Macmillan.

Robinson, Virginia. 1921. Analysis of process in the records of family case working agencies. In *Proceedings of the National Conference of Social Work,* 253–56. Chicago: University of Chicago Press.

———. 1926. Case studies of the family for research purposes. *The Family* 6(10): 298–300.

———. 1930. *A changing psychology in social case work.* Chapel Hill: University of North Carolina Press.

Roof, Judith, and Robyn Wiegman. 1995. *Who can speak? Authority and critical identity.* Urbana: University of Illinois Press.

Rose. 1991. *From client to individual: Rose's story.* Milwaukee: Family Service America.

Rose, Henry. 1906. Discussion of needy families in their homes. In *Proceedings of the National Conference of Charities and Correction,* 504–14. N.p.: Fred Herr Press.

Ross, Dorothy. 1991. *The origins of American social science.* New York: Cambridge University Press.

Ross, Ellen. 1993. *Love and toil: Motherhood in outcast London, 1870–1918.* Oxford: Oxford University Press.

Routzahn, Evart, and Mary Swain Routzahn. 1918. *The ABC of exhibit planning.* New York: Russell Sage Foundation.

———. 1928. *Publicity for social work.* New York: Russell Sage Foundation.

Routzahn, Mary Swain. 1920. *Traveling publicity campaigns.* New York: Russell Sage Foundation.

———. 1928. Presenting mountain work to the public. *Mountain Life and Work* 4(July): 27–31.

———. 1931. Interpreting the social worker to the public. In *Proceedings of the National Conference of Social Work,* 541–50. Chicago: University of Chicago Press.

Russell, Mary. 1921. Possibilities of casework with colored families. *The Family* 2(3): 59–62.

Ryan, Mary. 1981. *Cradle of the middle class: The family in Oneida County, New York, 1790–1865.* New York: Cambridge University Press.

Sacks, Oliver. 1986. Clinical tales. *Literature and Medicine* 5(2): 16–23.

Said, Edward. 1979. *Orientalism.* New York: Vintage.

Saleebey, Dennis. 1994. Culture, theory, and narrative: The intersection of meanings in practice. *Social Work* 39(4): 351–61.

Salem, Dorothy. 1990. *To better our world: Black women in organized reform, 1890–1920.* New York: Carlson Publishing.

Salsberry, Pearl. 1927. Techniques in case work. *The Family* 8(5): 153–57.

———. 1933. The Family Welfare Association of Minneapolis. *Opportunity: Journal of Negro Life,* Oct., 294.

Salvation Army. 1912. Salvation Army world's mirror: What it is doing is shown by story of Diamond Dolly. *Social News* 2(6): 6–7.

Sayles, Mary, ed. 1932. *Child guidance cases.* New York: Commonwealth Fund.

Schafer, Roy. 1981. Narration in the psychoanalytic dialogue. In *On narrative,* 25–50. Edited by W. J. T. Mitchell. Chicago: University of Chicago Press.

Schlossman, Steven, and Stephanie Wallach. 1978. The crime of precocious sexuality: Female juvenile delinquency in the progressive era. *Harvard Educational Review* 48(1): 65–93.

Schneider, Eric. 1980. In the web of class: Youth, class, and culture in Boston, 1840–1940. Ph.D. dissertation, Boston University.

Scudson, Michael. 1978. *Discovering the news: A social history of American newspapers.* New York: Basic Books.

Sears, Amelia. 1921. Outline of the first interview. In *Proceedings of the National Conference of Social Work,* 249–52. Chicago: University of Chicago Press.

Sekula, Alan. 1986. The body and the archive. *October* (Winter):3–65.

Shaw, Clifford. 1930. *The jack roller: A delinquent boy's own story.* Chicago: University of Chicago Press, Behavior Research Fund Monographs.

Shaw, Edward. 1908. Publicity in charitable work from the newspaper point of view. In *Pro-

ceedings of the National Conference of Charities and Correction, 267–75. Fort Wayne: Fort Wayne Printing.

Sherman, Corinne. 1923. Racial factors in desertion. *The Family* 3(9): 221–24.

Sheffield, Ada Eliot. 1920. *The social case history: Its construction and content.* New York: Russell Sage Foundation.

———. 1921. Identifying clue-aspects in social case work. In *Proceedings of the National Conference of Social Work,* 242–47. Chicago: University of Chicago Press.

———. 1922. *Case study possibilities.* Boston: Boston Research Bureau on Social Case Work.

———. 1931. Gestalt and case study: The situation as a unit of family case study. *Social Forces* 9(4): 465–74.

———. 1937. *Social insight in case situations.* New York: D. Appleton-Century.

Shostak, Marjorie. 1983. *Nisa: The life and words of a Kung woman.* New York: Vintage Books.

Showalter, Elaine. 1990. *Sexual anarchy: Gender and culture at the* fin de siecle. New York: Penguin Books.

Shuman, Cora. 1915. The good girl with a first baby, who is not feeble-minded. In *Proceedings of the National Conference of Charities and Correction,* 114–15. Chicago: Hildmann Publishers.

Sklar, Kathryn Kish. 1991. Hull-House maps and papers: Social science as women's work in the 1890s. In *The social survey in historical perspective, 1880–1940,* 111–47. Edited by Martin Bulmer, Kevin Bales, and Kathryn Kish Sklar. Cambridge: Cambridge University Press.

Slingerland, W. H. 1919a. *Child placing in families: A manual for students and social workers.* New York: Russell Sage Foundation.

———. 1919b. *Child welfare work in Louisville: A study of conditions, agencies, and institutions.* Louisville: Welfare League.

Smith, Carrie Weaver. 1920. The unadjusted girl. In *Proceedings of the National Conference of Social Work,* 180–83. Chicago: University of Chicago Press.

Smith, Dorothy. 1990. *The conceptual practices of power: A feminist sociology of knowledge.* Boston: Northeastern University Press, 1990.

———. 1992. Sociology from women's experience: A reaffirmation. *Sociological Theory* 10(1): 88–98.

Smith, Virginia. 1891. The co-operation of women in philanthropic and reformatory work. In *Proceedings of the National Conference of Charities and Correction,* 230–41. Boston: Geo. H. Ellis Press.

Smith-Rosenberg, Carroll. 1986. *Disorderly conduct: Visions of gender in Victorian America.* Oxford: Oxford University Press.

Solenberger, Edwin. 1906. Relief work of the Salvation Army. In *Proceedings of the National Conference of Charities and Correction,* 349–66. N.p. Fred Herr Press.

———. 1910. Record of child placing agencies. In *Proceedings of the National Conference on Charities and Correction,* 123–31. Fort Wayne: Fort Wayne Printing.

Southard, E. E. 1919. The individual versus the family as a unit of interest in social work. In *Proceedings of the National Conference of Social Work,* 582–87. Chicago: Rogers and Hall.

Southard, E. E., and Mary Jarrett. 1922. *The kingdom of evils.* New York: Macmillan.

Spaulding, Edith. 1923. *An experimental study of psychopathic delinquent women.* New York: Published for the Bureau of Social Hygiene by Rand McNally.

Spivak, Gayatri. 1988. Can the subaltern speak? In *Marxism and interpretation of culture,* 271–313. Edited by Cary Nelson and Lawrence Grossberg. Urbana: University of Illinois Press.

Stadum, Beverly. 1987. Maybe they will appreciate what I done and struggled: Poor women and their families—charity cases in Minneapolis, 1900–1930. Ph.D dissertation, University of Minnesota.

———. 1990. A critique of family caseworkers 1900–1930: Women working with women. *Journal of Sociology and Social Welfare* 17(3): 73–102.

———. 1992. *Poor women and their families: Hard-working charity cases.* Ithaca: SUNY Press.

Stallybrass, Peter, and Allon White. 1986. *The politics and poetics of transgression.* Ithaca: Cornell University Press.

Stange, Maren. 1992. *Symbols of ideal life: Social documentary photography in America, 1890–1950.* New York: Cambridge University Press.

Stansell, Christine. 1987. *City of women: Sex and class in New York, 1789–1860.* Urbana: University of Illinois Press, 1987.

Steele, H. Wirt. 1908. Publicity in social work. In *Proceedings of the National Conference of Charities and Correction,* 262–67. Fort Wayne: Fort Wayne Printing.

Steiner, Jesse Frederick. 1921. *Education for social work.* Chicago: University of Chicago Press.

Stern, Leon. 1922. Heredity and environment: The Bilder clan. In *Proceedings of the National Conference of Social Work,* 179–89. Chicago: University of Chicago Press.

Stern, Leon, and Elizabeth Gertrude Stern. 1923. *A friend at court.* New York: Macmillan.

———. The one white lamb. In *A friend at court,* 162–74. New York: Macmillan.

Stewart, Henry. 1916. Elementary requirements of standardization and chief obstacles to be encountered. In *Proceedings of the National Conference of Social Work,* 329–36. Chicago: Hildmann Publishers.

Stillman, Charles. 1927. *Social work publicity: Its message and its methods.* New York: Century.

———. 1935. Responses of social work to changing conditions affecting it. *Journal of Social Forces* 13(4): 544–53.

Stott, William. 1973. *Documentary expression and thirties America.* New York: Oxford University Press.

Stowe, Steven. 1996. Seeing themselves at work: Physicians and the case narrative in the mid-nineteenth-century American south. *American Historical Review* 101(1): 41–79.

Street, Elmwood. 1919. Current methods of social service publicity (stereopticon illustrations). In *Proceedings of the National Conference of Social Work,* 679–82. Chicago: Rogers and Hall.

Strong, Howard. 1910. The relation of commercial bodies to our charitable and social standards. In *Proceedings of the National Conference of Charities and Correction*, 247–52. Fort Wayne: Fort Wayne Printing.

Swift, Linton. 1928. Can the sociologist and social worker agree on the content of case records? *Social Forces* 6(4): 535–38.

Swift, Sarah. 1934. *Training in psychiatric social work at the Institute for Child Guidance, 1927–1933*. New York: Commonwealth Fund.

Taft, Jessie. 1918. The limitations of the psychiatrist. *Medicine and Surgery* 2: 365–69.

———. 1922. The social worker's opportunity. In *Proceedings of the National Conference of Social Work*, 371–75. Chicago: University of Chicago Press.

———. 1924. The use of transfer within the limits of the office interview. In *Proceedings of the National Conference of Social Work*, 307–11. Chicago: University of Chicago Press.

Taylor, Graham. 1912. Qualifications of the social worker. *The call of the new south: Proceedings of the Southern Sociological Congress*. Nashville: Brandau-Craig Dickerson.

Terry, Jennifer. 1990. Lesbians under the medical gaze: Scientists search for remarkable differences. *Journal of Sex Research* 27(3): 317–39.

———. 1991. Theorizing deviant historiography. *Differences* 3(2): 55–74.

Theis, Sophie Van Senden, and Constance Goodrich. 1921. *The child in the foster home*. New York: Studies in Social Work, Child Welfare Series, New York School of Social Work.

Thom, Douglas. 1922. Results and future opportunities in the field of clinics, social service, and parole. In *Proceedings of the National Conference of Social Work*, 375–81. Chicago: University of Chicago Press.

Thomas, Mrs. W. I. 1910. The five cent theater. In *Proceedings of the National Conference of Charities and Correction*, 145–49. Fort Wayne: Fort Wayne Printing.

Thomas, William I. 1923 [reprint 1925]. *The unadjusted girl*. Boston: Little, Brown.

Thomas, William I., and Dorothy Swaine Thomas. 1928. *The child in America: Behavior problems and programs*. New York: Alfred A. Knopf.

Thomas, William I., and Florian Znaniecki. 1927. *The Polish peasant in Europe and America*. New York: Alfred A. Knopf.

Thrasher, Frederick. 1927. *The gang: A study of 1,313 gangs in Chicago*. Chicago: University of Chicago Press.

Tice, Karen. 1992. Battle for benevolence: Scientific disciplinary control vs. indiscriminate relief: Lexington Associated Charities and the Salvation Army, 1900–1918. *Journal of Sociology and Social Welfare* 19(2): 59–77.

Tice, Karen, and Dwight Billings. 1991. Appalachian culture and resistance. *Journal of Progressive Human Services* 2(2): 1–18.

Todd, Arthur J. 1919. *The scientific spirit and social work*. New York: Macmillan.

Tousley, Clare. 1920. Publicity in case work. *The Family* 1(2): 15–19.

———. 1927. Interpretation of case work by the case work method. *The Family* 8(6): 175–82.

Towle, Charlotte. 1941. *Social case records from psychiatric clinics.* Chicago: University of Chicago Press.

Trachtenberg, Alan. 1989. *Reading American photographs.* New York: Hill and Wang.

Tufts, James H. 1914. The ethics of the family. In *Proceedings of the National Conference of Charities and Correction,* 24–37. Chicago: University of Chicago Press.

———. 1923. *Education and training for social work.* New York: Russell Sage.

Valverde, Mariana. 1990. The rhetoric of reform: Tropes and the moral subject. *International Journal of the Sociology of Law* 18: 61–73.

Van Dyke, John C. 1909. *The new New York: A commentary on the place and the people.* New York: Macmillan.

Van Maanen, John. 1988. *Tales of the field: On writing ethnography.* Chicago: University of Chicago Press.

Waite, Florence. 1926. How to study a case record. *The Family* 7(6): 186–93.

Walker, Sydnor. 1928. *Social work and the training of social workers.* Chapel Hill: University of North Carolina Press.

Walker, Wilma. 1937. *Child welfare case records.* Chicago: University of Chicago Press.

Walkowitz, Daniel. 1990. The making of a feminine professional identity: Social workers in the 1920s. *American Historical Review* 95(4): 1051–76.

Walkowitz, Judith. 1992. *City of dreadful delight: Narratives of sexual danger in late-Victorian London.* Chicago: University of Chicago Press.

Wallerstein, Helen. 1920a. Jane Clegg: A case history. *The Family* 1(5): 12–13.

———. 1920b. Purposeful investigation. *The Family* 1(7): 17–19.

———. 1925. The homemaker. *The Family* 6(4): 113–14.

———. 1930. A literary case history. *The Family* 11(1): 26–28.

Wannamaker, Claudia. 1925. Social treatment from the standpoint of a client. *The Family* 6(2): 31–36.

Warner, Amos. 1922. *American charities.* 3d ed. New York: Thomas Y. Crowell.

Warner, Amos, Alfred Queen, and Ernest Harper. 1930. *American charities and social work.* 4th ed. New York: Thomas Y. Crowell.

Watson, Frank Decker. 1922. *The charity organization movement in the United States.* New York: Macmillan.

Wead, Margaret. 1932. Recent changes in record writing. *The Family* 13(3): 74–79.

Weick, Ann, Charles Rapp, W. Patrick Sullivan, and Walter Kisthardt. 1989. A strengths perspective for social work practice. *Social Work* 34(4): 350–54.

Weller, Charles. 1908. Publicity from the point of view of a social worker. In *Proceedings of the National Conference of Charities and Correction,* 276–79. Fort Wayne: Fort Wayne Printing.

Wenocur, Stanley, and Michael Reisch. 1989. *From charity to enterprise: The development of American social work in a market economy.* Urbana: University of Illinois Press.

Wheeler, Mary. 1925. Some tests for the evaluation of case work methods. In *Proceedings of the National Conference of Social Work*, 252–58. Chicago: University of Chicago Press.

Whipple, Leon. 1927. The magic gift of style. In *Proceedings of the National Conference of Social Work*, 675–85. Chicago: University of Chicago Press.

———. 1930. The philosophical basis of educational publicity in social work. In *Proceedings of the National Conference of Social Work*, 569–82. Chicago: University of Chicago Press.

White, Hayden. 1987. *The content of the form.* Baltimore: Johns Hopkins University Press.

White, Michael, and David Epston. 1990. *Narrative means to therapeutic ends.* New York: Norton.

Wichenden, Homer. 1920. Examples of case treatment. In *Proceedings of the National Conference of Social Work*, 258–63. Chicago: University of Chicago Press.

Williams, J. Harold. 1922. The scientific attitude in social work. *Journal of Applied Sociology* 7(2): 65–69.

Witmer, Helen. 1930. Increasing the research value of case records. *Journal of Sociology and Social Research* 15(2): 116–25.

Witmer, Lightner. 1915. Clinical records. *The Psychological Clinic* 9(1): 1–17.

Wood, Arthur Evans. 1925. Cultural values in the social service curriculum. In *Proceedings of the National Conference of Social Work*, 643–51. Chicago: University of Chicago Press.

Woodberry, Laura. 1924. The modern case work exchange: A source book for case workers. *The Family* 5(3): 51–56.

Woods, Robert. 1898. *The city wilderness.* New York: Arno Press.

Young, Erle. 1930. The scientific study of social case records. *Sociology and Social Research* 4(March-April): 358–64.

Young, Pauline. 1930. Should case records be written in the first person? *The Family* 11(5): 153–54.

———. 1935. *Interviewing in social work: A sociological analysis.* New York: McGraw-Hill.

———. 1939. *Scientific social surveys and research.* New York: Prentice-Hall.

Index

KAREN W. TICE is an assistant professor at the University of Kentucky, where she teaches education and women's studies. She has also been a practicing social worker and a social work educator. She holds a master of social work degree and also a Ph.D. from the University of Kentucky.